T5-AEX-052

Exchange Rate Theory

Exchange Rate Theory

Chaotic Models of
Foreign Exchange Markets

Paul De Grauwe, Hans Dewachter
and Mark Embrechts

BLACKWELL
Oxford UK & Cambridge USA

First published 1993

Blackwell Publishers
108 Cowley Road
Oxford OX4 1JF
UK

238 Main Street, Suite 501
Cambridge, Massachusetts 02142
USA

British Library Cataloguing in Publication Data
A CIP catalogue record for this book is available from the British Library.

Library of Congress Cataloging-in-Publication Data

Grauwe, Paul de.
    Exchange rate theory: chaotic models of foreign exchange markets / Paul De Grauwe, Hans Dewachter, and Mark Embrechts.
      p.   cm.
    Includes bibliographical references and index.
    ISBN 0-631-18016-8
    1. Foreign exchange rates – Econometric models.   I. Dewachter, Hans.
II. Embrechts, Mark.   III. Title.
HG3823.G735   1993
332.4'56 – dc20   92-25472   CIP

Typeset in 11 on 13 pt Times
by Best-set Typesetter Ltd., Hong Kong
Printed in Great Britain by T.J. Press Ltd, Padstow, Cornwall

This book is printed on acid-free paper

Contents

Contents

Tables

Figures

Figures

Preface

Since the inception of floating exchange rates in the beginning of the 1970s, economists have attempted to develop theories that explained what was going on, and that could be used to make predictions about future exchange rate movements. After almost twenty years of frenetic research one is forced to admit that success has been limited.

During the 1970s there was a lot of confidence in simple *purchasing power parity* theories and *monetary* explanations of the exchange rate. Today these theories have all been abandoned as instruments to explain the movements of the major exchange rates, let alone to predict future movements. Although these models remain useful to explain the exchange rates of countries with hyperinflation, they hardly play a role in explaining the movements of the dollar/Deutschmark or the dollar/yen, except as a very long run theory.

During the first half of the 1980s old Keynesian theories were brushed up. The Mundell–Fleming model was resuscitated, and it was said that the dollar strengthened during 1980–5 because the USA had budget deficits. When the dollar collapsed in 1985 this Mundell–Fleming model was abruptly thrown away. New models were introduced, predicting that the only way the USA could stop the decline of the dollar was by reducing the budget deficit.

All this has led to a situation where theories are developed to fit the exchange rate cycle in which we live. It also implies that a different theory seems to be needed for every different cycle. The usefulness of a theory is thereby drastically reduced. An important effect of this is that market participants have become sceptical about the usefulness of economic models in exchange rate forecasting. This has led to a predominance of technical (chartist) analysis as a tool for forecasting the exchange rate.

In this book we present a very different approach to the modelling of the exchange markets. We will start from the proposition that the interaction of agents using different information sets (for example, chartists and fundamentalists) introduces a sufficient number of nonlinearities to make chaotic motion in the foreign exchange markets possible. This idea will be developed systematically in the context of simple and well-known models of the exchange markets. One of the surprising things that will come out of this is that very simple exchange rate models are capable of generating extraordinarily complex exchange rate movements, which appear to be white noise. Yet it will also be shown that short-term forecasting is possible in such a chaotic environment.

The book is organized as follows. In the first chapter we present the basics of chaos theory. Many of the concepts developed in this chapter will be used later in the book. In the second chapter we present a brief survey of the exchange rate theories, and we highlight the unsatisfactory state of exchange rate theorizing. In the following three chapters we present simple theoretical models incorporating nonlinearities, based on the interaction of "chartists" and "fundamentalists". We use these models to generate exchange rates, and we show that they are capable of mimicking some important empirical regularities observed in exchange markets.

In the following chapters we present more rigorous empirical tests of chaotic models in the foreign exchange markets. Chapter 6 presents the basic statistical tools to analyze the data. Finally, chapters 7 and 8 present the empirical results.

This book owes a lot to the many discussions we have had with colleagues. In particular we are grateful to Casper De Vries, Daniel Gros, Guido De Bruyne, and Christopher Capraro. We also thank Francine Duysens for the dedication and the precision with which she typed consecutive drafts of this book.

1

Introduction to Chaos Theory

1 INTRODUCTION

There was a time when scientists felt comfortable with the idea that our universe and its developments are completely deterministic. This view was preached by Pierre-Simon de Laplace (1749–1827) in the nineteenth century. Laplace thought that if we only had the skill and the patience to write down the differential equations defining the universe (and set the proper initial conditions), any future event in the universe (including stock prices and exchange rates) could be predicted with absolute certainty. Since the time of Laplace, successful scientific theories have come along and wrecked this view of a predefined universe. These theories relate to quantum mechanics, Gödel's incompleteness theorem, and the theory of chaos.

Several excellent textbooks and review articles on chaos have been written. The purpose of this chapter is to provide a self-consistent introduction to chaos with a minimal of mathematical diversions. A more or less intuitive picture of chaos will be developed, and the reader will be referred to the technical literature for a more rigorous and exact approach. There is no commonly agreed definition of chaos; we will therefore join the majority view of what constitutes chaos, and refrain from more technical aspects in areas that require a delicate mathematical exposé.

Our approach to introducing chaos has three main tiers. In this chapter we will introduce the fundamental concept of chaos. In the chapter on empirical analysis and methodology (chapter

6) we will introduce techniques to recognize and analyze chaotic signals and finally we will apply these techniques to exchange rates. We will try to explain the various aspects of chaos intuitively by studying examples and test cases.

Various authors have already hinted at examples where a series of economic data might fit within the paradigm of the chaos models that originated from mathematical physics. The theory of chaos is establishing itself as a maturing discipline in its own right and several physical and geological data have proven to respond well to this theory. Chaos implies that a time series of data in a chaotic regime can be predicted or extrapolated to the future for a limited time only. The chaotic regime has several generic properties, and identifying a chaotic regime is important in order that these generic properties can be utilized.

2 EXAMPLES OF CHAOTIC SYSTEMS

2.1 The Lorenz system

Several scientists have been aware of what we now call *chaotic phenomena* for nearly a century. In particular, the brilliant French mathematician, Henri Poincaré (1854–1912), anticipated the science of chaos in several of his publications. One of his many endeavors elaborates on the gravitational effects between three planets ("celestial bodies" to put it in his words). Poincaré realized for the first time that very small perturbations in this three-body problem could lead to entirely different planetary orbits (Poincaré, 1899).

The credit for the modern theory of chaos is attributed to Edward Lorenz, who was a meteorologist at MIT. He simulated a simple weather evolution model on a computer in 1960 and obtained some strangely behaving results from his model: a small change in the initial conditions would lead to a drastically different weather evolution a few days later (Lorenz, 1963). The model of Lorenz eventually boiled down to a set of three coupled nonlinear differential equations of the type

$$\begin{cases} \dfrac{dX}{dt} = 10(Y - X) \\[2mm] \dfrac{dY}{dt} = 28X - Y - XZ \\[2mm] \dfrac{dZ}{dt} = XY - \dfrac{8}{3}Z \end{cases}$$

The variables X, Y and Z bear no relation to temperature, pressure, humidity or any other characteristic of the weather as we know it, but for the time being the reader could interpret them as such in order to visualize the system. These equations are *differential equations*, because they involve the derivatives of X, Y, and Z with respect to time, they are coupled, and they are nonlinear. We say that a set of coupled differential equations of the type above is *nonlinear* when the right hand side contains terms in powers of X, Y, or Z (such as X^2 or $Y^{1/3}$, and/or cross-product terms (such as XY, YZ, YX, $\sqrt{XY}$, $X\sqrt{Z}$, ...). Nonlinear systems have properties and solutions that are very different from linear systems. Linear systems obey the *superposition principle*, meaning that if A and B are solutions to a differential equation, then $A + B$ is a solution as well. This superposition rule does not apply to nonlinear systems. While we can find analytical solutions for linear systems, nonlinear systems in general need to be solved numerically. In order to solve a set of coupled differential equations a set of initial conditions for the variables is required. For the Lorenz system this implies that in order to solve these equations one has to be supplied with values for X, Y, and Z at one particular time (usually at time $t = 0$). We will note such a set of initial conditions at time $t = 0$ as (X_0, Y_0, Z_0).

Lorenz solved the above differential equations numerically on a computer and found that his results became very different in time when the initial conditions were slightly different. Such very different solutions for slightly different initial conditions are shown for the X and Z coordinates in figure 1.1.

Figure 1.1 was obtained by numerically solving the Lorenz system. The continuous lines correspond to the initial conditions $(X_0, Y_0, Z_0) = (10, 10, 10)$, whereas the dashed line resulted from the initial conditions $(X_0, Y_0, Z_0) = (10.01, 10, 10)$. Note

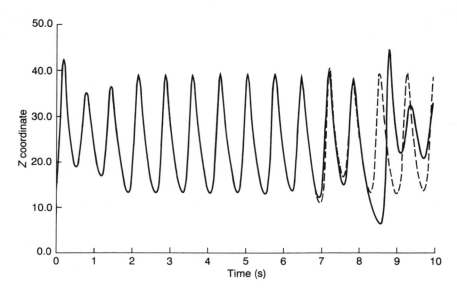

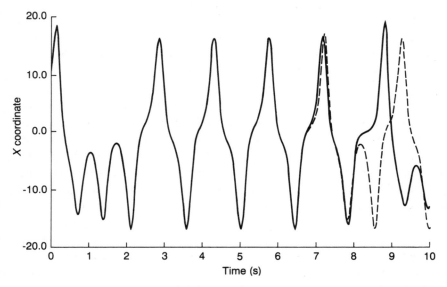

Figure 1.1 Sensitivity to initial conditions for the Lorenz attractor: Z and X are plotted versus time (t) for two slightly different sets of initial conditions. The continuous lines are for initial conditions $X_0 = 10$, $Y_0 = 10$, $Z_0 = 10$; the dashed lines are for initial conditions $X_0 = 10.01$, $Y_0 = 10$, $Z_0 = 10$.

that after 7 seconds the solutions for the two sets of initial conditions start diverging from each other, and that they become entirely different from each other after about 8 seconds. This phenomenon is called *sensitivity to initial conditions (SIC)*. Sensitivity to initial conditions is a first indication that the system is *chaotic*. Intuitively we would not like to rely on a model for weather prediction that exhibits such a sensitivity to the initial conditions: we certainly would not feel very comfortable with a weather forecasting model that would predict rain and hail when the average temperature the day before was 35°C, but would predict tropical weather if the average temperature the day before was 35.0001°C. In fact, if the answer given by the weather forecasting model is so sensitive to the values of the initial conditions, different computers will yield different answers, because computers work with a finite precision, causing the binary notation for numbers in different types of computers to be slightly different. While Lorenz was initially puzzled and perplexed by such an ambivalent model, he became fascinated by its dynamics and discovered several interesting characteristics for what is known as the *Lorenz model*.

Figure 1.2 shows the $X-Z$ projection of time evolution of the solution of the Lorenz system for two sets of initial conditions: a, $(X_0, Y_0, Z_0) = (10.0, 10.0, 10.0)$; and b, $(X_0, Y_0, Z_0) = (10.01, 10.0, 10.0)$. We noticed in figure 1.1 a divergence between the solutions for different initial conditions. After a while the evolution of the solution became entirely different. Figure 1.2, however, shows that the qualitative overall picture remains pretty much the same, in spite of the differences in figure 1.1. Figure 1.2 shows the $X-Z$ projections of the time evolution of the solution to the Lorenz system. Such a solution was obtained numerically, starting from a given set of initial conditions, and its time evolution is called a *trajectory*. In reality these trajectories move in a three-dimensional XYZ space, and will never cross each other. Different initial conditions will yield different trajectories in XYZ space. The boundaries and overall shape of figure 1.2a and b are roughly the same. We could extrapolate the similarities between a and b in the context of our weather prediction model by stating that even though we do not know and (could not know) what the exact values for

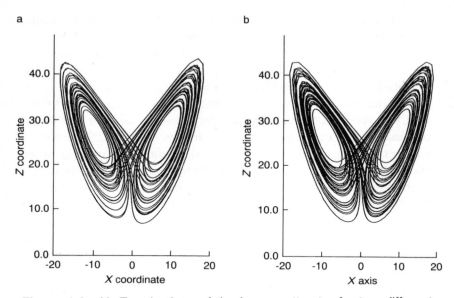

Figure 1.2 *X–Z* projections of the Lorenz attractor for two different sets of initial conditions: (a) $X_0 = 10$, $Y_0 = 10$, $Z_0 = 10$; (b) $X_0 = 10.01$, $Y_0 = 10$, $Z_0 = 10$. The first 5000 points are not plotted. Notice that even though the individual values are very different, the overall shape of the Lorenz attractor does not depend on the initial conditions.

temperature and pressure are going to be in a model with sensitivity to initial conditions, values for their ranges can still be estimated. Furthermore, we could say that even when we cannot predict the weather with the Lorenz model in the same sense that the weatherman predicts the weather on television, because of the sensitivity to initial conditions, the model would still lead to different seasons with very different weather regimes. In this idealized Lorenz model the reader could think of every "curly elliptic" part of the trajectory as one weather excursion in either the winter season (left wing) or the summer season (right wing). Of course this still would not make a lot of sense for this particular example, because the non-periodic solution would not correspond to an orderly evolution of the seasons: we would have two summer cycles following four winter cycles following one summer cycle and so on. Even when we are unable to provide for reliable weather predictions in the traditional sense due to the sensitivity to the initial conditions, we can still extract useful information from this chaotic model.

The trajectory of a solution to the Lorenz system in XYZ space has two wings (these wings do not fall in planes). Coincidentally with the resemblance of this trajectory to the wings of a butterfly, the phenomenon of sensitivity to the initial conditions (SIC) is referred to in popular terms as the *"butterfly effect,"* because (at least in theory) a butterfly flapping its wings in China (causing a change in the initial conditions to the Lorenz system) could trigger a tornado in Indiana.

We will call systems that exhibit sensitivity to the initial conditions and that show a seeming randomness or irregularity in their trajectory *chaotic systems*. Strictly speaking, more conditions will have to be met in order to call such systems chaotic. We will touch on some of these conditions later on, but refer the reader to the literature (Schuster, 1989; Baker and Gollub, 1990) for a more rigorous mathematical discussion. Chaos implies that we are dealing with nonlinear phenomena, but not all nonlinear systems will lead to chaos. The Lorenz system with the factor 28 replaced by 12 in the second equation would not exhibit sensitivity to the initial conditions and would therefore not be called a chaotic system. All possible solutions to the Lorenz system (but corresponding to different initial conditions) could be represented by trajectories in the XYZ space. Each point on such a trajectory would represent the value of X, Y, and Z at a particular time for a specific set of initial conditions. A space that allows us to represent all possible solutions of a system is defined as the *phase space* for this system.

Let us conclude this subsection by noting that because seemingly simple sets of equations such as the Lorenz system can show a rich behavior in their solutions (depending on the parameters of the system, and the initial conditions) it should come as no surprise to the reader that extremely complex nonlinear models dealing with economics, ecology, biology, or sociology might lead to phenomena that can also exhibit a sensitivity to the initial conditions. Changing initial conditions can also yield an entirely different type of solution to a nonlinear system.

James Gleick (1987) and Ian Stewart (1989) go to great lengths in their books highlighting the discovery of the science of chaos from a historical perspective.

2.2   The logistic equation

The growth-dynamics of a population could be described with a differential equation of the type

$$\frac{dp(t)}{dt} = r \cdot p - f(p)$$

where p is a normalized population that will take values between 0 and 1. This differential equation indicates that the change of population with time is the difference between a birth rate and a death rate. In the differential equation, r is a parameter indicating the birth rate and $f(p)$ is a non-specified function of p describing the death rate. If $f(p)$ is a linear function, the solution of this (now linear) differential equation will be an exponential increase or decrease of the population, depending on whether the death rate is larger or smaller than the birth rate. A Malthusian population model would assume a linear $f(p)$, and a birth rate exceeding the death rate. In order to come up with more pleasant scenarios for population growth studies, the Belgian professor Pierre-François Verhulst (1804–49) chose a quadratic (i.e. nonlinear) function for $f(p)$, and showed in 1837 that the now nonlinear and continuous differential equation could be reduced to a (discrete) difference equation of the type

$$X_{t+1} = \lambda X_t (1 - X_t)$$

In this equation X_t is a measure for the normalized population at time t and λ is a parameter. An expression that relates a variable X at time $(t + 1)$ to the variable X at time (t), or prior times, is called a *map*. Because the right hand side contains higher powers of X, the above map is nonlinear. Values for X at a particular time (t) can be derived from the map by an iterative procedure. The above equation is commonly referred to as the *logistic equation* or the *Verhulst equation*. A steady state solution (i.e. the solution $X_t = X_{t-1} = X_{t-2} \ldots$) for X (indicated by X^*) could be found by solving

$$X^* = \lambda X^* (1 - X^*)$$

This equation has two solutions, the trivial solution $X^* = 0$, and $X^* = 1 - 1/\lambda$. So, regardless of the initial value X_0 or the

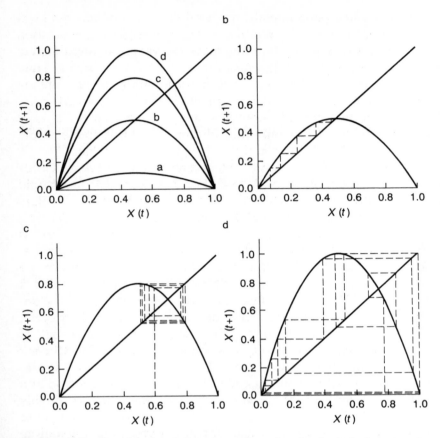

Figure 1.3 Graphical solution procedure for the logistic function for $\lambda = 0.5$ (a), $\lambda = 2.0$ (b, fixed point), $\lambda = 3.2$ (c, limit cycle), $\lambda = 4.0$ (d, chaotic).

starting guess for this mapping, we would naively expect to end up in either one of these two possible solutions after applying the mapping numerous times. The dynamics of the logistic equation are, however, more complex than just stated because the stability of the two solutions has not yet been investigated.

Figure 1.3 shows the graphical solution procedure for the logistic function for curve (a) $\lambda = 0.5$; curve (b) $\lambda = 2.0$; curve (c) $\lambda = 3.2$; curve (d) $\lambda = 4.0$. The solution procedure is shown explicitly for $\lambda = 2.0$, $\lambda = 3.2$, and $\lambda = 4.0$. The logistic equation maps the unit interval into itself for λ between 0 and 4. A computer simulation reveals that for $0 < \lambda < 1$, the mapping will always (regardless of the initial value) converge to the solution $X^* = 0$; for $1 < \lambda < 3$ the mapping yields as steady state solution $X^* = 1 - 1/\lambda$; while for $3 < \lambda < 4$ no steady state solution can be observed. The interpretation of the steady state solution for $0 < \lambda < 3$ is straightforward. One could verify that of the two possible solutions only one solution is stable in this region: for $\lambda < 1$ only the solution $X^* = 0$ is stable, while for $1 < \lambda < 3$ only the solution $X^* = 1 - 1/\lambda$ is stable.

The logistic map becomes interesting when we take a closer look to the solutions for $\lambda > 3$. For $3 < \lambda < 3.45$ we would observe that after a while the solution for X would oscillate between two values X_1^* and X_2^*. Such an oscillation is called a *limit cycle*, in our case, a *two-cycle*. What has happened here is that the second solution to the mapping has become unstable as soon as λ exceeds 3. Such a change in the stability behavior for the solution to a map or a differential equation is called a *bifurcation*. For larger values of λ the two-cycle becomes unstable and one observes the development of a four-cycle, eight-cycle, sixteen-cycle. . . . This sequence or cascade of *period-doubling bifurcations* was studied in detail by Mitchell Feigenbaum when he was at the Los Alamos National Laboratory. He proved that the cascade of bifurcations would stop at a finite value for λ which we will note as λ_∞ and which is roughly equal to 3.570. For $\lambda > \lambda_\infty$ the solution becomes even more complex. The successive values for X derived from the logistic map for (a) $\lambda = 0.5$, (b) $\lambda = 2.0$, (c) $\lambda = 3.2$ and (d) $\lambda = 4.0$ are shown in figure 1.4. All the solutions are for a starting value $X_0 = 0.3$.

The asymptotic behavior for the logistic map for $0.0 < \lambda < 4$ is shown in figure 1.5. By asymptotic behavior we mean here that we only consider the values for X after many iterations. Figure 1.5 was obtained by scanning the region for λ, starting with $\lambda = 0$, taking a starting value for X (e.g. $X_0 = 0.3$), doing 5000 iterations in the logistic equation, and plotting the next 100 values; λ is then slightly increased, let's say $\lambda = 0.01$, and the whole iteration process is repeated (i.e. doing 5000 dummy iterations and plotting the values of X obtained in iterations 5001 to 5100). This procedure is repeated for different values of

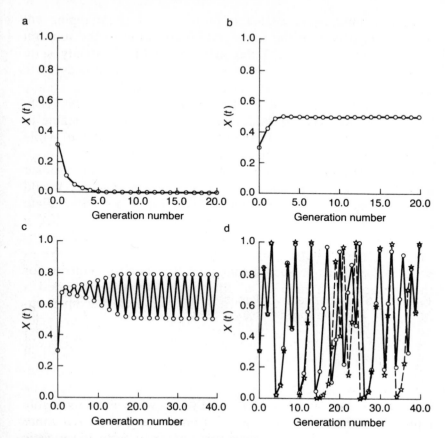

Figure 1.4 Successive values for X derived from the logistic map for: (a) 20 iterations, $\lambda = 0.5$, fixed point, $X^* = 0$; (b) 20 iterations, $\lambda = 2.0$, fixed point, $X^* = 0.5$; (c) 40 iterations, $\lambda = 3.2$, period 2 limit cycle; (d) 40 iterations, $\lambda = 4.0$, chaotic regime. All the solutions are for a starting value $X_0 = 0.3$. In (d) the mapping sequence for $X_0 = 0.30001$ is also shown (dashed line), illustrating SIC for this region.

λ. For each sequence of points λ was increased by 0.01 until λ had reached the value 4. The successive bifurcations are very clear in figure 1.5. This figure is also called the *Feigenbaum bifurcation diagram* for the logistic equation. Feigenbaum found that this bifurcation scenario was general, and that several different maps would follow this scenario. For $\lambda > \lambda_\infty$ we generally cannot predict what value the mapping will yield after

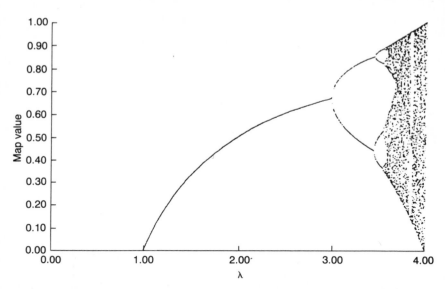

Figure 1.5 Feigenbaum bifurcation diagram. The asymptotic behavior for X of the logistic map is shown for $0 < \lambda < 4$. Note the chaotic region for $\lambda > \lambda_\infty$. In this region we can generally not make any predictions for X^* due to the sensitivity of the mapping results with regard to the initial value for X_0.

a finite number of iterations and the mapping exhibits a sensitivity to the initial value for X_0. Except for the narrow bands where the solutions would oscillate on an n-cycle again (e.g. $n = 3$ for $3.83 < \lambda < 3.86$), there are an infinite number of possible values for X and the mapping is called *chaotic*.

Figure 1.6 shows the sequence of values of X after 5000 iterations for λ ranging from 2.8 to 4. The successive bifurcations show up more clearly on this extended scale than in figure 1.5.

A possible sequence of mapping results in the chaotic regime for λ is shown in figure 1.4d. Only for maps in the chaotic regime will different initial conditions lead to a different solution, or will sensitivity to initial conditions be observed. The dashed line on figure 1.4d shows the results from the mapping if one starts with $X_0 = 0.30001$ instead of $X_0 = 0.3$ (continuous line). Even when the curve in figure 1.4d looks quite random to

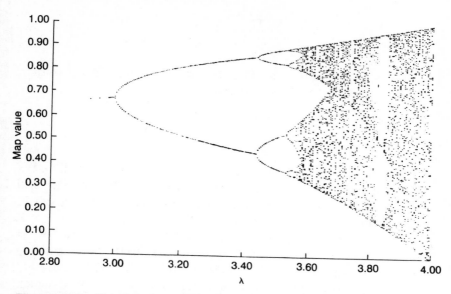

Figure 1.6 Feigenbaum bifurcation diagram. The asymptotic behavior for X of the logistic map is shown for $2.8 < \lambda < 4$.

us on first sight, techniques do exist (and will be introduced in this book) that allow us to distinguish a chaotic signal from a purely random signal. Several books and articles can be cited that describe the logistic map in all its mathematical detail and beauty (Feigenbaum, 1978, 1980; Schuster, 1989). It is surprising indeed that a simple mapping such as the logistic equation can exhibit such a rich dynamic behavior. The notion that purely deterministic equations such as the logistic map can yield a seemingly random solution speaks even more strongly to our imaginations.

2.3 The Hénon map

The logistic map is a one-dimensional map. It would be straightforward to expand the idea of a map to more dimensions. A widely cited example of a two-dimensional map was first encountered by the French astronomer M. Hénon in 1974 and is appropriately named the *Hénon map* (Hénon, 1976). This map has the following form:

$$\begin{cases} X_{t+1} = 1 + Y_t - aX_t^2 \\ Y_{t+1} = bX_t \end{cases}$$

a and b are parameters. The evolution of the Hénon map is usually described for $a = 1.4$ and $b = 0.3$, leading to

$$\begin{cases} X_{t+1} = 1 + Y_t - 1.4X_t^2 \\ Y_{t+1} = 0.3X_t \end{cases}$$

Hénon proved that the solutions (i.e. the values for X and Y after numerous successive iterations through the system) will tend either to infinity or to the structure shown in figure 1.7, depending on the choice of the initial conditions.

The structure in figure 1.7 is called the Hénon attractor. It was obtained by iterating the Hénon map 50 000 times starting from $(0, 0)$, ignoring the first 5000 iterations. Successive enlargements show that the Hénon map has a band structure which repeats itself after successive magnifications. Such a figure, where part of the figure resembles the total figure (and vice versa) is called *fractal*. The term fractal was coined by the Polish-born French-raised American mathematician, Benoit Mandelbrot. The Hénon attractor is chaotic in the sense that the solution sequence to the Hénon map will be very different for slightly different initial conditions. However, the overall shape of the Hénon attractor will always be the same (as illustrated in figure 1.8). Figure 1.8 shows two plots for the first 5000 points of the the Hénon map: one with initial conditions $(0, 0)$ (a) and one with initial conditions $(1, 1)$ (b). Figure 1.8c and d show the values for X versus iteration number. Both maps in figure 1.8 look very similar, which again is an indication that even when there is sensitivity to the initial conditions, the overall collection of points which result from the map remains similar. The Hénon attractor is called a strange attractor because of its sensitivity to initial conditions and the fractal nature of the map. We can develop here an intuitive understanding that a map consisting of two simultaneous equations is sufficient to produce a chaotic system with a strange (i.e. fractal) attractor.[1]

Looking at the Hénon map or the trajectory of the Lorenz

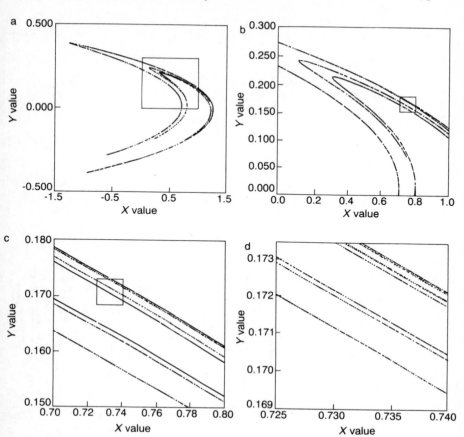

Figure 1.7 Hénon map for A = 1.4 and B = 0.3. Various magnifications are shown: (a) −1.5 < X < 1.5 and −0.6 < Y < 0.6; (b) 0 < X < 1 and 0 < Y < 0.3; (c) 0.7 < X < 0.8 and 0.15 < Y < 0.18; (d) 0.725 < X < 0.74 and 0.1685 < Y < 0.173.

attractor one notices that each part of the chaotic domain receives repeated visits by the trajectory. This observation can be rephrased and expanded by noting that in any immediate neighborhood of any value (X_i, Y_i) obtained from the map, sooner or later a new value (X_{i+N}, Y_{i+N}) arbitrarily close to (X_i, Y_i) will be

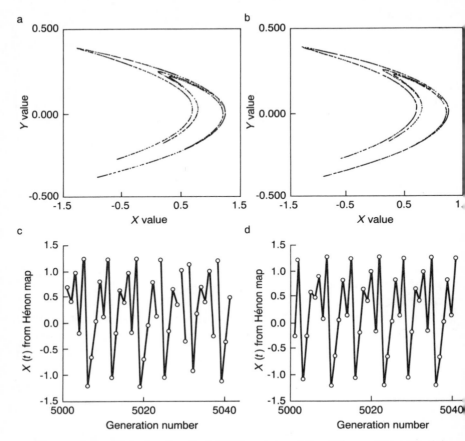

Figure 1.8 Plots for the first 5000 points of the Hénon attractor, (a) with initial conditions $(0, 0)$ and (b) with initial conditions $(1, 1)$. (c) and (d) show the values for X versus iteration number for iterations 5000 to 5040 corresponding with initial conditions $(0, 0)$ and $(1, 1)$ respectively. The maps in (a) and (b) look very similar even though the X values are very different.

found. This observation relates to the *ergodic* properties of a chaotic signal. However, this does not imply that the distribution of the points is uniform, Gaussian, or consistent with any other known distribution function. As a matter of fact, the points on a strange attractor are distributed in a fractal manner.

3   FRACTALS

3.1   What is a fractal?

In the preceding paragraph we introduced the concept of a strange attractor and briefly alluded to the fractal nature of such an attractor. Several excellent books have recently been published that provide the reader with a careful definition of what exactly constitutes a fractal (Barnsley, 1988; Falconer, 1990; Mandelbrot, 1983; Feder, 1989). Fractals were introduced in the 1970s by Benoit Mandelbrot. He introduced the concept of a fractal as a new geometric concept to describe irregular shapes such as mountains, clouds, wiggly lines, and coagulations of points. We are familiar with geometric structures such as points, lines, and surfaces. These structures can be categorized according to their (topological) *dimension*, which is 0 for a point, 1 for a line, and 2 for a surface. We would say that a wiggly line or a circle has a topological dimension of 1, because we could stretch the wiggly line or the circle (after cutting it) to yield a straight line. The branch of mathematics that deals with stretching wiggly lines and surfaces is called *topology*, and is sometimes lucidly referred to as rubber sheet mathematics. Mathematicians have defined several separate types of dimensions that are different from the (topological) dimension that we are intuitively familiar with. One different type of dimension is the *Hausdorff dimension*, which has the interesting characteristic that it can also take non-integer values. The figures that Mandelbrot was studying could be assigned such non-integer Hausdorff dimensions (e.g. 1.32). Bear in mind that these dimensions are not the topological dimension, but could be interpreted as a more generalized type of dimension. Fractals are figures with a non-integer (fractured) value for the Hausdorff dimension. One of the definitions that Mandelbrot introduced in his 1983 book *The Fractal Geometry of Nature* can be formulated as follows:[2]

> A fractal is a figure for which the Hausdorff dimension strictly exceeds the topological dimension.

We will not provide an exact definition of the Hausdorff dimension in this book. However, we will approximate the

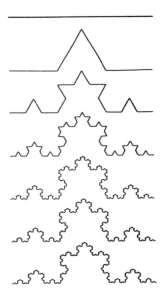

Figure 1.9 The Koch set. The first step is a straight line segment. In the second step the middle third has been replaced by two pieces, each as long as the middle third. At each succeeding stage in the construction of the Koch curve each line segment is replaced by a miniature copy of the figure in the second stage.

Hausdorff dimension by what we call the *fractal dimension*. By the fractal dimension we mean a *box-counting dimension* or a *correlation dimension*. The box-counting dimension and the correlation dimension will be introduced in this section. One has to keep in mind that these dimensions are strictly speaking not the same. However, for the type of strange attractors encountered in this book, and for our purposes, the box-counting dimension and the correlation dimension will generally be reasonably close approximations to the Hausdorff dimension.

An example of a fractal figure is the *Koch set*. The steps taken to obtain such a figure are shown explicitly in figure 1.9. The first step is a straight line segment. In the second step the middle third has been replaced by two pieces, each as long as the middle third. At each succeeding stage in the construction of the Koch curve each line segment is replaced by a miniature copy of

Figure 1.10   The Sierpinski triangle.

the figure in the second stage. In order to have a true fractal the process should be repeated over and over again indefinitely. Let us point out here that fractals bring several idiosyncrasies with them that will defy the familiar concepts of Euclidean geometry. For our purposes it will be sufficient to define a fractal as a mathematical object that can be produced by a simple repetitive mathematical operation.

A different example of a fractal is the *Sierpinski triangle* shown in figure 1.10. The notion that a fractal object exhibits self-similarity is very clear from this example. The whole figure is a magnification of its parts, and details in the figure are reductions of the whole figure. For such self-similar fractals the Hausdorff dimension will be exactly equal to the box-counting dimension and the correlation dimension. There is a very simple formula for estimating the fractal dimension of a self-similar fractal such as the Sierpinski triangle. Without proof we will state that the fractal dimension for a purely self-similar fractal is now equal to the *similarity dimension*, D_{sim}, according to:

$$D_{sim} = \frac{\log \text{ (no. of copies)}}{\log \text{ (reduction)}}$$

For the Sierpinski triangle we see that there are three copies of the original figure at each subsequent generation stage, while the length of a side of the triangle is reduced by a factor of 2. According to our definition the similarity dimension for the Sierpinski triangle would be $\log(3)/\log(2) = 1.58496$. It is

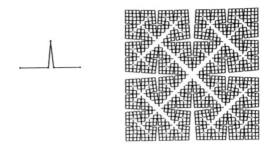

Figure 1.11   Space-filling Koch set.

interesting to note here that the fractal dimension of the Sierpinski triangle is smaller than the dimension of the embedding plane (2), but larger than 1 (the topological dimension of a line). The more "busy" the fractal figure is, or the more space-filling the fractal, the better the fractal dimension will approximate the dimension of the embedding space. To illustrate this concept more clearly consider the space-filling fractal in figure 1.11.

This figure results from arranging four (narrow triangle) Koch sets in a square. A Koch set is a set generated by the figure shown in the inset. At each stage of the generation we would replace the straight lines by a miniature copy of the figure in the inset. In the limit for α going to 90 degrees, the Koch set will fill part of its embedding space completely and its fractal dimension will be equal to 2. This concept shows that in certain special cases the fractal dimension can equal the dimension of the embedding space and be an integer. Space filling curves in a plane have a fractal dimension 2 and are also called *Peano curves*, in honor of the Italian mathematician Giussepe Peano (1858–1932). Figure 1.12 shows two stages in the creation of a Sierpinski tetrahedron. The embedding dimension is 3, and the fractal dimension according to the definition for the similarity dimension is $\ln(4)/\ln(2) = 2$. This again is a special case where the fractal dimension is an integer number. What makes the case of the Sierpinski tetrahedron very interesting here is that a fractal dimension of 2 does not necessarily imply that the fractal figure could be embedded in a plane. The fractal dimension is just a

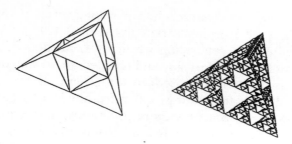

Figure 1.12   The Sierpinski tetrahedron.

gross measure indicating to what degree the embedding space is occupied by the fractal, and the embedding space for the Sierpinski tetrahedron is three-dimensional.

So far we have an intuitive idea of what constitutes a fractal. The notion of fractals has been expanded to fractal poetry and fractal painting. The concept of fractals is mirrored beautifully in the etchings of the Dutch artist Maurits Cornelis Escher (1898–1972). Escher in a sense was the prophet who announced the birth of fractal geometry.

To make some different connections between chaotic maps and fractals let us point out here that there are several interesting ways to obtain a Sierpinski triangle. One way would be to consider the following three maps:

$$\begin{cases} X_{t+1} = 0.5X_t + 0.05 \\ Y_{t+1} = 0.5Y_t + 0.05 \end{cases}$$

$$\begin{cases} X_{t+1} = 0.5X_t + 0.45 \\ Y_{t+1} = 0.5Y_t + 0.05 \end{cases}$$

$$\begin{cases} X_{t+1} = 0.5X_t + 0.05 \\ Y_{t+1} = 0.5Y_t + 0.45 \end{cases}$$

If we applied one mapping step for the X and the Y coordinates from one of the three maps selected at random, performed an additional mapping step with a different map randomly chosen from the three mappings, and built up a sequence of such random selected map steps, we would end up with a set of points that again looks like the Sierpinski triangle (figure 1.13).

This procedure for generating fractals was introduced by the mathematician Michael Barnsley and is called an *iterated function system*. He also calls this procedure for generating fractals the *chaos game*. In his fascinating and refreshingly original book *Fractals Everywhere*, Barnsley diligently builds up the necessary mathematical concepts to view fractals from the point of view of such iterated function systems. Note that the type of fractals obtained with iterated function systems consists of a collection of points, contrary to the fractals that we considered in the previous figures.

Our interest in fractals comes from a different angle to Barnsley's treatment. We are interested in the time evolution of exchange rates. We will show that models for the time evolution of exchange rates can be developed that can exhibit chaotic behavior. The chaotic systems that we consider will lead to strange attractors with a fractal structure. The fractal dimension of these fractals will provide us with a measure for the complexity of the dynamics that are involved in the evolution of this time series. We will use the concept of a fractal dimension in a phase space trajectory as a signature for detecting chaos.

3.2   The fractal dimension

The classical example for introducing a fractal dimension relates to measuring the length of a "wiggly" line with various different measuring sticks. It turns out that the length of a wiggly line actually depends on the length of the measuring stick. This odd fact was first observed empirically by Lewis Fry Richardson in 1961, and his results are described by Mandelbrot (1983) under the heading "How long is the coast of Britain?" While various authors adapt this example to their country of birth or favorite river from childhood, we will follow Mandelbrot's treatment here. The fractal nature of a coastline is illustrated in an intuitive way in figure 1.14a, where we can see that various enlargements of a bay give qualitatively similar pictures. This notion of a fractal is more general than the fractals that were introduced

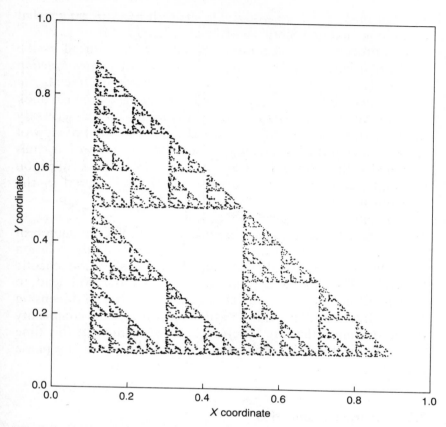

Figure 1.13 A Sierpinski triangle obtained from the "chaos game."

before, and that were all of the strictly self-similar type. The
length of a coastline could be measured by counting how many
times (N) one could fit a measuring stick with a known length
along the coastline and multiplying this number by the length of
the measuring stick. While this seems to be a very obvious way
to reach the objective, we will come to some startling conclusions
by applying this procedure: we will illustrate that the length of a
"wiggly line" depends on the length of the measuring stick.

The length of the coastline (L) is a function of the length of
the measuring stick δ according to

a

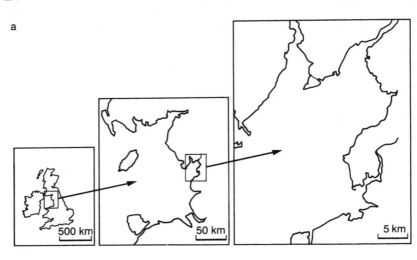

b

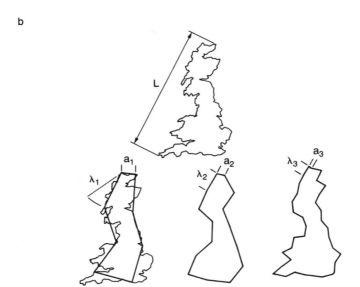

Figure 1.14 Illustration of the "coastline dimension." (a) The fractal nature of the coastline of Britain. (b) Measuring the length of a coastline by counting how many times one could fit a measuring stick with a known length along the coastline and multiplying this number by the length of the measuring stick.

$$L = N(\delta) \times \delta$$

where $N(\delta)$ is the number of times that we can fit the measuring stick around the coastline (figure 1.15b). For a familiar Euclidean shape, the number of times the measuring stick can be fitted around the perimeter is inversely proportional to the length of the measuring stick, or

$$N(\delta) \propto \frac{1}{\delta}$$

or, if we call the proportionality constant A,

$$N(\delta) = A \cdot \frac{1}{\delta}$$

For a Euclidean shape the length of the perimeter is independent of the length of the measuring stick, δ, because

$$L = A \cdot \frac{1}{\delta} \cdot \delta = A$$

For a fractal curve, the measuring procedure turns out to be different. We now observe that the number of times we can fit the measuring stick around the perimeter is not just proportional to $1/\delta$, but is proportional to $1/\delta^D$. The length can now be expressed as:

$$L(\delta) = N(\delta) \times \delta$$

which by using

$$N(\delta) \propto \frac{1}{\delta^D}$$

becomes

$$L(\delta) \propto \frac{1}{\delta^D} \times \delta$$

or

$$L(\delta) \propto \delta^{1-D}$$

By plotting the length of the coastline against the length of the measuring stick on a log–log scale one would obtain roughly straight lines (figure 1.16) because

$$\log[L(\delta)] = Ct + (1 - D) \log(\delta)$$

The length of the curve is now a function of the length of the measuring stick. The lengths of various coastlines (Australia, South Africa, Great Britain), the German and Portuguese land frontiers and the length of a circle are shown as a function of the length of the measuring device on a log–log scale in figure 1.15. On a log–log scale these measurements would roughly lead to straight lines with slope $1 - D$. The proportionality constant D is a measure of the jaggedness or non-smoothness of the coastline and corresponds to the fractal dimension. The more wiggly the coastline, the higher the fractal dimension D, the steeper the slopes on figure 1.16. The method just described for determining the length of a wiggly curve is also called the *coastline method* for determining the fractal dimension. The log–log plot for the perimeter of a circle shows a horizontal line indicating that $1 - D = 0$, or $D = 1$. For the perimeter of a circle the fractal dimension coincides with its topological dimension. This means that a circle is not a fractal (using Mandelbrot's definition) and that the perimeter of a circle is a smooth line. One can see from figure 1.16 that the fractal dimensions for the various coastlines and land frontiers range between 1 and 2. For many coastlines and land frontiers Mandelbrot's definition is satisfied, and we could call them fractals. Of course, strictly speaking the notion of a fractal would only be valid in the limit of the length of the measuring device going to zero. In practice there will be two limits to the length of the measuring device that can be used: there will be an upper limit, when the length of the measuring stick approximates the size of the object to be measured, and there will be a lower limit for natural objects, because the scenario of increasing resolutions will eventually have to be terminated. This upper limit explains why for larger lengths of the measure in figure 1.15 the plot for the perimeter of the circle will start deviating from a horizontal line.

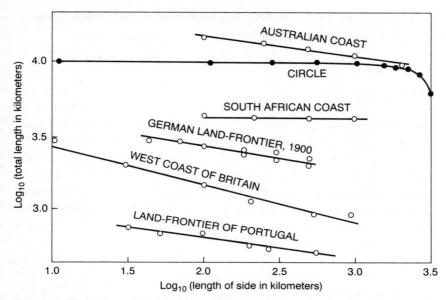

Figure 1.15 Lengths of various coastlines, land frontiers and the perimeter of a circle as a function of the length of a measuring device on a log-log scale. The slopes are equal to $1 - D$. (After Mandelbrot, 1983.)

3.3 The box-counting method for fractal dimensions

So far, the coastline method for determining the fractal dimension of a wiggly curve works fine. What about a fractal that consists of a set of points like the Sierpinski triangle of figure 1.13, or the *Cantor set* shown in figure 1.16?

The Cantor set can be obtained by starting from a line segment, and removing the middle third(s) of the line segment(s) after each step. This mechanism will lead to a collection of points arranged on a straight line. This set is named after the Russian-born German mathematician Georg Cantor (1845–1918), who was the founder of set theory and laid the basis for what can now be called the mathematics of fractals. Cantor was one of the most original mathematical minds of the nineteenth century, but his work was not widely appreciated at that time. A direct application of the coastline method would not work for

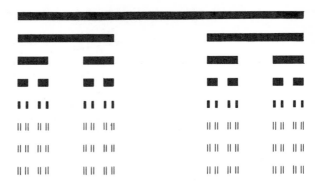

Figure 1.16 The Cantor set can be obtained by starting from a line segment and removing the middle thirds of the line segments after each step.

the Cantor set. A widely applied method for determining the fractal dimension for such fractals, that applies to wiggly curves as well, is known as as the *box-counting method*. Here is how it works. Consider the Cantor set superimposed on a grid as shown in figure 1.17. One could count how many boxes of the grid are covered by the fractal Cantor set, and keep track of that number as a function of the grid size. For each finer meshing the grid size is reduced by a factor of 2. In order to determine the fractal dimension one has to keep track of the number of boxes of the grid covered by the fractal as a function of the grid size reduction step (table 1.1).

The slope in the plot of the natural logarithm of the number of boxes of figure 1.17 versus $n \log 2$ (where n is the grid size reduction step) is the *box-counting dimension*. This process is illustrated for the Cantor set in figure 1.18. One can prove that the similarity dimension is a special case of the box-counting dimension. For fractals that are not strictly self-similar, such as coastlines and land-frontiers, the box-counting dimension will generally be slightly different from the coastline dimension or the Hausdorff dimension. We would estimate that the box-counting dimension of the Cantor set is about 0.8, while the exact result for the fractal dimension of the Cantor set is $\log(2)/\log(3) = 0.63093$. A higher resolution and a more refined imple-

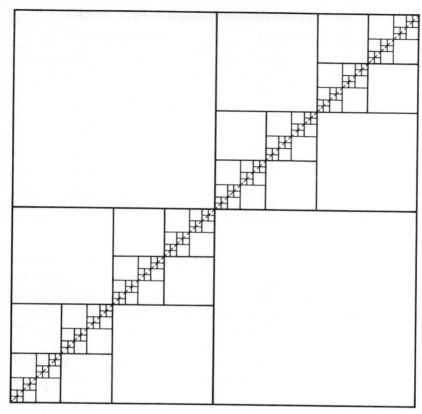

Figure 1.17 Illustration of the box-counting method for determining the fractal dimension of the Cantor set.

mentation of the box-counting algorithm would provide a better estimate of the fractal dimension, but requires a computerized system. Because the Cantor set consists of a number of points its topological dimension is the dimension of a point, or zero. The Cantor set is embedded in a straight line, and its embedding dimension is therefore equal to 1. The fractal dimension of the Cantor set lies somewhere in between the topological dimension and the dimension of the embedding space. The Cantor set therefore abides by Mandelbrot's definition of a fractal. Notice that the application of the box-counting method for determining the fractal dimension of a wiggly line is straightforward. The

Table 1.1   Grid size reduction step versus number of boxes to cover fractal

Grid reduction (n)	No. of boxes	n log2	log (no. boxes)
0	1	0	0
1	2	0.69	0.69
2	4	1.38	1.38
3	6	2.08	1.79
4	10	2.77	2.30
5	16	3.46	2.77
6	26	4.16	3.26
7	36	4.85	3.58

Hausdorff dimension is the true measure of the fractal dimension but is not very practical to estimate. We refer readers to the appropriate literature for a rigorous definition of the Hausdorff dimension (Barnsley, 1988; Feder, 1989; Mandelbrot, 1983). For the type of fractals that will be encountered in this book and for our purposes, the box-counting dimension and the coastline dimension will be acceptable approximations to the Hausdorff dimension. We will call all these dimensions the *fractal dimension*.

3.4   The correlation dimension

The concept of the *correlation dimension* will lead to an elegant way for estimating the fractal dimension of a set of n-dimensional datapoints. This method consists of centering a hypersphere about a point in *hyperspace* or phase space (figure 1.19), letting the radius (r) of the hypersphere grow until all points are enclosed and keeping track of the number of datapoints that are enclosed by the hypersphere as a function of the hypersphere radius. The slope of the log–log plot will then be an estimate of the fractal dimension of the set of datapoints. In practice, since the number of points (M) is finite, many spheres are used (centered on different points of the data-set) and the results are ensemble averaged. A first step in determining the correlation

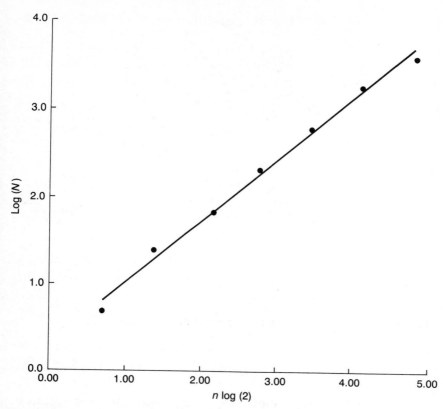

Figure 1.18 The fractal dimension of the Cantor set by the box-counting method ($Y = 0.69 + 0.34$). The box-counting dimension is the slope of the log-log plot of the number of covering boxes versus reduction number multiplied by log 2.

dimension for an n-dimensional signal $\vec{x}(t)$ requires the evaluation of the *two-point correlation function* on the set of M vectors (or datapoints) for various values of r

$$N(r) = \frac{1}{M(M-1)} \sum_{i=1}^{M} \sum_{i<>j}^{M} \theta\left[r - d(\vec{x}_i - \vec{x}_j)\right]$$

where θ is the Heavyside function defined by

$$\theta = 1 \quad \text{if} \quad d(\vec{x}_i - \vec{x}_j) < r$$
$$\theta = 0 \quad \text{if} \quad d(\vec{x}_i - \vec{x}_j) > r$$

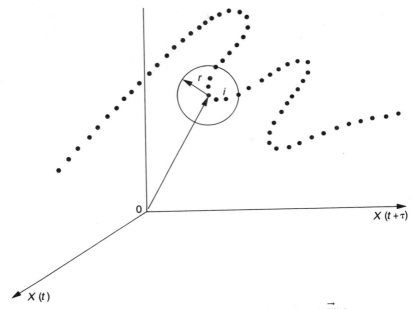

Figure 1.19 Phase space representation of a signal $\vec{X}(t)$.

In the above expression $d(\vec{x}_i - \vec{x}_j)$ represents the distance between two n-dimensional vectors. Several different measures for the distance between two points in an n-dimensional vector space can be defined. For a three-dimensional space we are intuitively familiar with the Euclidean distance, and the generalization of the Euclidean distance to higher dimensions works just fine. To gain computation speed different measures for calculating the distance between vectors could be used.

It has been found that in the limit as $r \rightarrow 0$,

$$N(r) = C_1 r^{D_c}$$

so that

$$\log(N) = D_C \log(r) + C_2$$

If we plot $N(r)$ versus r on a log–log plot the *correlation dimension*, D_C, can be determined as the slope of the line.

The concept of the correlation dimension is introduced here in a rather abstract manner. We will introduce several very powerful applications of the correlation dimension concept in chapter 6, which deals with empirical methods for analyzing chaos.

The mathematically inclined reader would notice here that the correlation dimension is nothing but a generalization of the box-counting dimension, whereas the box-counting dimension is a generalization of the similarity dimension.

To visualize the concept of hyperspace and hyperspheres we will mention a hyperspace view of our universe described by Rudy Rucker (1983). To the inhabitants of the earth, the earth's surface looks flat and two-dimensional. To travel to the two-dimensional surface of another planet or the moon, we have to cross the third dimension in space. The presence of this third dimension is not entirely obvious when we are at the surface of the earth. It would be even less obvious if our atmosphere was always clouded, so that we could not actually see the planets or the moon in the sky. Rucker makes the point here that extending this concept to higher dimensions is straightforward, and that it should not be inconceivable that there are other three-dimensional universes similar to our own three-dimensional universe, but that one has to cross a fourth dimension in order to reach such a universe. The generalization of this concept of a four-dimensional universe to even higher dimensions is a nice way to look at hyperspace.

4 WHAT IS CHAOS?

4.1 Introduction

Simple nonlinear maps or coupled differential equations can exhibit very complicated dynamics in a *chaotic regime*. These deterministic models can lead to seemingly random and highly irregular signals or trajectories. So far three examples of chaotic systems have been introduced: the Lorenz system, the logistic equation and the Hénon map. The concept of chaos was introduced intuitively by pointing out the irregularity of

the evolution of the variables of the system, the sensitivity to the
initial conditions and the fractal nature of the overall long-term
evolution of the solution. This section will further expand on the
concept of chaos.

From the examples of chaotic systems we observed some
typical characteristics. Several regimes, such as a fixed point,
periodic solution and the so-called chaotic regime, were identified. It depends on the values of one or more parameters of the
system whether or not the regime is chaotic. The dispersion of
these various modes for different values of a parameter of the
system can lead to a visually fascinating bifurcation diagram.

The concept of chaos was introduced by some simple examples
of maps and a nonlinear set of differential equations. The most
intriguing aspects of chaos discussed so far are threefold:

1   In the chaotic regime seemingly random, or highly irregular,
    signals were produced from a completely deterministic
    process.
2   In a chaotic regime there is sensitivity to initial conditions.
    This means that for most practical purposes we cannot know
    the exact answer. However, the overall dynamic behavior of
    the process is more robust and does not depend on the initial
    conditions. Sensitivity to initial conditions does not mean
    that we cannot predict the outcome of a chaotic system. It
    means that we can predict the results for a relatively short
    time only, and that we can predict the overall long-term
    evolution of the system in a general sense.
3   In a phase space of at least three variables for a set of
    differential equations, and at least two variables for a map,
    the chaotic regime is characterized by a fractal phase space
    plot: the strange attractor. Such a strange attractor can be
    characterized by a fractal dimension.

Strange attractors and chaos can lead to spectacular .pictures.
A philosophical exposé of the implications of the chaos concept
can be found in several publications (Gleick, 1987; Stewart, 1989).

There is no commonly agreed definition of chaos. We will
define chaos as a seemingly random and irregular signal generated by a deterministic process with some additional properties. The first of these properties is that the deterministic

process that generated a chaotic signal must show sensitivity to initial conditions. A second property is that a chaotic signal is associated with a strange attractor (i.e. that the phase space shows a figure or distribution of points that is characterized by a fractal or non-integer dimension). In this chapter we will add characteristics that are necessary for chaos and further expand on them. They are:

4   A continuous broadband Fourier power spectrum.
5   At least one positive Liapunov exponent.
6   Ergodicity.

The presence of some of the above characteristics can occur for a non-chaotic signal as well. All of the above points have to be observed simultaneously in order to have a chaotic system.

4.2   Characteristics of irregularity and randomness

Figure 1.20 shows the evolution of the Z variable of the Lorenz system during the first 80 time units. The first identification of a chaotic system is its irregular and erratic appearance. In order to have a chaotic signal a seemingly random evolution of the signal is required. If one were to ask whether figure 1.20a was the plot of a random signal the answer would be likely to be "no." There is a periodic component in this signal that eludes our intuitive concept of randomness because the spacing between the local maxima seems to be quite regular. On a larger timescale there seems to be an additional almost re-petitive cycle present in figure 1.20a. We have not yet defined what exactly we mean by seemingly random behavior. A defini-tion of randomness is more complicated than one would expect at first sight, and we will not attempt to provide such a definition here. For our purposes we will accept the irregularities in figure 1.20 as a sufficient indication of randomness. The first require-ment for chaos,

chaos is a seemingly random time series of data generated by a deterministic process,

would therefore be satisfied for the Lorenz system. Let us note here that the generation of pseudo-random numbers, which are certainly not intended to be chaotic, would satisfy that condition as well, but they will not satisfy the other requirements we will pose for a chaotic process. Figure 1.21a shows the first 80 time units in the evolution of the X variable of the Lorenz system. The periodicity is no longer there. The presence of a seemingly random ingredient is more pronounced. What we mean by the randomness requirement for chaos is a mere indication of randomness resulting from a deterministic process.

The presence of a random component might become more obvious when we look at the distribution function for the X and Z variables of the Lorenz system (figures 1.20b and 1.21b). The distributions are not Gaussian, Student t, or any other well known probabilistic distribution functions. A further check would show that these distribution functions are also stationary, meaning that they do not change in time. Other chaotic phenomena, such as the Hénon attractor, also have a stationary but irregular distribution (figure 1.22b). The logistic map (which does not show a strange attractor) shows a seemingly irregular development (figure 1.23a), but does not yield an erratic distribution function (figure 1.23b). Figure 1.24a shows 200 points chosen from a series of random data with a Gaussian distribution. The bell shape of the Gaussian distribution function is shown in figure 1.24b. The distribution functions presented in this section were obtained from 10 000 datapoints evaluated in 20 equally spaced bins. The distribution for the logistic map was evaluated in 100 equally spaced bins in order to show the sudden change at the edges.

4.3   Sensitivity to initial conditions

Simple nonlinear maps and nonlinear sets of differential equations can exhibit sensitivity to the initial conditions (SIC). This means that for a slightly different choice of initial value, X_0, the trajectory of the solution or map would initially remain very close to the original trajectory in phase space, but eventually diverge away from the initial trajectory. This phenomenon is called sensitivity to the initial conditions and is illustrated for the Lorenz system in figure 1.1 (and table 1.1), and for the Logistic equation (with $\lambda = 4$) in figure 1.4d.

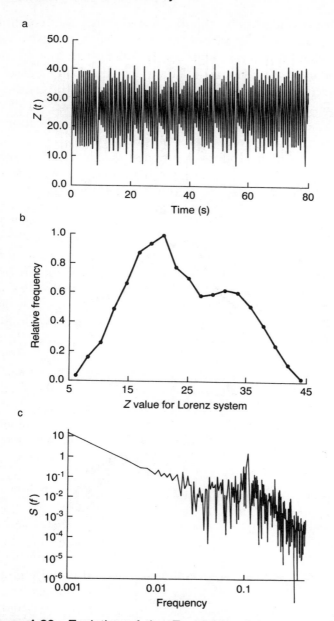

Figure 1.20 Evolution of the *Z* variable of the Lorenz system. (a) Evolution after the first 80 time units; (b) relative distribution function; (c) Fourier power spectrum on a log-log scale.

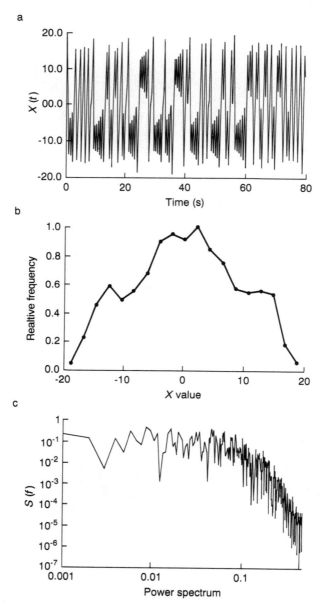

Figure 1.21 Evolution of the *X* variable of the Lorenz system. (a) Evolution after the first 80 time units; (b) relative distribution function; (c) Fourier power spectrum on a log-log scale.

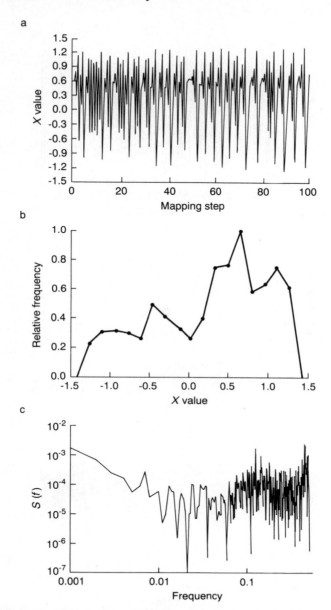

Figure 1.22 Evolution of the X component of the Hénon map. (a) Evolution after the first 200 time units; (b) relative distribution function; (c) Fourier power spectrum on a log-log scale.

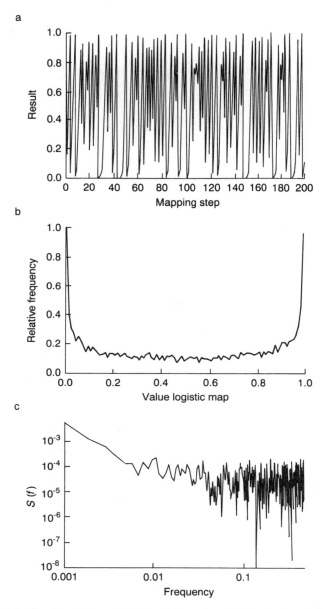

Figure 1.23 Evolution of the logistic map. (a) Evolution after the first 200 time units; (b) relative distribution function; (c) Fourier power spectrum on a log-log scale.

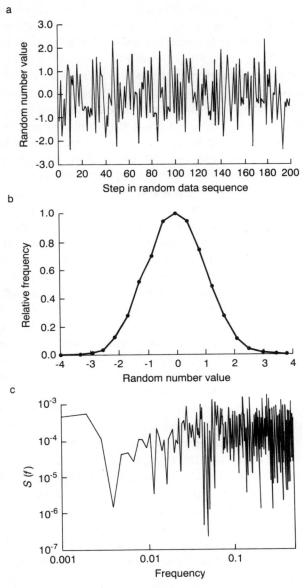

Figure 1.24 Random noise with a Gaussian distribution. (a) 200 random data; (b) relative distribution function; (c) Fourier power spectrum on a log-log scale.

Even when it seems to be straightforward to determine what the value of X will be after 30 steps for the logistic map, estimating this value with any reasonable degree of accuracy will lead to a problem. Digital computers only approximate the numbers, and these approximations are generally different for different computers or for different compilers. This implies that the initial conditions for a map or a differential equation will be approximated as well. Different computers will give a very different answer for the phase space trajectory (read numerical solution) of a chaotic system due to SIC. Only computers with infinite precision could possibly provide the correct answer. It will therefore be nearly impossible to determine within two significant digits what X will be for the logistic map in the chaotic regime after, let's say, 30 mapping projections. In the non-chaotic regime (even when several bifurcations have occurred), achieving this accuracy would pose no problem. However, it is important to note here that, even when all the computer results are incorrect, the overall dynamics and probabilistic properties of the map should be the same on different computers. The distribution function will also remain the same on different computers (in fact the initial conditions could even be very different from each other). It is meaningless to speak of the correct answer for a nonlinear chaotic map or a nonlinear chaotic set of differential equations. For chaotic systems, the correctness of the answer will become "fuzzier" as the number of time steps increases. Sensitivity to the initial conditions leads to a trade-off between the precision of the computer and the time required to carry out the computation: there seems to be a numerical equivalent here to the uncertainty principle in physics.

The implications of sensitivity to the initial conditions are less dramatic than would be expected at first sight, considering that the overall shape of the trajectory and the distribution function do not generally change with a small change in the initial conditions. Sensitivity to initial conditions for a chaotic signal has fascinating implications, however. The most intriguing aspect of SIC is that a chaotic signal, which seems to have ingredients of randomness and irregularity, can be predicted in the short term. SIC implies that if it can be proven that the time evolution of an economic indicator is chaotic, short-term predictions might be possible.

4.4   Strange attractors

The most appealing visual aspect of chaos is the emergence of strange attractors. Points on the trajectory of a strange attractor never repeat themselves. Yet the strange attractor is very different from a mere random distribution of points. The definition of what exactly constitutes a strange attractor is controversial. A strange attractor manifests itself in phase space. Phase space is the space of all possible trajectories of the system. In the case of a map, a phase space trajectory can be obtained by plotting the mapping sequence in phase space. In the case of a coupled set of differential equations we can proceed in a similar way. Strange attractors relate to the long-term dynamic behavior of a system. It is therefore customary to ignore the first few thousand points in a simulation. The Hénon map and the Lorenz butterfly are examples of strange attractors. These intriguing figures occupy only a fraction of the available phase space. One can attribute a fractal (i.e. a non-integer) dimension to this fraction of the phase space. We will define a strange attractor as an intriguing phase space trajectory plot with fractal properties. A strange attractor requires at least two dimensions for the phase space of a map, and three dimensions for the phase space of a set of differential equations. The fractal dimension of a strange attractor can be determined by applying the correlation dimension algorithm.

4.5   Fourier power spectrum for a chaotic signal

Fourier analysis is an established technique to analyze the periodicity characteristics of a signal. The basis of Fourier analysis is the fact that a signal or a function can be approximated by a summation of sine and cosine functions with different amplitudes and with different periods or frequencies. For example, one term in such a sum might be $A \cos(\omega t)$, where A is the amplitude and ω the frequency. Chaos implies a seemingly random highly irregular and aperiodic time series. However, this statement does not yet uniquely define chaos, because *quasiperiodic signals* can also look irregular (figure 1.25). Quasiperiodic signals are signals that are composed of several components with several different frequencies, f_i, for which any two frequencies are incommensurable, or

$$\frac{f_i}{f_j} \neq \frac{m}{n}$$

with m and n integer numbers. These quasiperiodic signals can be distinguished from a chaotic signal by looking at the *power spectrum* of the *Fourier transform* of the signal. The Fourier transform, $x(\omega)$, at a particular frequency ω of a signal $f(t)$, is

$$x(\omega) = \lim_{T \to \infty} \int_0^T dt\, e^{j\omega t} f(t)$$

The $x(\omega)$ will be complex numbers. We will generally deal with the magnitude of these complex numbers, which is the square root of the sum of the squares of the real and the imaginary part. The magnitude of a complex number is therefore a real number that we note as $|x(\omega)|$. The power spectrum is defined as the plot of the magnitude of the Fourier components, $|x(\omega)|$, versus the frequency, ω (usually on a double logarithmic or log–log scale). These definitions for the Fourier transform and the power spectrum are valid for a continuous analytical function $f(t)$, and they can easily be generalized for a discrete time series of datapoints. Caution is required, however, because of the possibility of introducing numerical artefacts when Fourier-transforming a finite discrete time series. An excellent reference describing methods for finding the Fourier transform for discrete data sets can be found in Flannery et al. (1985). Figures 1.20c, 1.21c, 1.22c, 1.23c, and 1.24c show the Fourier power spectrum on a log–log scale for the Z and X variables of the Lorenz system, the Hénon map, the logistic map and Gaussian noise. Figure 1.25 shows the time series, relative distribution function, and power spectrum for the quasiperiodic signal

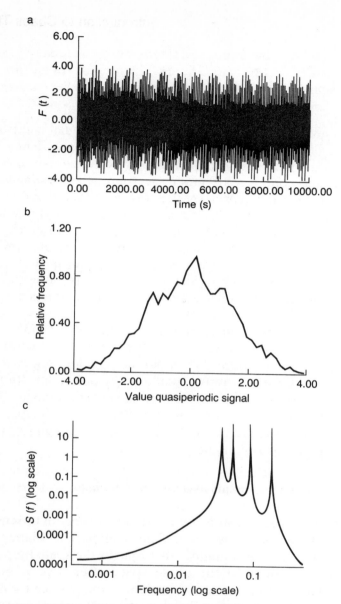

Figure 1.25 Time series (a), relative distribution function (b), and Fourier power spectrum (c) for the quasiperiodic signal

$$f(t) = \cos\left(\frac{2\pi}{18}t\right) + \cos\left(\frac{2\sqrt{11}\pi}{18}t\right) + \cos\left(\frac{2\sqrt{3}\pi}{18}t\right) + \cos\left(\frac{2\sqrt{2}\pi}{18}t\right)$$

$$f(t) = \cos\left(\frac{2\pi}{18}t\right) + \cos\left(\frac{2\sqrt{11}\pi}{18}t\right) + \cos\left(\frac{2\sqrt{3}\pi}{18}t\right)$$
$$+ \cos\left(\frac{\sqrt{2}\pi}{18}t\right)$$

The power spectrum for the quasiperiodic signal consists here of four discrete peaks, whereas the chaotic signal has a broad continuous spectrum of frequencies. We characterize such an irregular and continuous Fourier spectrum as a *broadband spectrum*. The Fourier power spectrum of a chaotic signal can also show peaks (e.g. the Z component of the Lorenz system in figure 1.20c). Such a peak indicates a trace of periodicity in an otherwise irregular chaotic signal. The initially straight downward trend of the power spectrum on a log–log plot is characteristic for a fractal (i.e. possibly chaotic) signal. Gaussian noise has all frequencies equally represented and has a more or less horizontal power spectrum (figure 1.24).

Looking at the Fourier power spectrum of a chaotic signal, chaos implies the presence of a broadband, i.e. continuous, Fourier power spectrum. When plotted on a log–log scale there will be a straight downward trend for the power spectrum. It is possible to estimate the fractal dimension of the strange attractor from the slope of the straight line (Peitgen and Saupe, 1988). This initial downward trend also allows us to distinguish a chaotic signal from a quasiperiodic time series.

4.6   Liapunov exponents as a measure of chaos

The *Liapunov exponent* is a measure of the degree of sensitivity to the initial conditions for a chaotic map. The Liapunov exponent for a map is a number that reflects the spatial separation of adjacent points in the phase space after several mapping steps. The concept of the Liapunov exponent can easily be introduced by considering the chaotic logistic map:

$$X_{t+1} = 4X_t(1 - X_t)$$

which leads to a chaotic time series in a one-dimensional phase space. Two points X_0 and $(X_0 + \varepsilon)$, that were initially close to each other, will not be close in the phase space after N repeated mapping steps (figure 1.4d). N repeated applications of a map starting from X_0 will be noted as $f^{(N)}(X_0)$, where the superscript (N) stands for the number of mapping steps.

The Liapunov exponent, $\lambda(X_0)$, is defined as

$$|f^{(N)}(X_0) - f^{(N)}(X_0 + \varepsilon)| = \varepsilon e^{N\lambda(X_0)}$$

in the limit for N approaching infinity and ε approaching zero. The Liapunov exponent is generally independent of the choice for X_0.

The Liapunov exponent, according to this definition, is just a measure for the average exponential separation of two adjacent points which become separated under the action of a map: two points with separation ε will (on average) after one mapping projection be separated by that same ε multiplied by the exponent of the Liapunov exponent. In other words: $e^{\lambda(X_0)}$ is the average factor by which the distance between adjacent points becomes stretched after one iteration (figure 1.26).

The Liapunov exponent for a map can be made explicit (from the definition above) as:

$$\lambda(X_0) = \lim_{N\to\infty} \lim_{\varepsilon\to 0} \frac{1}{N} \log\left|\frac{f^{(N)}(X_0) - f^{(N)}(X_0 + \varepsilon)}{\varepsilon}\right|$$

or

$$\lambda(X_0) = \lim_{N\to\infty} \frac{1}{N} \log\left|\frac{\mathrm{d}f^{(N)}(X_0)}{\mathrm{d}X_0}\right|$$

It can also be shown that the Liapunov exponent measures the average loss of information after one iteration (Schuster, 1989). In order to do so one has to rearrange the expression for the Liapunov exponent as

$$\lambda(X_0) = \lim_{N\to\infty} \frac{1}{N} \sum_{i=0}^{N-1} \log|f'(X_i)|$$

where $f'(X_i)$ represents $\left.\dfrac{\mathrm{d}f}{\mathrm{d}X}\right|_{X=X_i}$

The Liapunov exponent versus the bifurcation parameter for the logistic map is shown in figure 1.29. Note that the Liapunov

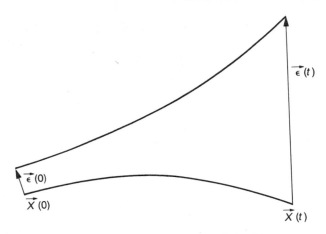

Figure 1.26   Illustration for the definition of the Liapunov exponent.

exponent is negative for the periodic regime, zero at the bifurcation points, and positive in the chaotic regime.

A two-dimensional mapping will have two different Liapunov exponents. We will now make some arguments that chaos for a 2-D map implies that one of the two Liapunov exponents is positive, while the other is negative, and the sum of the Liapunov exponents is negative. Figure 1.27 illustrates the concept of the Liapunov exponent for the Hénon map. Sensitivity to initial conditions implies that at least one Liapunov exponent is positive. The shrinking area of the small circle illustrated in figure 1.27 is proportional to $\lambda_1 + \lambda_2$. If the sum of the Liapunov exponents was positive, the area of the ellipse of figure 1.27 would grow after each mapping step, and ultimately the entire phase space would be filled. This would not lead to a fractal. In order to have sensitivity to initial conditions, and a fractal filling of the phase space, it is therefore necessary that one of the Liapunov exponents is positive, and that the sum of the Liapunov exponents is negative. The positive Liapunov exponent will cause a stretching of the attractor in the corresponding direction of phase space, while the negative Liapunov exponent (with $|\lambda_{neg}| > |\lambda_{pos}|$) indicates a general contraction in phase space, which can only be achieved by a folding. This repeated stretching and

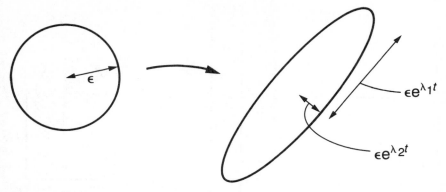

Figure 1.27 Liapunov exponents for the Hénon map.

folding operation is illustrated for the *Smale horseshoe attractor* in figure 1.28.

The definition of the Liapunov exponent for a one-dimensional map, $\vec{X}^{(n+1)} = \vec{G}(\vec{X}^{(n)})$, can be expressed as

$$e^\lambda = \lim_{N \to \infty} \left(\prod_{n=0}^{N-1} \left| \frac{dG}{dX_n} \right| \right)^{1/N}$$

and can generalized to m dimensions leading to m separate Liapunov exponents given by

$$\{e_1^\lambda, e_2^\lambda, \ldots e_n^\lambda\} = \lim_{N \to \infty} \left\{ \text{eigenvalues of } \prod_{n=0}^{N-1} J(\vec{X}_n)^{1/N} \right\}$$

where $J(\vec{X}_n)$ is a matrix consisting of elements J_{ij}, with $J_{ij} = dG_i/dX_j$, or

$$J(\vec{X}) = \left[\frac{\partial G_i}{\partial X_j} \right]$$

represents the *Jacobian* matrix of the map

$$\vec{X}^{(n+1)} = \vec{G}(\vec{X}^{(n)})$$

So far only Liapunov exponents for "discrete" maps have been discussed. The concept of a Liapunov exponent can also be introduced for a "continuous" differential equation and a set of

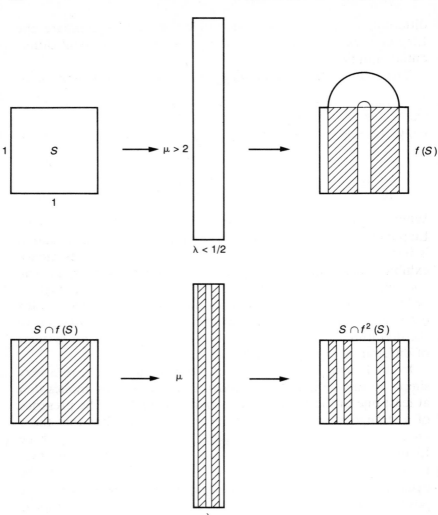

Figure 1.28   Smale horseshoe attractor, illustrating repeated stretching and folding in a strange attractor map.

differential equations. In order to do so, let us compare the Liapunov exponent for a simple map with its equivalent differential equation:

The solution for a simple map, $X_{t+i} = aX_t$, can be written as

$$X_{t+1} = aX_t \rightarrow X_t = e^{T \log a} X_0$$

while the corresponding differential equation, $dX/dt = aX$, leads to:

$$\frac{dX}{dt} = aX \rightarrow X(t) = e^{at}X(0)$$

Whereas the Liapunov exponent for the map is log (a), the Liapunov exponent for the corresponding differential equation is just a. Of course these linear one-dimensional systems cannot exhibit chaos, because the folding component is missing. The concept of Liapunov exponents can easily be expanded to higher-order systems of differential equations. Because our models for exchange rates will involve maps only, the reader is referred to the literature for a discussion of Liapunov exponents for systems of differential equations (Schuster, 1989).

In the language of Liapunov exponents one could give a very simple formal definition for a chaotic system. Chaos implies that at least one of the Liapunov exponents is positive. The presence of a strange attractor in a nonlinear system requires that there are at least two Liapunov exponents for a map and at least three Liapunov exponents for a set of differential equations. In order to have chaos, the sum of the Liapunov exponents has to be negative, and at least one of the Liapunov exponents has to be positive. Several mathematical formulations exist that propose relationships between the Liapunov exponents and the fractal dimension of the attractor. The Kaplan–Yorke conjecture gives the following relationship between the Hausdorff dimension of a strange attractor and the Liapunov exponents (Kaplan and Yorke, 1979).

$$D = j + \frac{\sum_{i=1}^{j} \lambda_i}{|\lambda_{j+1}|}$$

where D is the Hausdorff dimension, and j is the largest integer for which $\Sigma_{i=1}^{j} \lambda_i > 0$, assuming that the Liapunov exponents are ordered according to $\lambda_1 > \lambda_2 > \ldots \lambda_j$. To obtain the strange attractor for a coupled set of nonlinear differential equations would furthermore require that one of the Liapunov exponents was exactly equal to zero. In that case the strange attractor would show up at the crossings of the trajectories with a hyper-plane, which would be just that subset of the phase space for which the zero Liapunov exponent had been eliminated.

The concept the Liapunov exponent allows us to estimate the time over which the outcome of a chaotic system can be pre-dicted. This can be illustrated by considering the logistic map. After N mapping projections an initial small interval δ has been increased to Δ, according to

$$\Delta = \delta e^{\lambda N}$$

Obviously predictions for $\Delta > 1$, are impossible, because the mapping would have folded on itself (in order to remain between 0 and 1). The maximum number of mapping projections for which a prediction would be possible can be estimated by setting Δ equal to unity leading to

$$1 = \delta e^{\lambda N}$$

so that

$$N = \frac{1}{\lambda} \log \frac{1}{\delta}$$

In the above formula δ can be interpreted as the precision with which the initial state is located. It has been shown (Schuster, 1989) that for higher dimensional maps the Liapunov exponent has to be replaced by the *Kolmogorov* or *K entropy* to estimate *prediction times*, leading to

$$N = \frac{1}{K} \log \frac{1}{\delta}$$

where K is the Kolmogorov entropy. For one-dimensional systems the K entropy is equal to the Liapunov exponent. The concept for estimating a prediction time could be generalized to chaotic systems resulting from a set of nonlinear differential equations. One would now have that the time, T, for which the outcome of a chaotic system can be predicted, is

$$T = \frac{1}{K} \log \frac{1}{\delta}$$

The reader is referred to the literature for methods of estimating the K entropy (Farmer and Sidorowich, 1988).

Figure 1.29 shows the Liapunov exponent for the logistic map as a function of the bifurcation parameter of the logistic map. This Liapunov exponent was calculated directly from the following expression:

$$\lambda = \lim_{N \to \infty} \frac{1}{N} \sum_{i=0}^{N-1} \log |f'(X_i)|$$

where

$$f'(X_i) = a \left| 1 - 2X_i \right|$$

Note that in order to avoid an ambivalent notation, the free parameter for the logistic map is represented by a in the above expression. Note in figure 1.29 that the Liapunov exponent is positive in the chaotic regions, and exactly equal to zero at the bifurcations.

4.7 Ergodicity

One of the more difficult concepts relating to chaos is the *ergodic* property of a chaotic system. Ergodicity refers to the property of a chaotic system in which the averages computed from a data sample over time converge, in a probabilistic sense, to spatial ensemble averages. It is just this property of ergodicity that causes chaotic systems, which give very different responses in time for different initial conditions, to converge to a statistically similar strange attractor in phase space. This concept is illustrated for the Lorenz attractor in figure 1.2 and for the Hénon attractor in figure 1.8. The time invariant distribution functions in figures 1.20 to 1.23 are also a consequence of this ergodic property.

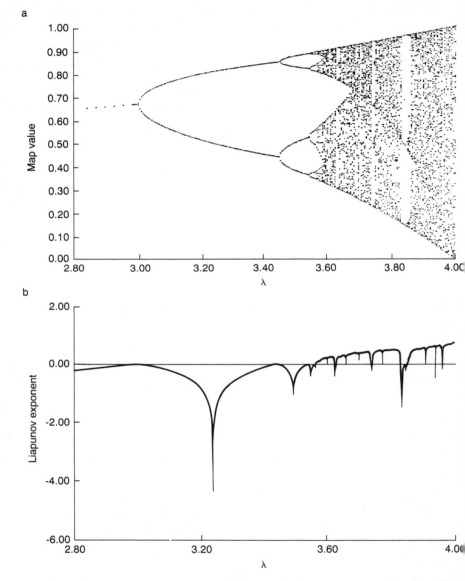

Figure 1.29 Liapunov exponent for the logistic map as a function of the bifurcation parameter (λ). (a) Feigenbaum bifurcation diagram (2.80 $< \lambda <$ 4); (b) Liapunov exponent versus λ (2.80 $< \lambda <$ 4).

NOTES

1 Note that this is not the case in a system of *coupled* differential equations (e.g. the Lorenz system) where one needs at least three differential equations to obtain a strange attractor.
2 The more precise definition is: "A fractal is a set for which the Hausdorff Besicovitch dimension strictly exceeds the topological dimension."

2

Exchange Rate Theories

1 INTRODUCTION

In this chapter a brief overview is given of the exchange rate theories that have become popular and that aim to explain the large fluctuations in the foreign exchange market. We will analyze the question of whether these theories are satisfactory as instruments for understanding the basic features of the workings of the foreign exchange market. The purpose of the present chapter is not to provide a complete survey of all existing theories. The reader who is interested in a more exhaustive analysis of exchange rate theories should consult Baillie and MacMahon (1989), McDonald (1989), and Mussa (1991).

2 THE "NEWS" MODEL

The exchange rate theories developed during the 1970s and 1980s have been based on two important new insights. The first is that the exchange market can best be modelled as an asset market (like the stock market, for example). This means that the exchange rate must be seen as a price that equilibrates the demand and supply of *stocks* of domestic and foreign currencies. This insight was new because before the 1970s the exchange rate was typically modelled as a price that equilibrates the *flow* demand and supply of foreign currency.

A second new insight came from the rational expectations theory. This says that agents who have to forecast the future price will take all relevant information into account, including the information embodied in the model that the economist is using.

The simplest possible way to illustrate how these new insights were incorporated in exchange rate models is provided by the following model (which was first presented by Mussa, 1979). This model has also been called the "news" model for reasons that will be clear shortly.

Let us start from the basic equation determining the exchange rate

$$S_t = X_t E_t(S_{t+1})^b \tag{1}$$

where S_t is the exchange rate in period t (i.e. the price of the foreign currency in units of the domestic currency) and X_t can be thought of as a reduced form equation describing the structure of the model and the exogenous variables that drive the exchange rate in period t. $E_t(S_{t+1})$ is the expectations held today (period t) in the market about next period's $(t + 1)$ exchange rate; b is the discount factor that speculators use to discount the future expected exchange rate $(0 < b < 1)$.

Alternatively, one could express this equation in log form as follows:

$$s_t = x_t + bE_t(s_{t+1}) \tag{2}$$

where lower case letters are used to express logarithms. The reader should be aware that these two forms are equivalent. In this chapter we will use the logarithmic form.

The asset market view of the exchange rate can be seen in the discount factor b. Currencies are assets, like stocks or houses, etc. The current price of these assets depends on the expected price in the future. This is in the nature of assets that do not deplete: since the asset will still exist in the future, and therefore will have a price in the future, this price must affect today's price. The parameter b also measures the speed with which the asset depletes. The faster an asset depletes, the smaller is b. In other words, when the asset depletes quickly, the future price will have a smaller effect on the current price.

The rational expectations assumption has the following implication. If expectations are rational they must be consistent with the model as specified in equation (2), and this must be the case for all periods. Therefore, when agents forecast the exchange rate for period $t + k$ they must do so according to the following rule:

$$E_t(s_{t+k}) = E_t(x_{t+k}) + bE_t(s_{t+k+1}) \tag{3}$$

where it is understood that the information used by the speculators is information available in period t.

It can now be seen that equation (3) is a difference equation of the first order with characteristic root equal to $1/b$. Since $b < 1$, this characteristic root is larger than one, implying that the solution will be explosive.

The solution can be written in the following form:

$$E_t(s_{t+k}) = \sum_{j=0}^{\infty} b^j E_t(x_{t+k+j}) + C_t(1/b)^k \tag{4}$$

where C_t is an arbitrary constant satisfying:

$$C_t = (1/b)C_{t-1} \tag{4'}$$

Solution (4) consists of two parts. The first part is obtained by solving equation (3) forward. The procedure is as follows: $E_t(s_{t+k+1})$ can be written as

$$E_t(s_{t+k+1}) = E_t(x_{t+k+1}) + bE_t(s_{t+k+2}) \tag{5}$$

This expression is substituted back into equation (3). We now have an expression in which $E_t(s_{t+k+2})$ appears. This can be expressed in a similar way as in (5) and substituted into (3). If we do this *ad infinitum*, we obtain that

$$E_t(s_{t+k}) = \sum_{j=0}^{\infty} b^j E_t(x_{t+k+j}) \tag{6}$$

Thus the expectation held in period t about the exchange rate in period $t + k$ is equal to the expected future path of the exogenous variable x_t driving the exchange rate. This future path is discounted at rate b.

The second part of the solution, as represented in equation (4), is the solution to the homogeneous part of the difference equation (2). It can be seen that this is explosive, i.e. since $1/b > 1$ the exchange rate moves to plus or minus infinity depending on the value of C_t. This has been called the rational speculative bubble, which is implicit in all rational expectations models.

It has been customary in the rational expectations literature to set $C_t = 0$ so that the explosive speculative bubble disappears from the solution. This procedure, however, is highly problematic. We will return to this problem in section 5, where we criticize the rational expectation assumption.

This difficulty has not prevented economists from closing their eyes and proceeding further with these models. In the context of the exchange rate model, this has led them to eliminate the bubble component of the solution. This then yields the following solution for s_t:

$$s_t = \sum_{j=0}^{\infty} b^j E_t(x_{t+j}) \tag{7}$$

This solution implies that the exchange rate today is equal to the present value of the whole expected future path of the exogenous variables x_t (also called fundamental variables), driving the exchange rate.

This model now has an important implication. It allows us to decompose the change in the exchange rate from period t to period $t + 1$ into two components, an expected and an unexpected change. The expected change results from an expectation that the fundamentals will change from t to $t + 1$. The unexpected change in the exchange rate results from changes in the fundamentals that come as a surprise. This is called the "news" component. To the extent that the changes in the fundamentals are difficult to predict and that the largest part of these changes is news, the exchange rate will also be driven mainly by the news component.

3   STRUCTURAL MODELS

A whole class of models has gone a step further than the model discussed in the previous section by specifying explicitly the economic structure underlying X_t. We consider three such structural models here.

3.1   Monetary models with flexible prices

The monetary model of the exchange rate was developed by Mussa (1976, 1979), Frenkel (1976), and Bilson (1978a, b, 1979). The flexible price monetary model can be represented by three equations:

- The money market equilibrium condition

$$ms_t = p_t + \alpha_1 y_t - \alpha_2 r_t \tag{8}$$

  where ms_t is the log of the supply of money, p_t is the log of the price level, y_t is the log of the output level and r_t is the log of 1 plus the nominal interest rate. The right hand side represents the demand for money.
- The open interest parity condition

$$r_t - r_{ft} = E_t s_{t+1} - s_t \tag{9}$$

  where r_{ft} is the log of 1 plus the foreign interest rate. This equation says that when the exchange rate is expected to increase in the future ($E_t s_{t+1} > s_t$) the domestic interest rate must be higher than the foreign interest rate in order to compensate holders of domestic assets for the expected future capital loss.
- Purchasing power parity (PPP)

$$s_t = p_t - p_{ft} \tag{10}$$

  where p_t and p_{ft} are the logs of the domestic and foreign price levels. This PPP equation can be interpreted as the equilibrium condition in the goods market. It is assumed in this model that prices are perfectly flexible so that there can be no deviation from purchasing power parity.

Substituting r_t from (9) into (8) and (8) into (10) yields

$$s_t = \frac{1}{1 + \alpha_2} [ms_t - \alpha_1 y_t + \alpha_2 E_t(s_{t+1}) + \alpha_2 r_{ft} - p_{ft}] \tag{11}$$

This solution corresponds to equation (2), where X_t is set equal to $1/(1 + \alpha_2)[ms_t - \alpha_1 y_t + \alpha_2 r_{ft} - p_{ft}]$. The solution of this model is thus equivalent to the solution of (2), i.e.

$$s_t = \sum_{i=0}^{\infty} \left[\left(\frac{\alpha_2}{1 + \alpha_2} \right)^i E_t[ms_{t+i} - ms_{ft+i} - \alpha_1(y_{t+i} - y_{ft+i})] \right] \quad (12)$$

where we have added a money market equation for the foreign country equivalent to (8). Note that we have excluded the possibility of a bubble solution. This model then says that the exchange rate today is the discounted value of future expected money stocks and output levels in the home and foreign countries.

3.2 Monetary model with sticky prices

The most celebrated monetary model is the Dornbusch model (Dornbusch, 1976a,b), which has become the classroom model *par excellence*. The difference between this model and the flexible price monetary model is basically the modelling of short run price behavior. While prices adjust immediately in the monetary model, they only adjust with some lag in the Dornbusch model. The purchasing power parity condition in (10) is replaced by a long-run PPP and a price dynamics equation (10b). The price dynamics equation is determined by the excess demand in the goods market (10a):

$$ED = Z_1[s_t + p_{ft} - p_t] \quad (10a)$$

where ED represents the excess demand function. This equation states that when the exchange rate exceeds its PPP value ($s_t > p_{ft} - p_t$) there will be excess demand for the domestic goods (and vice versa). This is so because when $s_t > p_{ft} - p_t$ domestic goods are cheap expressed in foreign currency, thereby increasing foreign demand.

$$p_t - p_{t-1} = \partial(ED) \quad (10b)$$

Equation (10b) says that with excess demand domestic prices increase (and vice versa).

Although the solution of this model was originally presented in a perfect foresight framework we will present the general rational expectations solution of Wickens (1984). We restrict ourselves to the final solution. The interested reader is referred to Wickens (1984) for the actual model and Pesaran (1988) and Minford and Peel (1983) for an overview of the methodology. The solution is again a variant of (2).

$$s_t = \theta_1 s_{t-1} + (\theta_2 \alpha_2)^{-1} \sum_{j=0}^{\infty} \theta_2^{-1} \underset{t-1}{E} x_{t+j} + \varepsilon_t \tag{13}$$

$$\theta_1 < 1 \quad \theta_2 > 1$$

$$x_{t+1} = [(ms_t - ms_{ft}) - \alpha_1(y_t - y_{ft})]$$
$$\quad - c_1[(ms_{t-1} - ms_{ft-1}) - \alpha_1(y_{t-1} - y_{ft-1})]$$

$$c_1 = \frac{1}{(1 + dZ_1)}$$

The exchange rate today depends on the expected future money stocks and output levels. However, the current exchange rate also depends on the past exchange rate. This is due to the assumption of price stickiness, which introduces inertia into the system. We will use this framework in later chapters when we construct the chaotic exchange rate models.

The Dornbusch model has been extended by many authors, in particular by Frankel (1979). This extension consists of allowing inflation to occur in the long run, and highlighting the importance of the real interest rate in the determination of the real exchange rate. In this extension, therefore, an increase in the *real* interest rate leads to a *real* appreciation of the domestic currency, and vice versa.

3.3 Portfolio balance model

Another approach, but still in the same framework, is used in the portfolio balance models developed by McKinnon and Oates (1966), Branson (1969, 1975, 1977), Allen and Kenen (1978), Isard (1980), and Dornbusch and Fischer (1980).

Portfolio balance models typically assume identical portfolio preferences for both home and foreign investors. These investors determine their relative positions between home and foreign investments on the relative return after taking consideration of the risk involved. This leads to another open interest parity condition:

$$(r_t - r_{ft}) = ES_{t+1} - S_t + RP(B_t/B_{ft}S_t) \tag{14}$$

$RP(\ )$ denotes the risk premium. B_t is the value of bonds outstanding at home; B_f is the (foreign currency) value of foreign bonds, so that $B_{ft}S_t$ is the (domestic currency) value of these bonds. In general one assumes that as the value of outstanding domestic bonds increases relative to foreign bonds, wealth owners demand an additional return (risk premium) on their domestic bond holdings. This means that RP increases.

If we replace (9) by (14), we obtain another variant of equations (11) and (12). More specifically, the only difference is that the wealth variables will enter in X_{t+i} as well.

4 EMPIRICAL TESTING OF EXCHANGE RATE MODELS

We have reviewed the different approaches to modelling the underlying structure of exchange rate fundamentals. In this section we present some estimation results for the different models.

The first generation tests of the exchange rate models consisted of specifying econometric equations that explain the exchange rate by the fundamental variables, as identified in the theoretical models. The most commonly used econometric specification (based on the Frankel (1979) extension of the Dornbusch model) is as follows:

$$S_t = \alpha_1(ms_t - ms_{ft}) + \alpha_2(y_t - y_{ft}) + \alpha_3(\pi_t - \pi_{ft})$$
$$+ \alpha_4[(r_t - \pi_t) - (r_{ft} - \pi_{ft})] \tag{15}$$

where π_t and π_{ft} are the expected rates of inflation in the domestic and foreign countries, and $(r_t - \pi_t)$ and $(r_{ft} - \pi_{ft})$ are the real interest rates in the domestic and foreign countries.

The different models can be separated by looking at the coefficients: if $\alpha_3 > 0$ and $\alpha_4 = 0$ we obtain the monetary model. For $\alpha_3 = 0$ and $\alpha_4 < 0$ we obtain the sticky price models and finally if $\alpha_3 > 0$ and $\alpha_4 < 0$ we obtain Frankel's model.

Table 2.1 presents estimation results taken from Baillie and Selover (1987). The results are very unsupportive of any of these structural models. In fact, generally speaking, the only significant coefficient is the autoregressive coefficient. This result is consistent with those of Driksell and Sheffrin (1981), Haynes and Stone (1981), and Frankel (1984). It must be stressed, however, that all three models find some support when applied to the early 1970s and the 1920s. The breakdown of these structural

Table 2.1 Estimation results of equation (15), sample 1973–1983

	c	α_1	α_2	α_3	α_4	R^2	ρ
£/$	0.2067	0.1618	−0.2278	−0.0002	0.0003	0.2	0.89
	(0.58)	(1.3)	(1.72)	(0.1)	(0.054)		
¥/$	−6.0163	−0.097	0.13	−0.004	0.006	0.92	0.97
	(15.12)	(1.25)	(0.63)	(1.7)	(0.8)		
DM/$	−0.9294	0.059	−0.098	−0.002	−0.0094	0.23	0.98
	(7.56)	(0.63)	(0.61)	(1.34)	(1.16)		
AM$/$	−0.1883	0.034	0.1	−0.004	0.007	0.05	0.98
	(1.34)	(0.75)	(1.27)	(2.2)	(2.3)		
FF/$	−1.7967	−0.10	−0.07	−0.0007	−0.002	0.14	0.99
	(7.03)	(1.05)	(0.56)	(0.28)	(0.33)		

Absolute T values in parentheses.
Source: Baillie and Selover (1987)

models is situated in the late 1970s. Supportive evidence for the model can be found in Bilson (1978a, b), Putnam and Woodbury (1979), Frankel (1979), and Bachus (1984).

As we indicated above, the portfolio balance models are very similar to the monetary models. The difference between the two types of models is that a risk premium enters in the latter. However, the ways in which authors insert the risk premium are very different. Some authors bring it in through a constant, others employ different definitions of wealth. We present estimation results of Hooper and Morton (1982), Hacche and Towned (1983), and Frankel (1984).

The reduced form equation estimated by these authors can be written as

$$S_t = \alpha_1(ms_t - ms_{ft}) + \alpha_2(y_t - y_{ft}) + \alpha_3(\pi_t - \pi_{ft})$$
$$+ \alpha_4[(r_t - \pi_t) - (r_{ft} - \pi_{ft})] + RP(w, w_f) \qquad (16)$$

Table 2.2 presents some estimations of the portfolio balance models as specified in (16). The results of Morton and Hooper appear to be the best. These authors assume that the risk premium is a function of accumulated current account surpluses (deficits). All variables have correctly signed coefficients and

Table 2.2 Estimation result for reduced form equation of the portfolio model

	A	B	C	D
α_1	0.77	0.032	0.15	−0.03
	(2.56)	(0.84)	(1.5)	(0.6)
α_2	−1.84	−0.114	0.06	0.03
	(2.72)	(1.01)	(1.2)	(0.75)
α_3	2.41	−0.005	−0.24	0.000
	(0.98)	(1.66)	(1.00)	
α_4	−0.15	−0.009	0.05	0.03
	(0.27)	(1.8)	(0.63)	
Current account	−1.69	0.033	−	
	(3.9)	(0.47)		
Premium	0.97	−0.095	−	
	(0.82)	(4.32)		
B/w	−	−	−0.06	−3.44
			(0.14)	(10.75)
wG/w	−	−	−2.21	2.26
			(6.9)	(5.14)
wUs/w	−	−	1.13	1.67
			(7.06)	(11.93)
c	4.5	3.73	−0.05	−2.07
	(131.9)	(28.78)	(0.22)	(8.63)
R^2	0.78	0.97	n.a.	n.a.
ρ	n.a.	0.78	0.98	1.0

A: Hooper and Morton (1982), effective dollar quarterly 1973–8.
B: Haecke and Towned (1983), effective sterling monthly 1977–81.
C: Frankel (1984), DM/$ monthly 1974–81.
D: Frankel (1984), £/$ monthly 1974–81.
B/w: ratio of US bonds to total wealth.
wG/w: ratio of German wealth to total wealth.
wUS/w: ratio of US wealth to total wealth.
Source: McDonald (1989)

moreover the risk premium is significant. Hacche and Towned estimated the same model for the effective pound exchange rate. Their results, as well as the results of Frankel, are very disappointing for the model as a whole.[1] In the latter case,

Table 2.3 Results of the out-of-sample forecasting performance, forecasting periods of 1, 6, and 12 months for period 1973–1981

	RW	FPM	SPM	PB	F_t
$/DM 1 month	3.72	3.17	3.65	3.50	3.2
6 months	8.71	9.64	12.03	9.95	9.03
12 months	12.98	16.12	18.87	15.69	12.6
$/¥ 1 month	3.68	4.11	4.4	4.2	3.72
6 months	11.58	13.38	13.94	11.94	11.93
12 months	18.31	18.55	20.41	19.20	18.95
$/£ 1 month	2.56	2.82	2.90	3.03	2.67
6 months	6.45	8.90	8.88	9.08	7.23
12 months	9.91	14.62	13.66	14.57	11.62

Note: The structural models are estimated with an AR(1) correction. RW is the random walk model, FPM is the flexible price monetary model, SPM is the sticky price monetary model, PB is the portfolio balance model and F_t is the forward rate. Performance is tested by the root mean squared error.
Source: Meese and Rogoff (1983)

however, the risk premium itself has some support. The very strong autocorrelation in B, C, and D is also remarkable.

The second generation empirical tests of the exchange rate models are based on the out-of-sample forecasting performance of these models. In a series of papers Meese and Rogoff (1983, 1984) have employed this methodology. The forecasting performance of the different models was compared to that of the very naive forecasting rule implied by the random walk model. Table 2.3 presents the results for the $/DM, $/¥, and $/£ rates. The methodology used is that of revolving regressions, i.e. the expectations of the future exogenous variables are replaced by their effective realizations. The general conclusion from these tests is that the performance of the structural models is not better than the performance of the random walk model (see table 2.3).

Meese and Rogoff (1984) repeated their experiment, this time controlling for possible biasedness of coefficients by imposing constraints on the coefficients of the model. Although the performance of the structural models improves for forecasting one year ahead or more, there is no improvement for the forecast performance at higher frequencies. The obvious conclusion is that structural exchange rate models do not work well as predictive instruments. What is striking in these results of Meese and Rogoff is that the forecasts with structural models use much more information than the random walk forecasts. In the former case it is assumed that the forecaster knows the future value of the exogenous variables. This information, however, does not help him at all.

These devastating results induced researchers to look at the problem from another point of view. The focus shifted away from the structural models, in which one tries to explain the exchange rate, to models in which this ambition is abandoned. This led resarchers to concentrate exclusively on the time series properties of the exchange rate.

In this connection there has been an enormous amount of research on the issue of whether or not the exchange rate follows a random walk. The random walk can be represented by equation (17)

$$s_t = s_{t-1} + \eta_t, \quad E\eta_t = 0 \tag{17}$$

where η_t is independently and identically distributed (i.i.d.) with $E\eta_t = 0$ and constant variance.

The consensus now is that the random walk model is rejected in favor of the martingale model. The martingale model can also be represented by (17) but is less stringent on the innovation η_t than the random walk model. In the martingale model one only imposes the restriction that all odd moments of η_t are zero. This means, for example, that the variance of η_t need not be constant.

Empirical tests of the random walk model have been performed by specifying an equation like

$$s_t = c + \alpha s_{t-1} + u_t \tag{18}$$

In general, one cannot reject the hypothesis that $\alpha = 1$ (there is a "unit root"). However, one also finds that u_t is not white noise. Baillee and Bollorslev (1989), for example, conclude that "all exchange rate series are well approximated by a martingale difference equation, but with time dependent heteroskedasticity."[2]

These results have been obtained by many other researchers for various frequencies (see, for example, Meese and Singleton, 1982; Baillie and McMahon, 1989; Corbae and Ouliaris, 1986). These results imply that the random walk model should be rejected. However, the exchange rate data exhibit unit roots.

From this survey of the empirical literature we conclude that the existing structural models of the exchange rate are rejected by the data. The problem with exchange rate models, however, runs deeper. Recent criticism has also been levied at the rational expectation assumption underlying these models. To this criticism we now turn our attention.

5 DIFFICULTIES WITH THE RATIONAL EXPECTATIONS NEWS MODEL

The rational expectations news model faces several difficulties. We discuss two of these difficulties. A first problem has to do with the existence of speculative bubbles in the rational expectations model. As indicated earlier, the rational expectations models produce an infinite number of explosive paths (speculative bubbles). It is customary in the rational expectations literature to ignore these bubbles (technically $C_t = 0$ in (4)). This procedure is highly problematic. It is not clear why speculators will set $C_t = 0$. One rationalization has been that since all (observed) bubbles explode at some time, rational agents, with perfect foresight, will be able to forecast the exact timing of this future explosion. Since this would allow them to make infinite profits by taking the right speculative position just prior to the explosion of the bubble, all speculators would do this, thereby bringing the time of the burst in the bubble closer to today. Repeating this reasoning, one arrives at the conclusion that the bubble cannot start.

This rationalization is unsatisfactory because it brings into the model an idea that is external to the functioning of the model, i.e. that every bubble must burst. The solution of the model as represented in equation (4), however, does not contain a mechanism leading to a burst in the bubble. In fact, the model predicts that the bubble must go on forever. It follows that the argument that rational agents will not allow the bubble to materialize (i.e. they set $C_t = 0$) because they observe that in reality each bubble bursts, implies that these agents use information not consistent with the underlying model. The latter predicts everlasting bubbles.

This problem is a very general one and appears in all rational expectations models. In all these models there is an infinity of possible solutions, most of which are unstable. The need then arises to select one particular solution. This selection will necessarily be based on information not contained in the model. Thus, even in rational expectations models, *ad hoc* assumptions will be necessary. Fully consistent expectations appear to be impossible. In a sense it can be said that rational expectations models introduce *ad hoc* assumptions at a higher level of abstraction than non-rational expectations models. Put differently, the rational expectations approach can be considered as an attempt to develop models that are informationally self-contained. This attempt has not succeeded. At some point information from outside the model must be introduced.[3] *Ad hoc* assumptions cannot be avoided.

A second problem with the rational expectations news model relates to its empirical verification. Recent empirical tests have revealed several anomalies within the model. These anomalies have shown up in three sorts of studies.

First, Goodhart (1989) has looked at the effect of news on the exchange rates (i.e. the DM/$, £/$ and ¥/$ rates). His basic finding is that most exchange rate movements appear to occur in the absence of observable news. In other words, there seems to be an inherent exchange rate dynamics which is unrelated to the occurrence of news.

Second, the asset market approach together with the rational expectation assumption imply that there is a long-run equilibrium relationship between the exchange rate and its fundamentals. One way to test for the existence of such an equilibrium relationship is the cointegration test (see Engle and Granger, 1987). The results of the cointegration tests between the exchange rate and its fundamental performed by Baillie and Selover (1987), Adler and Lehman (1983), and Boothe and Glassman (1987) all reject the null hypothesis of a long-run equilibrium relationship between monetary fundamentals and the exchange rate.

Cutler et al. (1989a, b) report significant positive autocorrelation at short horizons (a month) but negative and significant serial autocorrelation at lower frequencies. Although we cannot definitely exclude rationality (Levich, 1979) they (and many others) interpret this as evidence of feedback trading at short horizons. At longer horizons, however, fundamentalists take over the market (i.e. there are negative correlations). This pattern, moreover, is found in other asset prices as well (stock, gold, and silver prices).

Finally there has been a lot of research on the expectation formation of active agents. Most of the literature is based on survey evidence (although some laboratory experiments have been done). Basically the result of these studies (Allen and Taylor, 1989; Frankel and Froot, 1988; Takagi, 1991) is that expectations are not rational. Expectations over short horizons tend to incorporate bandwagon effects, while at long horizons they display regressive properties. Moreover, Froot and Ito (1989) show that expectations are not consistent. Consistency implies that the forward iteration of expectations over short horizons corresponds to the observed long-run expectation. The consistency of expectations is a necessarily condition for rational expectations. The violation of this requirement necessarily implies the violation of rational expectations.

To conclude, a lot of evidence is accumulating against the rational expectations paradigm. However, unless it is replaced by another approach, there is little to gain in abandoning the paradigm. One fruitful way which is being explored (see De Long et al., 1990a; Cutler et al., 1989a, b) is the explicit modelling of the different types of agents in the markets. This is the direction we will take in the following chapters. We will leave the assumption of homogeneous agents and explicitly model the interactions between agents using different types of information.

6 CONCLUSION

In this chapter we have briefly reviewed the existing exchange rate models. We have also analyzed the problems these models face. The focus of the criticism in this chapter has been the rational expectations (perfect foresight) assumption. We have argued that these models cannot avoid bringing into the analysis *ad hoc* assumptions about the information economic agents use. Thus, the rational expectations models fail in their main objective, i.e. to impose as a condition that economic agents use only information which is consistent with the underlying model. In addition, we criticized the rational expectations models on empirical grounds. There are anomalies in the behavior of the foreign exchange markets that cannot be explained by these models.

All this makes it fruitful to develop models in which economic agents use information that is not fully consistent with the underlying model. Some *ad hoc* assumptions will have to be introduced. As was argued earlier, this is inevitable. It is also done in rational expectations models at a higher level of abstraction.

NOTES

1 Note that Frankel used a more elaborated equation for the risk premium: $-\alpha_1 + 1/b(B/w) - (\alpha_2 - \alpha_1)w_2/w + [\alpha_1 - \alpha_3](w_1/w)$. The theory predicts that $\alpha_2 \geq \alpha_1$ and $1/b > 0$. These models are known as the habitat models because they incorporate the idea that agents have a natural preference for domestic assets.

2 Baillie and Bollerslev applied an *m* test for conditional heteroskedasticity and found it to be highly significant. This implies that ε_t is not i.i.d. and thus that the random walk is rejected in favor of the martingale model.

3 This problem is reminiscent of Gödel's incompleteness theorem, which states that no logical system is informationally self-contained (see Hofstadter, 1979).

3

A Simple Chaotic Exchange Rate Model

1 INTRODUCTION

The purpose of this chapter is to develop a theoretical model of the foreign exchange market, and to ask the question of under what conditions chaotic behavior, as defined in chapter 1, is possible in such a model. It will be shown that under reasonable assumptions about the way speculators process information, chaotic behavior is possible. That is, the exchange rate exhibits a complex dynamics which is largely (but not completely) unpredictable. This theoretical analysis is important for the empirical study of later chapters. We must first be able to establish whether there are theoretical reasons why exchange rates should behave in a chaotic way, before we analyze the data to detect whether chaotic patterns exist.

2 A CHAOTIC MODEL OF THE EXCHANGE RATE

As pointed out in chapter 2, the amount of information economic agents are assumed to be able to process is unreasonably high in the news model with rational expectations. In this chapter we will start from the assumption that economic agents use a limited set of information and that, in addition, their information sets are different. In other words, contrary to the traditional model, we assume heterogeneous economic agents who use different pieces of information. We will add to that, however, that use of these different pieces of information is itself dependent on market conditions.

Let us start from the basic equation determining the exchange rate (note that the starting point is the same as in the news model):

$$S_t = X_t E_t(S_{t+1})^b \tag{1}$$

where S_t is the exchange rate in period t, and X_t can be thought of as a reduced form equation describing the structure of the model and the exogenous variables that drive the exchange rate in period t. $E_t(S_{t+1})$ is the expectations held today (period t) in the market about next period's ($t + 1$) exchange rate; b is the discount factor that speculators use to discount the future expected exchange rate $(0 < b < 1)$.

We now proceed to specify the information economic agents use when forecasting the future exchange rate. Our basic assumption is that there are two classes of speculators. One class is called "chartists" (noise traders, technical analysts), the other "fundamentalists".[1] Both classes of speculators will be assumed to use only partial information to forecast the future.

The "chartists" use the past of the exchange rates to detect patterns which they extrapolate into the future. This means that they do not use information embodied in the exchange rate model. The "fundamentalists" compute the equilibrium value of the exchange rate as given by the model, and consider that exchange rate to be the one to which the market exchange rate will move. Thus, if the market rate exceeds this equilibrium value, fundamentalists expect it to decline in the future (and vice versa).

One way to interpret this dual behavior is as follows. The "chartists" use the past movements of the exchange rates as indicators of market sentiments and extrapolate these into the future. Their behavior adds a "positive feedback" into the model. As will become clear, this is a source of instability. The "fundamentalists" have regressive expectations, i.e. when the exchange rate deviates from its equilibrium value they expect it to return to the equilibrium. The behavior of the fundamentalists adds a "negative feedback" into the model, and is a source of stability.

We now implement this speculative dynamics as follows. We write the change in the expected future exchange rate as consisting of two components, a forecast made by the chartists and a forecast made by the fundamentalists:

$$E_t(S_{t+1})/S_{t-1} = (E_{ct}(S_{t+1})/S_{t-1})^{m_t}(E_{ft}(S_{t+1})/S_{t-1})^{1-m_t} \qquad (2)$$

where $E_t(S_{t+1})$ is the market forecast made in period t of the exchange rate in period $t + 1$; $E_{ct}(S_{t+1})$ and $E_{ft}(S_{t+1})$ are the forecasts made by the chartists and the fundamentalists, respectively; m_t is the weight given to the chartists and $1 - m_t$ is the weight given to the fundamentalists in period t. The way m_t is determined will be analyzed later.

A note on the timing of the forecasts is important here. Chartists and fundamentalists take positions in the market in period t based on the forecasts they have made for period $t + 1$. They have made these forecasts using information available in period $t - 1$. This is the reason why in equation (2) S_{t-1} appears. We need this assumption because S_t is the solution of the model that we obtain when chartists and fundamentalists have taken their foreign exchange market positions. Thus this S_t is not observable by these agents at the moment they make their decisions. If we take short enough time periods, however, this assumption about the timing of the information set is not very restrictive.

We assume that the chartists extrapolate recent observed exchange rate changes into the future, using a univariate time series model:

$$E_{ct}(S_{t+1})/S_{t-1} = f(S_{t-1}, \ldots, S_{t-N}) \qquad (3)$$

Equation (3) is a very general description of different models used by chartists. As will be shown later, it encompasses most of the models used by chartists and technical analysts, which can all be rewritten as some weighted average of past exchange rates. Of course, it is also known that chartists use qualitative analysis of the past trends. These cannot easily be quantified, and are outside the scope of the present analysis. Thus, chartists use more complex forecasting rules than the one presented here. The use of simple rules, however, is not necessarily a disadvantage if we can show that very complex behavior of the exchange rate is possible even if our chartists use the relatively simple forecasting rule assumed here.

The fundamentalists are assumed to calculate the equilibrium exchange rate S_t^* (the steady state). The steady state can be calculated by imposing $E_{ft}S_{t+1} = S_t = S_{t-1}$. This implies that

$$S_t^* = (X_t)^{1/(1-b)} \qquad (4)$$

Thus S_t^* is the equilibrium exchange rate that is obtained given the value of the exogenous (fundamental) variable X, prevailing today and expected to prevail in the future. (In a following chapter we will specify detailed structural models. In these models, S_t^* will then be related to price levels and money stocks.) Fundamentalists then expect the market rate to return to that fundamental rate (S^*) at the speed α during the next period, if they observe a deviation today, i.e.

$$E_{ft}(S_{t+1})/S_{t-1} = (S_{t-1}^*/S_{t-1})^\alpha \qquad (5)$$

In order to simplify the analysis we will set X_t as a constant and normalize it to 1.

Note that our fundamentalists do not have rational expectations in the technical sense. Rational expectations would require them to take into account not only the information embodied in the structural model but also the behavior of the chartists and the dynamics that this behavior has for the exchange rate.

We now turn to the analysis of how the weight m_t is determined. The analysis is based on the assumption that the fundamentalists have heterogenous expectations. Suppose there are N fundamentalists who make different estimates of the equilibrium value of the exchange rate at time t. Suppose also that these estimates are normally distributed around the true equilibrium value S_{t-1}^*. We then obtain the picture in figure 3.1.

When the market exchange rate at time $t(S_{t-1})$ is equal to the true equilibrium exchange rate (S_{t-1}^*), half the fundamentalists will find that the market rate is too low, whereas the other half will find that it is too high compared to their own estimates of the equilibrium rate. If we assume that these fundamentalists have the same degree of risk aversion and the same wealth, the amounts of foreign exchange bought by the first half will be sold by the second half. Thus, when the market exchange rate is equal to the equilibrium (fundamental) exchange rate, the fundamentalists do not influence the market. It is as if they are absent

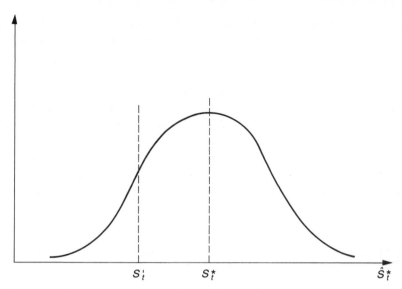

Figure 3.1 Frequency distribution of the estimated exchange rate.

from the market. The market's expectations will then be dominated by the chartists' beliefs.

As the market exchange rate starts to deviate from the true equilibrium value, fundamentalists become important again. Take the example of figure 3.1. When the market rate has declined to S_{t-1}^1, the number of fundamentalists believing that the market rate is too low compared to their own estimates of the equilibrium rate increases so that their expectations become more important in the market. The weight of the fundamentalists on the market's expectation tends to increase. The same happens when the market exchange rate increases relative to the true equilibrium value.

We conclude that in a world where there is uncertainty about the true fundamental value of the exchange rate, the weight of the fundamentalists' belief in the total market's expectation will increase when the market exchange rate departs from the true equilibrium value.

This leads us to postulate the weighting function as follows:

$$m_t = 1/(1 + \beta(S_{t-1} - S_{t-1}^*)^2) \tag{6}$$

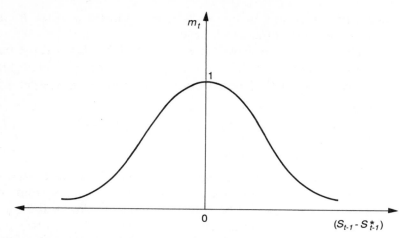

Figure 3.2 The weighting function of chartists.

where m_t is the weight given to the chartists, and $\beta > 0$.

Graphically we can represent this specification as in figure 3.2. From figure 3.2 it can be seen that when the market exchange rate is equal to the fundamental rate the weight given to the chartists attains its maximum value of one. It is as if there are no fundamentalists in the market. When the market rate deviates from the fundamental rate the weight of the chartists tends to decline. For very large deviations it tends towards zero. The market expectations will then be dominated by the fundamentalists.

Note that the parameter β determines the speed with which the weight of the chartists declines. It also measures the degree of divergence of the fundamentalists' estimates of the equilibrium exchange rate. With a high β the curve in figure 3.2 becomes steeper. This means that the estimates of the true equilibrium rate made by fundamentalists are very precise, i.e. there is little divergence in these estimations. As a result, relatively small deviations of the market rate from the true equilibrium rate lead to a strongly increasing influence of the fundamentalists in the market. The opposite is true when β is low. In that case there is a lot of uncertainty in the market concerning the true equilibrium rate. As a result, a movement away from the equilibrium rate induces little reaction from the fundamentalists, so that their weight in the market increases little.

We now proceed towards solving the model. This is done by substituting equations (3) and (5) into (2), and (2) into (1). After some rearranging one obtains the following system of equations:

$$S_t = [S_{t-1}f(S_{t-1}, \ldots, S_{t-N})^{m_t}(S^*_{t-1}/S_{t-1})^{\alpha(1-m_t)}]^b \tag{7}$$

$$m_t = 1/[1 + \beta(S_{t-1} - S^*_{t-1})^2] \tag{8}$$

This is the basic system of equations that will be used to detect chaos. Given its nonlinear nature, this higher order system of difference equation cannot be solved analytically. We will therefore have to use experimental (simulation) methods. The problem of that approach is that there are many possible combinations of parameters to be analyzed. Some choice limiting the range of parameters is necessary. In order to do so we first analyze some popular models used by chartists in forecasting the exchange rate. We will then select some of these popular models.

3 MODELS USED BY CHARTISTS

The most popular models used by chartists and technical analysts are the moving average model,[2] the momentum model, and the filter rule model. We discuss them consecutively and show how all these models can be rewritten in the form of equation (3), i.e. the forecasts are all based on some weighted average of past exchange rates, where the weights are determined by the specific model.

3.1 The moving average model

In this model chartists expect an increase in the future exchange rate when a short-term moving average of the past exchange rates crosses a long-term moving average of the past exchange rates from below. When the short-term moving average crosses the long-term moving average from above (B), chartists expect a future decline of the exchange rate. When the short-run average crosses the long-run average from below (A) a

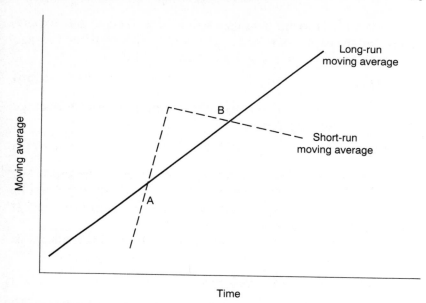

Figure 3.3 Moving average chart. A, chartists buy foreign exchange; B, chartists sell foreign exchange.

buy order is given by chartists. We show an example in figure 3.3.

This moving average model can be formalized in the following way:

$$E_{ct}(S_{t+1})/S_{t-1} = \left(\frac{SMA(S_{t-1})}{LMA(S_{t-1})}\right)^{2\gamma} \tag{9}$$

where $SMA(S_{t-1})$ is the short-term moving average of the past exchange rate and $LMA(S_{t-1})$ is the long-term moving average of the past exchange rate.

According to equation (9), when the short-term moving average exceeds the long-term one, the chartists expect a future increase of the exchange rate relative to the most recently observed exchange rate. When the short-term moving average is below the long-run one, chartists expect a future decline of the exchange rate. The factor with which they extrapolate the past into the future is represented by the parameter γ.

Very simple moving averages will be assumed in our experimental analysis. In particular, the short term moving average will be assumed to be a one-period change, i.e.

$$SMA(S_{t-1}) = S_{t-1}/S_{t-2} \qquad (10)$$

Similarly, we assume a very simple two-period moving average to represent the long-run, i.e.

$$LMA(S_{t-1}) = (S_{t-1}/S_{t-2})^{0.5}(S_{t-2}/S_{t-3})^{0.5} \qquad (11)$$

Clearly, more complicated moving averages could be used. We have performed sensitivity analyses to check whether our results are dependent on the specification of these moving averages. It turns out that they are not.

Manipulating equation (9), and using (10) and (11), allows us to rewrite it as:

$$E_{ct}(S_{t+1})/S_{t-1} = (S_{t-1}/S_{t-2})^{\gamma}(S_{t-3}/S_{t-2})^{\gamma} \qquad (12)$$

A comparison with equation (3) reveals that this is just a special case of the more general weighted average representation of past exchange rate changes.

3.2 The momentum model

In this model chartists expect a future increase in the exchange rate when the current observed change relative to n periods ago starts increasing. Formally we have

$$E_{ct}(S_{t+1})/S_{t-1} = \left(\frac{S_{t-1}/S_{t-n}}{S_{t-2}/S_{t-n-1}}\right)^{2\gamma} \qquad (14)$$

Here too we can rewrite the equation so that it becomes a special case of the general moving average representation. This yields another moving average model:

$$E_{ct}(S_{t+1})/S_{t-1} = (S_{t-1}/S_{t-n})^{2\gamma}(S_{t-2}/S_{t-n-1})^{-2\gamma} \qquad (15)$$

3.3 The filter rule model

In this model chartists expect a future increase (decline) in the exchange rate when the market rate has increased (declined) by

x percent above its previous low point (below its previous high point).

This rule can be formalized as follows:

$$E_{ct}(S_{t+1})/S_{t-1} = \left(\frac{S_{t-1}}{S'(1 + x)}\right)^{2\gamma} \tag{16}$$

if $S_{t-1} > S'$ $(1 + x)$ and S' is a low point
or $S_{t-1} < S'$ $(1 + x)$ and S' is a high point
otherwise $E_{ct}(S_{t+1})/S_{t-1} = 1$

It can immediately be seen that this rule can be interpreted as a moving average of past exchange rates, but with the length of the lags variable. This constrasts with the previous two chartists' models, where the length of the lag is constant. The filter rule model is also different from the previous two models in that the coefficients of the moving average switch from zero to positive numbers depending on the market situation.

In the following section we will use some of these chartists' models (in particular the moving average model) to investigate how they affect the dynamics of the exchange rate.

Under this particular chartist model, the system can be solved by replacing $f(S_{t-1}, \ldots,)$ by (12). The solution is given by (7') and (8'):

$$S_t = S_{t-1}^{\varphi_1} S_{t-2}^{\varphi_2} S_{t-3}^{\varphi_3} \tag{7'}$$

$$m_t = 1/[1 + \beta(S_{t-1} - 1)^2] \tag{8'}$$

$$\varphi_1 = b[1 + \gamma m_t - \alpha(1 - m_t)]$$

$$\varphi_2 = -2b\gamma m_t$$

$$\varphi_3 = b\gamma m_t$$

4 EXPERIMENTAL RESULTS: EXISTENCE OF CHAOS

The model represented by equations (7') and (8') was simulated using different parameter values. In the simulation results

Table 3.1 Characterization of asymptotic solutions of the model in γ–α space

γ \ α	0.05	0.1	0.15	0.2	0.25	0.3	0.35	0.4	0.45	0.5	0.55	0.6	0.65	0.7	0.75	0.8	0.85	0.9	0.95
10	CH	CH	CH	CH	CH	CH	CH	CH	CH	CH	CH	CH	CH	CH	CH	CH	CH	CH	CH
7	LC	CH	CH	CH	CH	CH	CH	CH	CH	CH	CH	CH	CH	CH	CH	CH	CH	CH	CH
6	LC	PH	CH	CH	CH	CH	CH	CH	CH	P10	CH	CH	CH	P16	CH	CH	CH	CH	CH
5	LC	LC	CH	CH	CH	CH	CH	CH	CH	P5	CH	CH	CH	P4	CH	CH	CH	P4	P4
4	LC	LC	CH	CH	CH	CH	P4	P4	CH	P4	PH	CH	CH	P4	P4	CH	CH	CH	P4
3.5	LC	LC	P5	P5	CH	P4	CH	CH	CH	CH	CH	CH	CH	CH	P4	P4	P4	P4	P4
3	LC	LC	P20	P10	P9	CH	PH	PH	CH	CH	CH	P7	CH	P4	P4	P4	P4	P4	P4
2.5	LC	LC	P5	P10	CH	CH	PM	CH	CH	CH	LM	P5	CH	CH	P4	P4	P4	P4	P4
2	LC	LC	LCL	P5	CH	CH	P11	P11	LC	P4	P5	P15	CH	P4	P4	P4	P4	P4	S
1.5	LC	LC	LC	P11	P15	CH	LC	LC	LC	LC	LC	P5	LC	P14	P28	S	S	S	S
1	S	S	S	S	S	S	S	S	S	S	S	S	S	S	S	S	S	S	S
0.75	S	S	S	S	S	S	S	S	S	S	S	S	S	S	S	S	S	S	S
0.5	S	S	S	S	S	S	S	S	S	S	S	S	S	S	S	S	S	S	S
0.25	S	S	S	S	S	S	S	S	S	S	S	S	S	S	S	S	S	S	S

S = stable solution. LC = limit cycle. Pi = cycle with periodicity i. CH = chaotic solution.

reported here we fixed the coefficient b (the discounting para-meter) to 0.95 and the coefficient β (the parameter measuring the degree of precision of the fundamentalists' estimates) to 10 000.[3] We then varied the two other coefficients of the model, α and γ, in order to find out for what parameter ranges one obtains chaotic solutions. It will be remembered that α is the coefficient measuring the speed with which the fundamentalists expect the exchange rate to return to its fundamental value, and γ is the coefficient measuring the degree of extrapolation of past exchange rate movements applied by chartists.

In table 3.1 we present the nature of the solutions obtained for different combinations of the parameters α and γ. The results of table 3.1 can be interpreted as follows. When the extrapolation parameter γ is less than or equal to one we obtain solutions that always converge (without cycles) to the fundamental value of the exchange rate. As γ increases above 1, we obtain cyclical movements of the exchange rate. These can be periodic or chaotic. For a sufficiently high extrapolation parameter, however, the solutions always become chaotic. (In the following sections we discuss different formal methods to detect chaos. Here it suffices to present the results.)

The parameter α also affects the nature of the dynamics. However, there seems to be as much likelihood of obtaining chaos with low as with high αs. (Note that we have restricted α to lie between 0 and 1. A value of α equal to 1 implies that fundamentalists expect the exchange rate to return to its funda-mental value in one period; a value above 1 implies that they expect some overshooting.

5 EMPIRICAL RESULTS: AN EXAMPLE

In this section we analyze an example of a chaotic solution of the exchange rate model. This will allow us to focus on some of the characteristics of chaotic models. We selected the following parameter combination, which yields results that are representa-tive of the chaotic solutions: $\alpha = 0.65$ and $\gamma = 3$.

We first present the time series of the simulated[4] exchange rate for the first 1000 periods in figure 3.4, and the phase

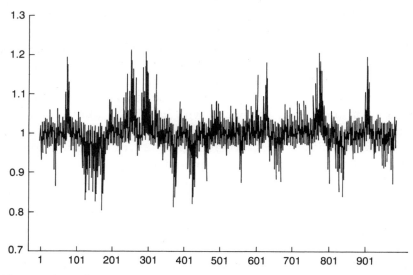

Figure 3.4 Simulated exchange rate in the time domain (1000 observations).

diagram of the same simulation in figure 3.5. The equilibrium exchange rate S_t^* has been normalized to be equal to 1. We observe the cyclical behavior of the exchange rate around the equilibrium value. However, each cycle is unique. That is, we never return through the same point in the phase diagram. This is, of course, a typical feature of chaotic solutions. It is also related to the fractal nature of the strange attractor.

The most spectacular feature of chaotic models is their sensitivity to initial conditions. We illustrate this in figure 3.6, where we compare two simulation runs. That in figure 3.6a is the base run and is exactly the same as the simulation of figure 3.4. Figure 3.6b is a simulation where we have changed the inititial exchange rate by 1 percent compared to the initial value used in the base run. We observe that after about 50 periods the two time series start to diverge. This divergence can be quite significant. This can be seen, for example, by comparing the movements of the two time series between periods 200 and 300.

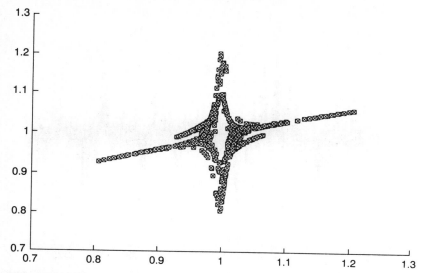

Figure 3.5 Phase diagram of the model in the S_t, S_{t-1} space (1000 observations).

During that period the exchange rate in the base run tends to be high compared to the fundamental value (which is 1), whereas the exchange rate in the other simulation is low compared to the fundamental. Comparing the two simulations creates the impression that the two series are drawn from quite different samples. Thus a trivial change in the initial conditions changes the whole future path of the exchange rate in a quite dramatic way. For the whole simulation period, the *average* deviation between the two series is 7 percent.

This sensitivity to initial conditions which is characteristic of chaotic models manifests itself in other, sometimes spectacular, ways. We highlight two of these manifestations here. First, we simulated exactly the same model with the same parameters and the same initial conditions on two different computers. One was an IBM PS/2 Model 70386 (with math coprocessor), the other and IBM PS/2 Model 40SX (portable). The results are given in figure 3.7. A comparison of the two figures shows that after

a

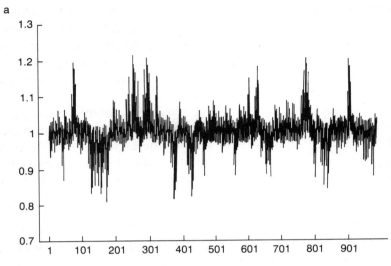

b

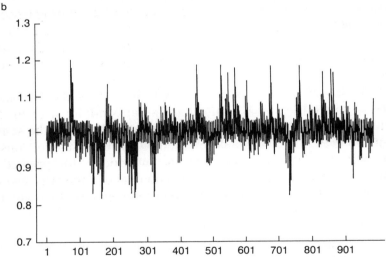

Figure 3.6 Sensitivity to initial conditions generated by a difference in the initial exchange rate. (a) Base run; (b) a 1 per cent change in the initial exchange rate compared to the base run.

approximately 150 periods the two series start to diverge. Quickly afterwards, the time paths of the two exchange rates are completely different. In fact, one obtains a result that is very much like the result obtained when the initial conditions were changed. The two series give the impression of having been drawn from different sample periods.

A second way in which the sensitivity to initial conditions manifests itself is by the manner a small change in the parameters of the model affects the time path of the exchange rate. In order to analyze how sensitive the model was to small changes in the parameters the following experiment was undertaken. We changed one of the parameters of the model (α) by 1 percent and kept all the other parameters (and initial conditions) unchanged. We then simulated this slightly altered model and compared it with the base simulation. The results are shown in figure 3.8. We observe that after about 70 periods the two series show a completely different history. For example, during periods 500 to 600 the model with the slight change in parameter "predicts" very low exchange rates compared to its fundamental value. In the base run the exchange rate moves very closely around the fundamental value.

The extreme sensitivity of the dynamic path of the exchange rate to small and trivial changes in initial conditions, or in the value of the parameters of the underlying model, and the sensitivity to the choice of computer used to solve the model, raises important issues concerning the use of models for predictive purposes. It also raises deeper questions about the way agents will use information in a chaotic environment. To these issues we now turn our attention.

6 PREDICTIONS AND INFORMATION IN A CHAOTIC WORLD

In order to interpret correctly the previous results it is important to be aware that while they have dramatic effects on the time path of the exchange rates, the small changes in the initial conditions in no way affect the underlying "order" which drives

a

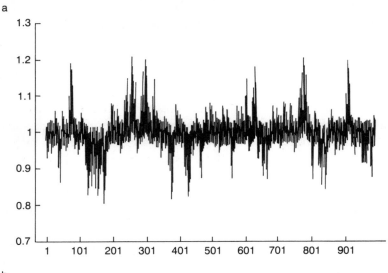

b

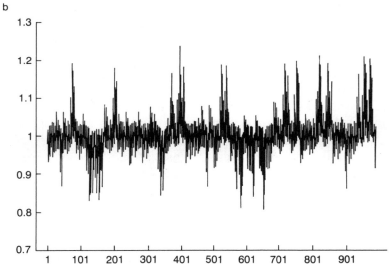

Figure 3.7 Sensitivity to initial conditions owing to the use of different computers. (a) Simulations on an IBM PS/2 Model 70; (b) simulations on an IBM PS/2 Model 40SX.

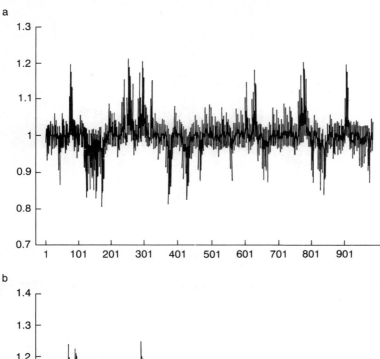

Figure 3.8 Sensitivity to initial conditions generated by a 1 percent difference in α. (a) $\alpha = 0.65$; (b) $\alpha = 0.66$.

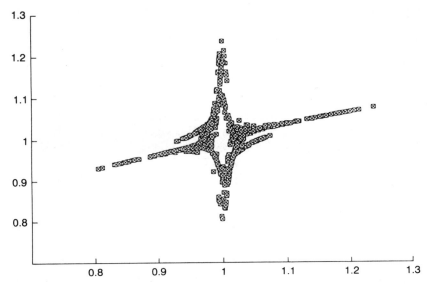

Figure 3.9 Phase diagram of the model simulated on an IBM PS/2 Model 40SX.

the exchange rate. This can be illustrated by comparing the phase diagram of the base run (figure 3.5) with the phase diagram of the model where some slight change in initial conditions has been made. We show this in figure 3.9. It can be seen that the two phase diagrams are identical in structure. This feature of chaotic models, which was also stressed in chapter 1, vividly illustrates the fact that there is a lot of order in the underlying structure driving the exchange rate. However, the question is how and whether this order can be exploited to make predictions.

The results of the previous sections suggest that in order to be able to exploit the knowledge of the underlying model for predictive purposes, our knowledge must be infinitely precise. Some small lack of precision (like, for example, the difference in precision due to the use of two different computers) leads *after some time* to very different predictions of the exchange rate.

This result has very strong implications for the use of econometric models in exchange rate forecasting. One way to interpret our results is as follows. Suppose the true structural model driving the exchange rate is the one that has produced the base simulation run (figure 3.3). The econometrician now estimates the model and manages to estimate all coefficients exactly, except for one where he makes a minuscule error of 1 percent (such a precision in the estimations of the underlying model would be a truly remarkable feat in econometrics). He then uses the model to make forecasts of the future exchange rate. This would produce the prediction as shown in figure 3.3. It can be seen that after some time the estimated model becomes completely useless as a predictive instrument.

The previous result also allows us to give a new interpretation to the well-known results that Meese and Rogoff (1983) obtained in their empirical tests of different exchange rate models. They found that (out-of-sample) forecasts of exchange rates using econometric models were less precise than "naive" forecasts based on the random walk model (see chapter 2). These empirical results have usually been interpreted as follows. Econometric models use observations of the past. When out-of-sample forecasts are made the underlying structure may already have changed. As a result, the model's forecasts produce systematic errors, which will typically be less pronounced when using the random walk model.

A second interpretation of the Meese and Rogoff results is also possible. It is quite possible that the underlying structure does not change, but that the precision with which we estimate this economic structure is not good enough to use the models for forecasting purposes. This interpretation follows from the results obtained in our nonlinear model. Note that this second interpretation is not in contradiction with the first one. In fact the two interpretations complement each other. The poor forecasting record with econometric models is likely to be the result of too little precision in estimation, and continuous changes in the underlying parameters of the model. Our results are also consistent with the view that changes in the structural parameters (however slight) are enough to ensure that forecasts with econometric models that base their estimation on the past are of limited usefulness.

The extreme sensitivity of the time path of the exchange rate to trivial changes in initial conditions and in parameters leads to deeper questions about how economic agents will use information. In the classroom models that are now in use and that rely on the rational expectations paradigm, economic agents are assumed to use all relevant information, including the information embodied in the structural model. Our results suggest that there might be situations in which it will not pay for economic agents to use the information embodied in such models to predict exchange rates. When economic agents realize that the degree of precision needed to use these models for predictive purposes is unattainable, they are likely to disregard that information. The rational expectations assumption, which has dominated academic thinking about the exchange rate, becomes a very shaky foundation for constructing exchange rate models.

7 ON SHORT-TERM PREDICTABILITY

The discussion of the previous section leads to quite a pessimistic view about the possibility of predicting exchange rates in a chaotic world. There is, however, one aspect of the chaotic model that can lead to a somewhat more optimistic view. As discussed in chapter 1, it appears from the dynamics of chaos that *short-term* forecasting can be undertaken with some reliability, provided that a sufficient degree of precision of the underlying model, and of the initial conditions, can be obtained.

This possibility of making reliable short-term forecasts is illustrated in the following way. We present the simulations of the base run and of the model where we have made an "estimation error" on one parameter (α) of 1 percent. We present the first 100 periods (see figure 3.10). We observe that during the first ten periods the predictions made with the model containing the estimation error come very close to the values predicted by the "true" model. Only after a sufficiently long period do the predictions of the model with the estimation error become very unreliable. Thus, with sufficient precision, predictions over the very short run can usefully be undertaken. In chapter 6 we return to this problem of predictions, and we will analyze whether this feature of chaos models can usefully be

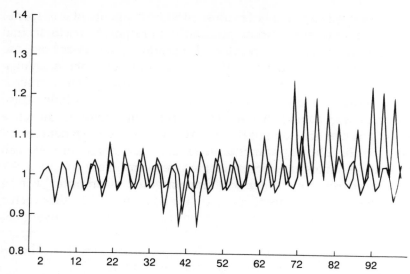

Figure 3.10   Short-term forecastability in chaotic regimes.

employed to make "real-life" predictions of exchange rates. We will also study the question of how short the short run is over which such predictions can be made. It will be shown that even if we do not know the underlying model, short-term predictions are possible.

8   FORMAL TESTS FOR THE EXISTENCE OF CHAOS

In this section we present formal tests for the existence of chaos in the exchange rate model. We will compute the correlation dimension and the power spectrum of the simulated exchange rate.[5] We take the same example as that discussed in the previous sections.

8.1   The correlation dimension

It will be remembered from the discussion of chapter 1 that if a time series is chaotic, a strange attractor can be identified that only occupies a (small) fraction of the available phase space. The computation of the correlation dimension allows us to find the dimension of this attractor. The higher this dimension, the more complex the structure of the data will be. If the exchange rate series is driven by white noise, the dimension of the attractor goes towards infinity; that is, it will tend to fill the whole phase space. Computation of the correlation dimension requires a large amount of datapoints. However, this requirement is no problem for the experimental data analyzed here since we can produce as many datapoints as are necessary.

The correlation dimension as computed in chapter 1 is a function of the embedding, i.e. the dimension of the vector space of the n-tuples x_i in the definition of $C(r)$. (For example, in two-dimensional phase diagrams like figure 3.3 we compute the distance between all the points in the phase diagram. The x_is then have a dimension 2 so that the embedding is 2).

We calculate the value of the correlation dimension D_C for various embeddings. When the value of the correlation dimension does not change further with increasing embeddings, it is assumed that the correlation dimension defined by the formula above has converged to its correct value.

We show the results of these calculations in figure 3.11. It can be see that for sufficiently small changes in r the correlation dimension converges towards (approximately) 1.4 for the various embeddings. We conclude that the correlation dimension is approximately 1.4. This also means that the dimension of the attractor is 1.4. The intuition behind this result is that the attractor can be fully represented in a two-dimensional phase diagram (like figure 3.4). In addition, since the dimension is less than 2, the attractor will not fill the whole two-dimensional phase space. This result, of course, is related to the fact that the model producing the simulated exchange rates consists of two equations, (7') and (8').

8.2 The power spectrum of the chaotic model

The spectral representation of the simulated exchange rate allows us to discover the fractal dimension of the model. In general, the fractal dimension can be inferred from the slope of

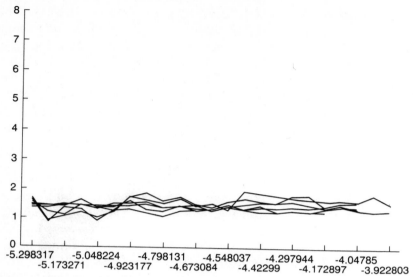

Figure 3.11   Correlation dimension estimates for embedding 2 to 7.

the power spectrum. When the data are white noise the power spectrum is flat (the slope is zero), and the fractal dimension is zero. A slope between 0 and -2 implies chaos (the fractal dimension is between 0 and 2). From this and the evidence presented before we conclude that the considered time series is chaotic.

In figure 3.12 we present the power spectrum of the simulated exchange rate. The initially straight downward slope of the power spectrum is characteristic for the fractal structure of the signal. With an increase in the frequency we obtain noise in the power spectrum. As indicated in chapter 1 this feature contrasts with Gaussian noise, which has all frequencies equally represented and a more or less horizontal power spectrum.

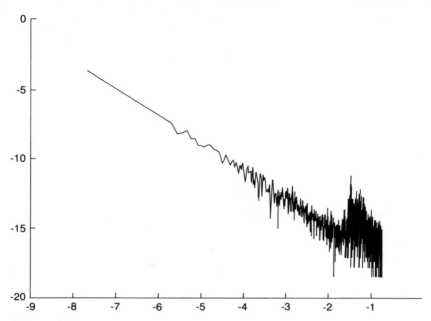

Figure 3.12   Log-log representation of the power spectrum.

9   ADDITIONAL CHARACTERISTICS OF CHAOTIC SOLUTIONS

The chaotic solutions of the model have other interesting features that we discuss in the present section. These results are important to an understanding of the workings of the foreign exchange market.

For sufficiently low values of the parameter α (which, as will be remembered, measures the speed with which fundamentalists expect the exchange rate to return to its fundamental value) we find that the exchange rate will fluctuate on one side of its fundamental value for long periods of time. The initial conditions determine on which side the exchange rate will fluctuate. After a sufficiently long period, however, the exchange rate will suddenly move to the other side.

We illustrate this feature of the chaotic model as follows. We simulated a model (with $\alpha = 0.15$ and $\gamma = 3.5$) assuming two different initial conditions, one below and another above the equilibrium exchange rate. The phase diagrams of these two simulations (for the first 700 periods) are presented in figure 3.13a and b. It appears that they are asymmetrically below and above the equilibrium value of 1. After a sufficiently long period, however, the exchange rate will switch to the other side. Thus, extending the simulation to more periods leads to a symmetric phase diagram (see figure 3.13c). This feature is known as *ergodicity*.

The time domain representation of the phase diagram of figure 3.13c is presented in figure 3.14a, from which we observe that the exchange rate moves above the equilibrium exchange rate for a long period, without seeming to converge to it. Suddenly, however, the exchange rate moves below its equilibrium value, again for quite some time. When this happens, the time series seems to reveal a sudden and permanent change in the fundamental exchange rate. It looks as if some important exogenous event has occurred, affecting the equilibrium value of the exchange rate. In fact nothing has changed in the underlying exogenous variables, nor in the structure of the model.

This result leads to the interesting implication that it will be very difficult to separate the movements of the exchange rate that come from the inherent dynamics of the model, and those that are due to exogenous shocks (news). In order to show this, we simulated the same model, and now introduced an unexpected shock in the exogenous variable X_t during periods 601 to 603 (the shocks were transitory: after period 603, the exogenous variable returned to its pre-period 601 value). This shock has the effect of pushing the exchange rate to the lower part of the phase diagram. We show the result in the time domain in figure 3.14b. Comparing figure 3.14b with figure 3.14a, we find exactly the same dynamics, i.e. after period 600 the exchange rate starts fluctuating around a value which appears to be a new equilibrium. (Note also that the shocks underlying the movements in figure 3.14 are temporary. They appear to have a permanent effect on the exchange rate, however.)

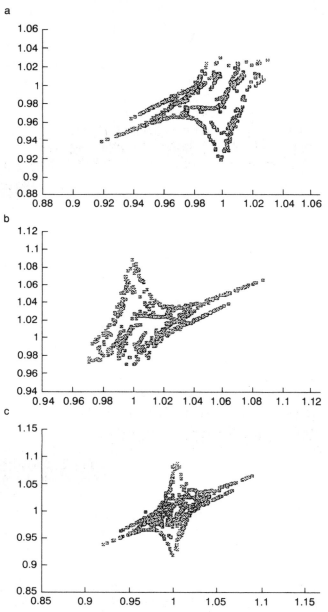

Figure 3.13 Phase diagram with differing initial condition and periods. (a) $S_{t-1} = 0.9$, 800 periods; (b) $S_{t-1} = 1.1$, 800 periods; (c) $S_{t-1} = 0.9$, 1000 periods. Other parameters were $b = 0.95$, $\beta = 10\,000$, $\alpha = 0.25$ $\gamma = 3.5$.

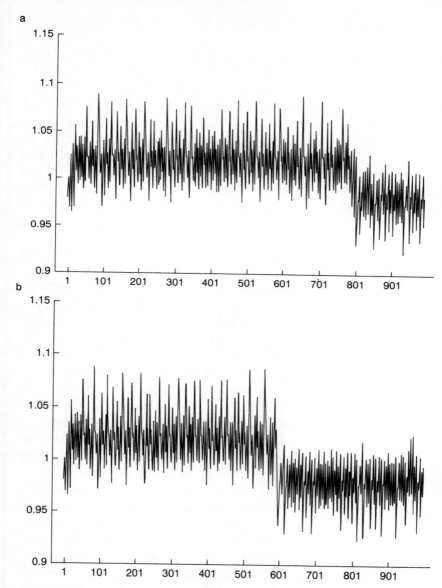

Figure 3.14 Time domain representation of the model. (a) Simulations without shocks; (b) simulation with shock in period 601, 602, 603. Other parameters were $b = 0.95$, $\beta = 10\,000$, $\alpha = 0.25$, $\gamma = 3.5$.

10 DETERMINISTIC CHAOS OR RANDOMNESS?

In the previous sections we presented a deterministic model capable of generating exchange rate movements that have the appearance of being random. However, the chaotic dynamics was obtained only for certain parameter configurations. For many other parameter values we obtained periodic solutions and limit cycles. In principle, these solutions are not subject to the sensitivity to initial conditions, and are predictable. In this section we show that by adding "infrequent" stochastic shocks to some of these periodic and limit cycle models we obtain solutions that are very close to the chaotic solutions, at least in the time domain (this is not the case, however, in the phase space).

The experiments were set up as follows. We selected a limit cycle model with a low α (it will be clear later why we did this), and then added random shocks in the fundamental variable. However, the random shock occurred "infrequently", that is (on average) every n periods (we selected $n = 5$ and $n = 2.5$). The period when the shock occurs was also determined randomly, i.e. the probability of a shock occurring in a particular period was $1/n$. The random shocks were calibrated such that the standard deviation of the random variable was equal to the standard deviation of the exchange rate obtained in the deterministic limit cycle model. By doing this, we made sure that half of the total variance of the simulated exchange rate came from the deterministic part of the model, and the other half from the stochastic part. We show the results in figures 3.15 and 3.16.

Figure 3.15 presents the phase diagram of the deterministic (limit cycle) model. An important feature of this model is that it has two limit cycles. Depending on the initial condition chosen, the exchange rate will move to the lower or to the upper part, and remain stuck there forever. In general, with an initial condition below (above) 1 (the fundamental value), the exchange rate moves to the lower (upper) limit cycle. Thus, there is no tendency for the exchange rate to converge to its equilibrium value: depending on the initial condition, it will fluctuate either above or below the equilibrium value forever.

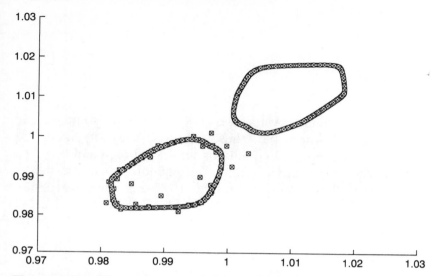

Figure 3.15 Phase diagram of the model for different initial values $S_{601} = S_{602} = S_{603} = 0.95$, $S_{t-1} = 1.1$. Other parameters were $b = 0.95$, $\beta = 10\,000$, $\alpha = 0.15$, $\gamma = 3.5$.

In figure 3.16 we present the exchange rate in the time domain after the addition of "infrequent" random shocks to the deterministic model ($n = 5$ and $n = 2.5$). We observe that the exchange rate fluctuates around 1. This means that the shocks regularly push the exchange rate from one limit cycle to the other.

In order to test for the *sensitivity to initial conditions* we first changed the initial condition by 1 percent, and simulated the new model assuming that exactly the same random shocks occur as in the model without the change in initial conditions (the base run). We show the results of these two simulations in figure 3.17 for the first 1000 periods. The remarkable feature is that we obtain the same "sensitivity to initial conditions" result as in the chaos models. The two time paths appear to be quite different. This feature is also illustrated by figure 3.18, where we have brought the two time series together in one graph for the last 200 periods. Figure 3.18 also illustrates another feature, which is

a

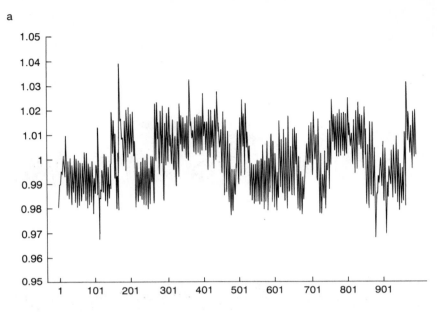

b

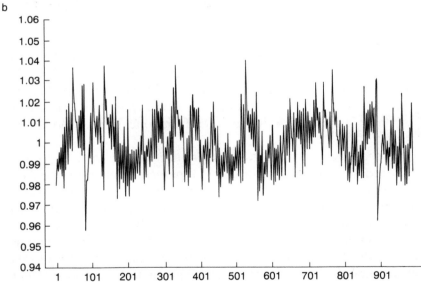

Figure 3.16   Time domain representation for the model with stochastic shocks. (a) Probability of shock = 0.2; (b) probability of shock = 0.4. Other parameters were $b = 0.95$, $n = 5$, $\beta = 10\,000$, $\alpha = 0.15$, $\gamma = 3.5$.

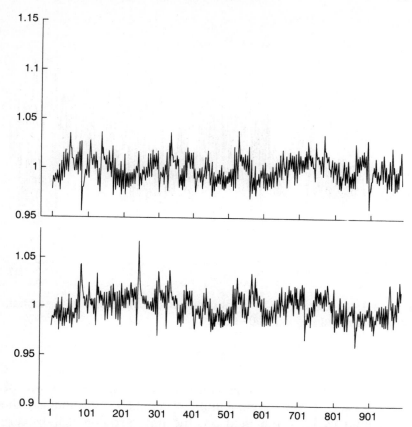

Figure 3.17 Sensitivity to initial conditions in the model with stochastic disturbances.

that the two series once in a while tend to coincide, whereafter they diverge again.

In order to understand why we obtain this sensitivity to initial conditions in a limit cycle model it is useful to look at the phase diagram of the deterministic part of the model (see figure 3.15). The difference in intitial conditions (however slight) will lead to a situation where the two series are out of step. The same exogenous shock will then move the two exchange rates in a different point off the limit cycle. There is a critical region

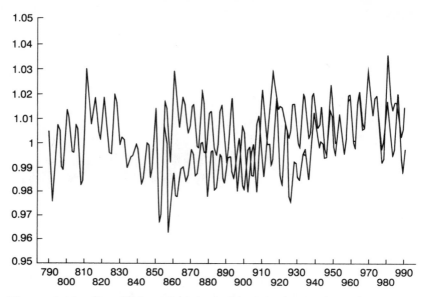

Figure 3.18 Sensitivity to initial conditions in the model with stochastic disturbances (period 790–990).

between the two limit cycles where one exchange rate will be pushed back to the original limit cycle, and the other to the other limit cycle. From then on, the time series will look very different.

In a second experiment we changed one parameter (α) of the limit cycle model slightly (i.e. by 1 percent), and simulated this new model assuming that exactly the same random shocks occur as in the model without the change in parameters (the base run). We show the results of these two simulations in figure 3.19 for the last 200 periods. In this experiment we also obtain a result similar to the chaos model. The two time paths are totally different. The two models, however, are identical except for the fact that in one simulation $\alpha = 0.15$ and in the other $\alpha = 0.16$. In addition, the stochastic disturbances to which the two models are subjected are identical in size and timing.

The nature of this result can be understood more easily by analyzing again the phase diagram of the deterministic part of

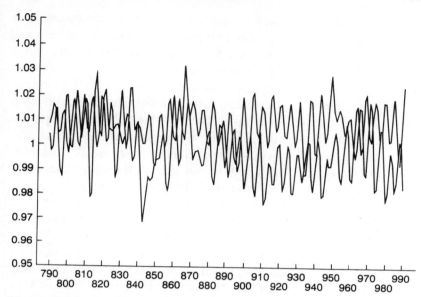

Figure 3.19 Sensitivity to initial conditions generated by a change in α. Other parameters were $b = 0.95$, $\beta = 10\,000$, $\gamma = 3.5$, probability of shock $= 0.2$.

the two models. Here the small change in parameter slightly affects the curvature of the limit cycle. As a result, when the same stochastic disturbance hits the two models the exchange rate is brought to a slightly different point off the limit cycle. If this happens in some critical region between the two limit cycles, the two exchange rates will be propelled to a different limit cycle.

We have performed similar experiments with *periodic* models, leading to analogous results, as long as the parameter α is kept low enough. The results are completely comparable to the results obtained with a limit cycle model.

11 EXCHANGE RATE INERTIA

The results of the previous section lead to the conclusion that a deterministic model producing predictable cycles in the exchange rate, together with "news" that occurs only infrequently, is capable of generating a very complex exchange rate dynamics, which has the same sensitivity to initial conditions as the chaos models. However, this feature depends on the size of the parameter α, which measures the speed with which the fundamentalists expect the exchange rate to return to its equilibrium value. If this parameter is large enough this feature disappears. We show this in figure 3.20, where we present the phase diagrams of the model when we progressively increase the value of α. We observe that with low α the phase diagram shows two limit cycles. When α is increased the limit cycles move closer together, then start overlapping. For some critical value the two limit cycles have merged into one. At that point the sensitivity to initial conditions under infrequent stochastic shocks is lost.

Thus, the dynamics of the model is very much influenced by the speed with which the fundamentalists expect the future exchange rate to return to its equilibrium value. As will be remembered, this was also the case with the chaotic solutions of the model. We found that with sufficiently low α, the exchange rate will remain above (or below) the equilibrium rate for long periods. The interpretation of this result can be formulated as follows. When α is low, fundamentalists expect that it will take a lot of time for the exchange rate to move towards its fundamental value. Put differently, they expect little change in the exchange rate in the near future. As a result, the short-term forecasts are dominated by the beliefs of the chartists. It follows that the pressures to move towards the fundamental value of the exchange rate will be weak. In the limit cycle models this can lead to a situation where the exchange rate moves permanently above (or below) the fundamental exchange rate, except if some exogenous shock propels it to the other side of the equilibrium value. In the chaotic solutions we have the same feature: the exchange rate stays on one side of its fundamental value for a long time. Here, however, it is propelled to the other side in an *endogenous* way. This has to do with the fact that in chaos models high turbulence is generated endogenously, thereby moving the exchange rate "to the other side" without the need of an exogenous disturbance.

This feature of the exchange rate dynamics, which one could

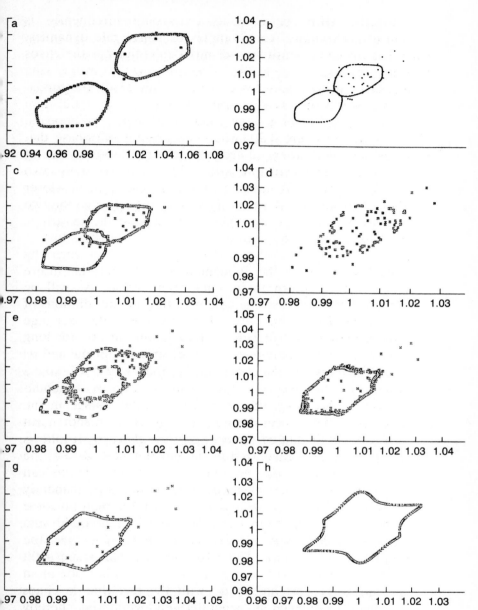

Figure 3.20 Phase space transitions generated by changes in α.

call *inertia*, tends to disappear when fundamentalists expect the exchange rate to move quickly to its fundamental value. In that case they expect a return movement in the near future, so that the fundamentalists' expectations matter for short-term forecasts. This will generally force the exchange rate to fluctuate around its fundamental value in the short run.

There is some empirical evidence indicating that the short-run movements of the exchange rate are dominated by the chartists' forecasts and that the fundamentalists' beliefs tend to be unimportant for the short-run forecasts. This indicates that the α parameter is likely to be small. Our model then predicts that the exchange rate behavior will show a lot of inertia, i.e. that the forces pushing the exchange rate to its fundamental value will be weak (at least in the short run).

12 CONCLUSION

The model developed in this chapter allows us to formulate an alternative view concerning the role of news in the foreign exchange market to the view which today prevails among exchange rate theorists. Our model implies that one does not need news in every period to explain complex exchange rate movements. Much of the movement observed in the exchange rates can be the result of an internal speculative dynamics. In this sense the model presented in this chapter explains a puzzle related to the news model, noted in the prevous chapter. There we observed that many exchange rate movements could not easily be traced to observable news. The news model, however, predicts that exchange rates can only move if there is some unexpected disturbance in one of the exogenous variables driving the exchange rate. The results of this chapter solve this puzzle.

The model presented in this chapter, of course, does not imply that news is unimportant. There are certainly many periods in which the occurrence of unexpected events drives the exchange rate. In addition, we have shown that unexpected disturbances, even if temporary in nature, can have quite dramatic and persistent effects on the future time path of the exchange rate.

NOTES

1 See Frankel and Froot (1987) for a first attempt at formalizing this idea. A recent microeconomic foundation of this assumption is provided by Cutler et al. (1989a, b). Empirical evidence about the importance of these types of speculators is found in Allen and Taylor (1989) and Froot and Frankel (1990).
2 Note that in the literature on chartism, the term "moving average model" is used in a very specific meaning, which is different from the meaning given to this term in the more formal statistical literature.
3 A sensitivity analysis on the coefficient β revealed that the qualitative nature of the results is not affected by the size of this coefficient. Thus, a smaller β still produces chaos if a larger β does. However, when β is small the variance of the exchange rate increases. We return to this in the next chapter.
4 We used the following values for the parameters for all simulations in this chapter: $b = 0.95$, $\beta = 10\,000$, $\alpha = 0.65$, $\gamma = 3$.
5 It will be remembered from the discussion of chapter 1 that an important characteristic of chaotic solutions is the sensitivity to initial conditions. Detecting such sensitivity can be considered as "proof" of the existence of chaos. We discussed this feature in the previous sections and will not repeat it here.

4

Additional Analysis of Chaos in a Simple Exchange Rate Model

---

1 INTRODUCTION

In chapter 3 a simple chaotic exchange rate model was presented that is capable of mimicking some important features of observed exchange rate movements. In this chapter we change the focus somewhat. We use the same exchange rate model with different parameter values, in order to illustrate some of the more complex features such a chaotic model can produce. We will attach less importance here to the question of whether the parameter values are realistic.

The model is the same as in chapter 3 except for the following features. First, we use a simpler moving average model for the chartists, i.e. it is assumed that when the chartists extrapolate the past exchange rates they use a two-period moving average. We now obtain the following solution for the exchange rate:

$$S_t = S_{t-1}^{3m_t b + (1-\alpha)(1-m_t)b} S_{t-2}^{-2m_t b}$$

$$m_t = \frac{1}{1 + \beta(S_{t-1} - 1)^2}$$

where

S_t is the exchange rate in period t;
S_{t-1} is the exchange rate in period $(t - 1)$;
S_{t-2} is the exchange rate in period $(t - 2)$;
m_t is the weight given to chartists;
α is a parameter expressing the fundamentalists' reaction;
b is the discount factor $(0 < b < 1)$;
β is a parameter for influencing m_t.

Table 4.1 Parameter space explored for the map

Parameter	Value	Description
X_0	0.95	initial value for X
Y_0	0.95	initial value for Y
Z_0	0.95	initial value for Z
T_0	0.50	initial value for T
a	variable	exponential parameter fundamentalists
b	0.95	discount factor
c	600	parameter for influencing m_t

To be consistent with the usual mathematical notations the variables S_t, S_{t-1}, S_{t-2} and, m_t will be replaced by X, Y, Z, and T. The parameters α, b, and β are replaced by a, b, and c, leading to the following map:

$$X = Y^{3Tb+(1-a)(1-T)b} Z^{-2Tb}$$

$$T = \frac{1}{1 + c(Y - 1)^2}$$

A second feature, making the model presented in this chapter different from the model of the previous chapter, has to do with the parameter values we assume here. We represent these parameters in table 4.1. We will allow the parameter a (which represents the fundamentalists' reaction to deviations between the market and the fundamental exchange rate) to exceed 1. This could mean that fundamentalists expect future overshooting of the exchange rate.

2 IS THERE CHAOS IN THE SIMPLE EXCHANGE RATE MODEL?

In order to examine the above mapping for signs of chaos, the parameter space for the map can be explored by varying a, b and c and the initial conditions. For several different parameter combinations, different types of strange attractors can be identified in the model. In this section we will mainly be exploring the overall mathematical form and dynamics of the map.

In order to check for chaos, a time series of data is generated from the map. The first 5000 data points of the time series are ignored to avoid transient effects, and the phase space trajectory is reconstructed in $XYZT$ space for the map. The dynamics of the mapping will be explored for the parameters of table 4.1. The initial values for X, Y, Z, and T are labeled with the subscript "0" in table 4.1. Only one parameter, a (the exponential parameter for the fundamentalists), is varied by letting a take values ranging from 0.2 to 2.

Figure 4.1 shows the $X-Y$ phase space projection plots for the values of a indicated in Table 4.2. This table also contains a brief description of the encountered phenomena. The $X-Y$ phase space projection was generated from 15 000 datapoints. Figure 4.1 is very instructive in the way chaos develops in this map. For values of a less than unity, the system evolves toward a limit cycle (quasiperiodic signal) (figure 4.1a). Figure 4.1b shows how this limit cycle gets gradually deformed and twisted for larger values of a ($a = 1.1$). Eventually sharp corners (and "horns") develop for this deformed limit cycle ($a = 1.2367$ in figure 4.1c). There is a gradual tendency for frequency locking in these sharp corners. This means that the sharp corners are visited more often by the mapping trajectories than the points in between. When the parameter a increases further, frequency locking occurs and eventually a perfect 8-cycle can be observed ($a = 1.24$ in figure 4.1d). With increasing values

Figure 4.1 First strange attractor from the simple exchange model for various values of the parameter a (exponential factor for fundamentalists). The strange attractor is fully developed for $1.391 < a < 1.43$. (a) limit cycle, $a = 0.7$; (b) deformed limit cycle, $a = 1.1$; (c) sharp-edged deformed limit cycle, $a = 1.2367$; (d) 8 cycle, $a = 1.24$; (e) 16 cycle, $a = 1.31$; (f) 32 cycle, $a = 1.357$; (g) n cycle after several bifurcations, $a = 1.36$; (h) partially developed chaos, $a = 1.37$; (i) n cycle, $a = 1.372$; (j) partially developed chaos, $a = 1.376$; (k) n cycle, $a = 1.382$; (l) recovering strange attractor, $a = 1.392$.

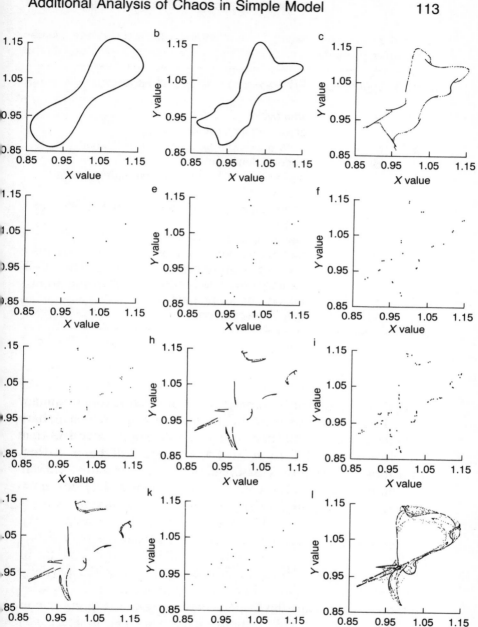

Table 4.2   Regime leading to first strange attractor in the simple exchange rate model

a value	Figure 4.1	Brief phenomenological description
0.700	a	limit cycle
1.100	b	deformed limit cycle
1.2367	c	severely deformed limit cycle with sharp edges
1.240	d	period 8 limit cycle
1.310	e	period 16 limit cycle after first bifurcation at $a = 1.306$
1.357	f	period 32 limit cycle after second bifurcation at $a = 1.356$
1.360	g	several bifurcations later
1.370	h	partially developed chaos
1.372	i	periodic behavior again
1.376	j	partially developed chaos
1.382	k	periodic behavior again
1.392	l	fully developed chaos

for a, this 8-cycle will be subject to several bifurcations, similar to the Feigenbaum scenario of the logistic map. A first period doubling bifurcation occurs for $a = 1.306$. Figure 4.1e shows a 16-cycle ($a = 1.31$). At $a = 1.356$, there will be a second bifurcation evolving to a 32-cycle (figure 4.1f for $a = 1.357$). This bifurcation process continues (e.g. figure 4.1g for $a = 1.36$), until eventually partially developed chaos manifests itself (figure 4.1h for $a = 1.37$). We use here the term *partially developed chaos* to distinguish figure 4.1h from the *fully developed chaos* of figure 4.1l. Both h and l are truly chaotic in the sense of chaos described in chapter 1. After the partially developed chaos regime, there is a rapid sequence of n-cycles alternated by partially developed chaotic regimes (e.g. n-cycle in figure 4.1i for $a = 1.372$; partially developed chaos in figure 4.1j for $a = 1.376$; 16-cycle in figure 4.1k for $a = 1.382$), until chaos eventually manifests itself over a relatively broad parameter

a

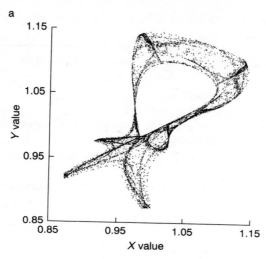

Figure 4.2 Simple exchange rate model. View of the "jellyfish" attractor for $a = 1.43$.

range for a (figure 4.1l, $a = 1.392$). This is what we call the first chaotic regime, which exists for a ranging from 1.391 to 1.43. There are small intervals in this chaotic region where the n-cycles will appear again, similar to the chaotic regime for the logistic map.

In the scenario just described, chaotic behavior evolves after several period doublings. This scenario is in fact very similar to the now classical phenomenon for finding chaos in the logistic map. Figure 4.2 shows a better view of the strange attractor for $a = 1.42$. This attractor is reminiscent of a jellyfish. Bifurcation diagrams similar to the bifurcation diagram of the logistic equation could be generated. Such a bifurcation diagram would now be three-dimensional, and does not show very nicely in a two-dimensional projection.

Figure 4.3 shows the XY, XZ, XT and TZ projections of the "jellyfish" attractor ($a = 1.392$). Strange attractors of this type can be constructed from the simple exchange rate model. They

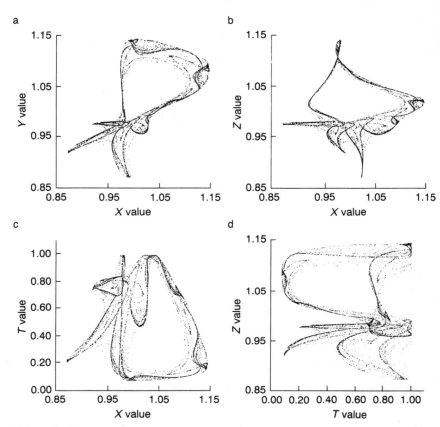

Figure 4.3 Various projections of the "jellyfish" attractor for $a =$ 1.392. (a) XY view; (b) XZ view; (c) XT view; (d) ZT view.

manifest themselves for a ranging from 1.39 to 1.43 and are labeled type I attractors (figure 4.4a).

There are several other parameter regimes for which strange attractors will appear in this simple model. Different types of strange attractors can be found in the range $1.46 < a < 1.64$ (type II attractor), and $2.01 < a < 2.86$ (type III attractor). Typical samples of the type I, type II, and type III attractors are shown in figure 4.4. The attractor regions are interspersed with regions of n-cycles and partially developed chaos. While the type I and type II attractors developed themselves from an 8-cycle with subsequent bifurcations, the type III attractor evolved from a 5-cycle after several bifurcations. Some of the pictures for partial chaos from this 5-cycle are revealing as well (e.g. partially developed chaos for $a = 1.81$, figure 4.4d). For $a > 2.86$, the mapping process leads to ever-increasing values for X, Y, Z, and very small values for T ($T < 0.00001$). The values for X, Y, and T eventually become infinity (i.e. the map *blows up*).

There are several other parameter regimes in this model that would lead to chaos. Varying c accomplishes only a scaling and makes very little difference in the dynamic behavior of the system. By varying b, other chaotic regimes can be found. So far, we only encountered strange attractors that look similar to the type I, II, or III attractors summarized in figure 4.4. An example of a type II attractor can be found by setting $b = 1.7$, and $a = 1.3$.

3 FRACTAL BASIN BOUNDARIES

The attractors described in the previous section were all found with the same initial conditions for the variables X, Y, Z, and T. Different initial conditions *can* also provide a different dynamic behavior. It is quite possible that a system would evolve to a chaotic attractor for a certain set of initial conditions, and to a limit cycle or a different type of chaotic attractor for a different set of initial conditions. The space of the dynamics of the exchange rate model will be explored by varying the initial conditions. Figure 4.5 shows the summary of such a study. This figure shows the parameter a on the vertical axis, and the initial condition for T, T_0, on the horizontal axis. The initial conditions for X, Y, and Z were scaled to the initial conditions for T according to

$$X_0 = Y_0 = Z_0 = 0.95 \times 2 \times T_0$$

The values for b and c were kept unchanged from those reported in table 4.1. Interpretation of figure 4.5 is a little tricky. Whenever the mapping process blows up (i.e. produces

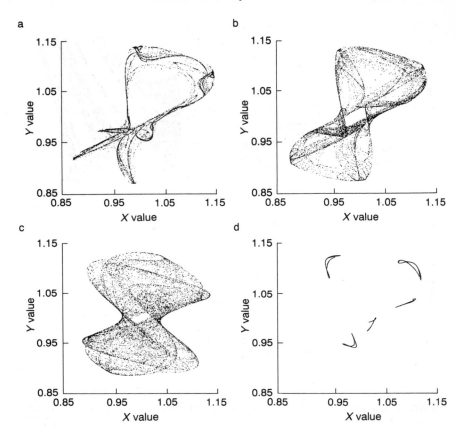

Figure 4.4 Typical representations for type I, type II, and type III attractors. (a) *XY* view for type I attractor (*a* = 1.392); regime extends for 1.391 < *a* < 1.43. (b) *XY* view for type II attractor (*a* = 1.53); regime extends for 1.47 < *a* < 1.64. (c) *XY* view for type III attractor (*a* = 2.7); regime extends for 2.01 < *a* < 2.86. (d) *XY* view for partially developed type III attractor (*a* = 1.81); notice the five different branches for this chaotic signal.

extremely large values for *X*, *Y*, and *Z*), a white point is plotted. If the values for the map remain finite, a black point is plotted.

In order to save computing time while producing the plots of figure 4.5, we actually applied a slightly different procedure. It

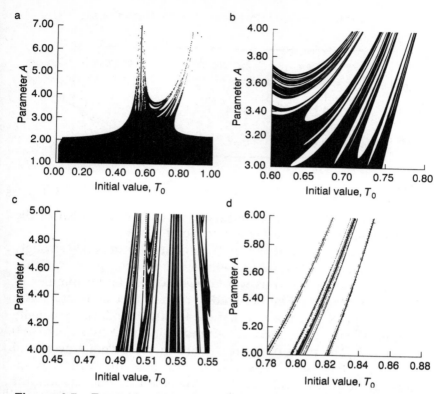

Figure 4.5 Fractal basin boundaries. (a) $0 < T_0 < 1$, $1 < a < 7$; (b) $0.6 < T_0 < 0.8$, $3 < a < 4$; (c) $0.45 < T_0 < 0.55$, $4 < a < 5$; (d) $0.78 < T_0 < 0.88$, $5 < a < 6$.

was noticed that future mapping steps will blow up as soon as a T value becomes smaller than 0.00001. To obtain the plots of figure 4.5, 15 iterations were performed. If a value for T became less than 0.00001 during these mappings, a white point was plotted; otherwise a black point was plotted. The plots in figure 4.5 are for several different intervals for T_0 and a (see Table 4.3). Such plots are referred to in the literature as *fractal basin boundary plots*. These fractal basin boundary plots are distant cousins of the now famous Mandelbrot set (Mandelbrot, 1983). The plots in figure 4.5 show a certain degree of (fractal)

Table 4.3 Parameter intervals for fractal basin boundary plots

Range for T_0	Range for a	Figure 4.5
0.00−1.00	1−7	a
0.60−0.80	3−4	b
0.45−0.55	4−5	c
0.78−0.88	5−6	d

self-similarity. Figure 4.5c and d are actually reminiscent of the fractal properties of the Hénon attractor.

The overall shape of the plots in figure 4.5 depends strongly on the number of iterations monitored. For the plots in figure 4.5 only 15 mapping steps were calculated. A larger number of mapping steps would be required to obtain the true fractal basin boundary plots. We noticed that the fractal boundaries gradually disappear when the number of iterations increases (e.g. 400 iterations). The plots of figure 4.5 are therefore not true fractal basin boundary plots. The fractal nature of these plots is intriguing, however, and they were included in this chapter for that very reason.

It would be possible to expand the scope of the plots of figure 4.5. This time one could monitor (in addition to the cases for which the map blows up) whether the system evolves to a strange attractor, to a limit cycle, or to an n-period cycle. Different regimes can be indicated by using different colors. A nice theoretical treatment of fractal basin boundaries can be found in Frame (1992).

4 ANALYSIS OF THE "JELLYFISH" ATTRACTOR

In this section the data that generated the "jellyfish" attractor will be further analyzed to verify more signatures for chaotic behavior. Sensitivity to the initial conditions will be verified, the power spectrum will be calculated, and the fractal dimension

4.2 Sensitivity to initial conditions

The dramatic appearance of the "jellyfish" attractor implies that we are dealing with a chaotic signal. If it were not for the visualization of this strange attractor, sensitivity to the initial conditions (SIC) would ultimately judge whether our strange creature (jellyfish) was actually a chaotic signal or an entirely different kind of animal.

Table 4.4 shows the first 79 datapoints for the X component of the attractor for two different sets of initial conditions: $X_0 = 0.95$ (series no. 1), and $X_0 = 0.951$ (series no. 2). The signals are almost identical initially, and slowly diverge to completely different values at later times. The diverging trend between the two time series indicates sensitivity to the initial conditions and is the most convincing argument for the chaotic nature of the datapoints.

Sensitivity to initial conditions is definitely one of the more decisive criteria for a chaotic time series. SIC implies that even when the signal is generated from a completely deterministic model, just changing one of the initial conditions slightly will eventually yield different values. Sensitivity to the initial conditions does not affect the overall probabilistic properties of the time series. Changing the initial conditions does not affect the distribution function or the Fourier power spectrum (as long as we remain in the same fractal basin). SIC seems at first sight to be incompatible with the finite precision of present day computers. Different computers would provide us with completely different answers for a time series generated from a chaotic map. However, because the general dynamics of the system are not affected, SIC actually has less impact on the overall signal characteristics than we would expect at first sight.

4.3 Fractal dimension for the "jellyfish" attractor

The correlation function is plotted as a function of the radii of the hyperspheres, for various embeddings ($n = 2$ to 11) of the vector space, in figure 4.7a. The plot is on a log–log scale, and the slopes of these curves converge with increasing embeddings

Additional Analysis of Chaos in Simple Model

Table 4.4 Sensitivity to the initial conditions for the "jellyfish" attractor

PT no.	Series no. 1	Series no. 2	PT no.	Series no. 1	Series no. 2
0	0.95000	0.95100	40	0.87469	0.87904
1	0.96599	0.96725	41	0.98806	0.98527
2	1.00729	1.00757	42	1.02549	1.02602
3	1.05119	1.05177	43	1.09020	1.09266
4	1.13194	1.13268	44	1.14302	1.14496
5	1.07490	1.07333	45	0.99557	0.99315
6	0.97323	0.97326	46	0.98161	0.98219
7	0.95949	0.95850	47	0.95710	0.96375
8	0.95913	0.95718	48	0.93069	0.94410
9	0.98745	0.98664	49	0.95729	0.95791
10	1.02427	1.02426	50	1.01529	1.00585
11	1.08718	1.08754	51	1.05897	1.04764
12	1.14367	1.14448	52	1.12219	1.12611
13	0.99924	0.99894	53	1.04307	1.08370
14	0.98122	0.98136	54	0.97623	0.97358
15	0.94879	0.94973	55	0.93646	0.96468
16	0.91348	0.91508	56	0.90537	0.96808
17	0.96000	0.95920	57	0.98006	0.99141
18	1.02282	1.02221	58	1.02732	1.02451
19	1.07065	1.06912	59	1.09526	1.08480
20	1.11576	1.11526	60	1.14254	1.13731
21	1.01521	1.01760	61	0.99023	1.00099
22	0.97701	0.97694	62	0.98222	0.98023
23	0.92095	0.92065	63	0.97011	0.94294
24	0.87177	0.87149	64	0.95863	0.90416
25	0.99098	0.99136	65	0.96526	0.96598
26	1.02499	1.02493	66	0.99655	1.02548
27	1.08661	1.08606	67	1.03438	1.08035
28	1.13844	1.13763	68	1.10746	1.12305
29	0.99898	0.99949	69	1.12396	1.00339
30	0.98060	0.98044	70	0.97972	0.97820
31	0.94757	0.94617	71	0.97965	0.93359
32	0.91288	0.91039	72	0.98585	0.89214
33	0.96243	0.96357	73	0.99980	0.97770
34	1.02350	1.02421	74	1.02395	1.02682
35	1.07387	1.07602	75	1.07020	1.09290
36	1.11943	1.12046	76	1.10950	1.14083
37	1.01143	1.00856	77	1.01344	0.99237
38	0.97743	0.97764	78	0.97647	0.98170
39	0.92336	0.92600			

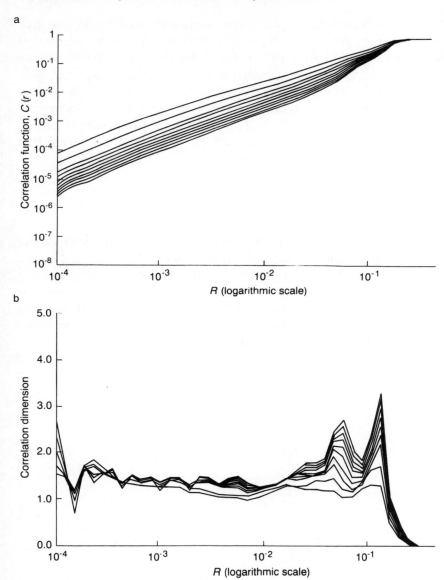

Figure 4.7 Estimating the fractal dimension of the "jellyfish" attractor. (a) $C(R)$ versus R on a log-log scale; (b) correlation dimension estimated from pointwise slope of $\log[C(R)]$ versus $\log(R)$.

to the correlation dimension (for small values of R). Figure 4.7b shows the slope of $\log[C(R)]$ versus $\log(R)$ as a function of $\log(R)$, for embeddings ranging from 2 to 11. Five thousand 11-tuple vectors were constructed for generating the curves in figure 4.7. From figure 4.7b we can conclude that the fractal dimension of the jellyfish attractor is about 1.47. The saturation of the curves and the extended region for constant slopes in figure 4.7b are clear indications that the time series that generated the "jellyfish attractor" is indeed chaotic.

5   CONCLUSION

In this chapter we used more advanced techniques to detect chaos in a simple exchange rate model. This allowed us to uncover a spectacularly complex behavior of the exchange rate in a model that is extremely simple. In the next chapter, we extend the model by adding more structure to it. This will also allow us to generate exchange rate movements that come closer to the ones observed in reality.

5

A Chaotic Exchange Rate Model
with Money

1 INTRODUCTION

In chapter 4 we developed a model of the exchange rate in which the structure of the underlying model and the exogenous variables were left unspecified. We summarized this structure by the exogenous X_t variable, which was identified as the fundamental value of the exchange rate. The drawback of this very simple model is that there is no feedback from the exchange rate to the underlying model. For example, in the previous model, the movements of the exchange rate do not affect the domestic price level. They therefore also leave the fundamental value of the exchange rate unaffected.

In this chapter we add some structure to the underlying model. This will make it possible to introduce an important interaction between the exchange rate and the domestic price level. We will keep the nature of the speculative behavior unchanged. It will become clear from this chapter that by adding structure to the underlying model we increase the complexity of the exchange rate dynamics.

2 THE MODEL

The model used in this chapter has frequently been used in the foreign exchange rate literature.[1] It consists of a money market equilibrium condition, the open interest parity condition, and goods market equilibrium.[2] We also discussed this model in chapter 2.

2.1 The money market equilibrium condition

Equilibrium in the money market is achieved when the demand for money is equal to the supply. We specify the demand for money in the traditional way, i.e.

$$M_{dt} = Y_t^a \cdot P_t \cdot (1 + r_t)^{-c} \tag{1}$$

where P_t is the domestic price level in period t, r_t is the domestic interest rate, Y_t is the (exogenous) level of domestic output. Note that if we take logarithms of this function we obtain the usual linear specification of the money demand function, which is often used in the literature (see chapter 2).

The process determining the supply of money, M_{st}, crucially depends on the policy regime. We will start by assuming that the monetary authorities follow a policy of rigidly controlling the supply of money. This, of course, is not a very realistic assumption. Such a policy of strict money supply targeting most often leads to a large short-term volatility of the interest rate, so that most central banks in the world apply some interest-rate smoothing procedure in the short run. In a second stage of our analysis we will analyze how interest-rate smoothing by the monetary authorities affects the dynamics in the market. The regime of money stock targeting, which implies that M_{st} is an exogenous variable, will be used as a benchmark for comparison with the effects of interest-rate smoothing.

Equilbrium in the money market now implies

$$M_{st} = M_{dt} \tag{2}$$

2.2 The open interest parity condition

Assuming that the domestic financial markets are completely open to the rest of the world, the open interest parity condition can be used. This condition implies absence of capital controls. We have

$$E_t(S_{t+1})/S_t = (1 + r_t)/(1 + r_{ft}) \tag{3}$$

where S_t is, as before, the exchange rate in period t (the price of the foreign currency in units of the domestic currency), $E_t(S_{t+1})$

is the forecast made in period t of the exchange rate in period $t + 1$, r_{ft} is the foreign interest rate.

The open interest parity condition is an equilibrium condition implying that if, say, the domestic interest rate exceeds the foreign interest rate, the price of the foreign currency must be expected to increase relative to the spot price today ($E_t(S_{t+1}) > S_t$). This is necessary in order to compensate holders of foreign assets for the unfavorable foreign interest rate.

There has been a lot of analysis of the conditions under which this parity relationship holds. An important condition is risk neutrality of speculators. We do not go into a discussion of the issues relating to the validity of the open interest parity condition. The interested reader can consult a very useful survey by MacDonald and Taylor (1990). We use this parity condition here mainly because this efficiency condition is used most often in theoretical exchange rate models.

2.3   Goods market equilibrium

The short-term price dynamics is assumed to be determined as follows

$$P_t/P_{t-1} = \left(\frac{S_t P_{ft}}{P_t}\right)^k \tag{4}$$

where $k > 0$. That is, when the real exchange rate increases (declines) upward (downward) pressure on the domestic price level is exerted. Put differently, when the domestic currency experiences a real depreciation this increases demand for the domestic good, tending to increase the price level. The opposite occurs when there is a real appreciation of the currency.

In the long run, purchasing power parity (PPP) is assumed to hold, i.e.

$$S_t^* = P_t^*/P_{ft}^* \tag{5}$$

where S_t^* is the equilibrium (PPP) exchange rate, P_{ft}^* is the foreign and P_t^* is the domestic steady state[3] value for the price level.

Note that we assume full employment, so that adjustment

towards equilibrium is realized through price changes. The parameter k measures the speed of adjustment in the goods market. In general the size of this parameter depends on the choice of the units of time. If the unit of time in the model is, say, a week, then k will be low compared to a model where the unit of time is a month or a quarter.

The model consisting of equations (1) to (5) fully describes the structure of the economy. It is a very simple structure, which, however, has some interesting features. In particular it can be seen that there is an interaction between the spot exchange rate and the price level.

One can easily solve this structural model as follows. P_t from equation (4) can be substituted into the money demand equation (1). Together with the money market equilibrium condition, this yields an expression determining the domestic interest rate. The latter is then substituted in the open interest parity condition (3). This yields the following expression for the exchange rate:

$$S_t = Z_t^{\psi} \cdot E_t(S_{t+1})^{\phi} \tag{6}$$

where $Z_t = M_{st} \cdot Y_t^{-a} \cdot P_{t-1}^{-\xi}$ $(\xi = 1/(1 + k))$, and

$$\phi = 1/(1 + k/((1 + k)c))$$
$$\psi = (1/c)\phi$$

It should be noted that equation (6) has a similar structure to the exchange rate equation we started out with in chapter 4. The difference from the previous exchange rate equation, however, is that underlying the variable Z_t there is a structural model. In addition the ϕ parameter expresses structural parameters of the model. Note, however, that as in the case of the simple exchange rate model of chapter 4 this parameter lies between 0 and 1. This means that the discounting parameter is itself determined by the structure of the underlying model.

2.4 Expectations formation

The way in which expectations are formed is assumed to be the same as in chapter 4, i.e. we assume that there are fundamentalists and chartists. The fundamentalists compute the equilibrium (fundamental) exchange rate, which in the present model is the PPP value of the exchange rate. If the fundamentalists observe a market rate above (below) the fundamental rate they expect it to decline (increase) in the future. The rate at which they expect the exchange rate to return to its fundamental value is related to the speed at which the prices in the goods market adjust (the parameter k). It will be assumed that the fundamentalists know this parameter and take that information into account to set their expectations.

As in chapter 4, we will assume that the chartists extrapolate the past exchange rate movements according to some moving average model. For the sake of convenience we repeat the equations that describe these expectational assumptions.

The change in the expected future exchange rate consists of two components, a forecast made by the chartists and a forecast made by the fundamentalists:

$$E_t(S_{t+1})/S_{t-1} = (E_{ct}(S_{t+1})/S_{t-1})^{m_t}(E_{ft}(S_{t+1})/S_{t-1})^{1-m_t} \qquad (7)$$

where $E_t(S_{t+1})$ is the market forecast made in period t of the exchange rate in period $t + 1$; $E_{ct}(S_{t+1})$ and $E_{ft}(S_{t+1})$ are the forecasts made by the chartists and the fundamentalists, respectively; m_t is the weight given to the chartists and $1 - m_t$ is the weight given to the fundamentalists in period t.

The chartists extrapolate recent observed exchange rate changes into the future, using a moving average procedure, i.e.

$$E_{ct}(S_{t+1})/S_{t-1} = f(S_{t-1}, \ldots, S_{t-N}) \qquad (8)$$

The fundamentalists are assumed to calculate the equilibrium exchange rate (the fundamental rate), S_t^*. This is obtained by solving equation (6) forward, given the current and the future values of the exogenous variables. For the sake of simplicity, we set all these exogenous variables equal to one. This implies that the equilibrium exchange rate is equal to 1. Note that PPP holds in equilibrium.

Fundamentalists then expect the market rate to return to that fundamental rate at speed α during the next period, if they observe a deviation today, i.e.

$$E_{ft}(S_{t+1})/S_{t-1} = (S_{t-1}^*/S_{t-1})^{\alpha} \qquad (9)$$

It will be assumed that the speed with which fundamentalists expect the exchange rate to return to its fundamental value is equal to the speed of adjustment in the goods market (k).

Finally, we make the same assumption as in chapter 4 about the weights to be given to chartists and fundamentalists. Thus,

$$m_t = 1/(1 + \beta (S_{t-1} - S_{t-1}^*)^2) \tag{10}$$

where m_t is the weight given to the chartists, and $\beta > 0$.

We can now solve the model consisting of equations (6) to (10). Substitute (8), (9), and (10) into (7), and (7) into (6). This yields the following expression for the exchange rate:

$$S_t = z_t^{\psi} S_{t-1}^{\phi_1} S_{t-2}^{\phi_2} S_{t-3}^{\phi_3} S_{t-1}^{*\phi_4} \tag{11}$$
$$\psi = (1/c)\phi$$
$$\theta = 1/(1 + k/(1 + k)c)$$
$$Z_t = m_{St} y_t^{-a} P_{t-1}^{-\xi}$$
$$\xi = 1/(1 + k)$$
$$\phi_1 = \phi[1 + \gamma m_t - \alpha(1 - m_t)]$$
$$\phi_2 = -2\phi\gamma m_t$$
$$\phi_3 = \phi\gamma m_t$$
$$\phi_4 = \phi\alpha(1 - m_t)$$

We analyze the characteristics of this solution in the next section, using simulation experiments, much in the same way as we did in chapter 4.

3   SIMULATION RESULTS: EXISTENCE OF CHAOS

Since the model used in this chapter has more structure than the one used in chapter 4, there are also more parameters that can potentially influence the dynamics of the model. Here we will concentrate on three parameters, i.e.

- the chartists' extrapolation parameter γ;
- the fundamentalists' "regression" parameter α;
- the interest elasticity of the demand for money c.

The other parameters of the model are fixed. The numerical values given to these parameters are shown here (in a later section we discuss how sensitive the results are to variations in these parameters):

Scaling factor of weight function	β	$= 10\,000$
Income elasticity of money demand	α	$= 0.2$
Exchange rate period $t - 1$	S_{t-1}	$= 1.02$
Exchange rate period $t - 2$	S_{t-2}	$= 0.99$

Exchange rate period $t - 3$ $S_{t-3} = 1.0$
Domestic money stock $M_{st} = 1.0$
Foreign money stock $M_{fst} = 1.0$
Domestic production $Y_t = 1.0$
Foreign production $Y_{ft} = 1.0$
Foreign interest rate $r_{ft} = 0.0$
Foreign price level $P_{ft} = 1.0$

In order to detect chaos we varied the three coefficients mentioned earlier. The results are presented in table 5.1, which shows three sub-tables. Each sub-table has a different value of the interest elasticity and shows the nature of the solution depending on the size of the γ and the α coefficients. We observe a varied pattern of solutions (periodic, limit cycles and chaos). In general, we find that as the degree of extrapolation by the chartists increases, the probability of obtainig a chaotic solution also increases. Similarly, when fundamentalists expect the exchange rate to move slowly towards its fundamental value (i.e. α is small), the occurrence of chaos becomes more likely.

In figures 5.1 to 5.3 we show some examples of chaotic solutions in the time domain and the phase space. Figure 5.1 shows the time series of a chaotic solution. We illustrate the sensitivity to initial conditions in figure 5.2, where two simulations of the same model are presented, the only difference being that the initial conditions are different. It can be seen that a small difference in the initial conditions (we changed the initial exchange rate by 1 percent) has a profound influence on the whole future time path of the exchange rate.

As in the model of chapter 4, the sensitivity to initial conditions also implies that very small changes in a parameter of the model produces, after some time, a completely different time path for the exchange rate. We show an experiment similar to the one used in chapter 4 in figure 5.4. This shows two simulations with the same model. However, one parameter has been slightly changed. It can be seen that after some time the two series seem to behave independently. This sensitivity to initial conditions has important implications for econometric analysis and forecasting. We discussed these in chapter 3, so we do not have to repeat them here.

An important feature of the dynamics of the exchange rate, which is visible with the naked eye in figure 5.2, is the strong

Table 5.1 Characterization of asymptotic solutions in $\gamma-\alpha$ space

Interest elasticity = 0.1

Gamma										
4	CH	P4	CH	CH	CH1	P4	P4	P4	P4	LC1
3	CH	P4	CH	CH	CH1	P4	P4	P4	P4	LC1
2	LC1	LC1	LCS	CH	P4	P4	P4	LC1	LC1	LC1
1	LC1	LC1	LC1	S	S	S	S	S	S	S
Alpha	0.05	0.1	0.15	0.2	0.25	0.3	0.35	0.4	0.45	0.5

Gamma									
4	P15	P11	P11	LC1	LC1	LC1	P18	P18	P18
3	P15	LC1	LC1	LC1	LC1	LC1	LC1	LC1	LC1
2	LC1	LC1	LC1	LC1	LC1	S	S	S	S
1	S	S	S	S	S	S	S	S	S
Alpha	0.55	0.6	0.65	0.7	0.75	0.8	0.85	0.9	0.95

Interest elasticity = 0.5

Gamma										
4	CH	CH	CH	P18	LC1	LC1	P4	P4	P4	CH
3	CH	CH	CH	P10	P24	P9	LC1	P4	P4	LC4
2	CHS	CHS	LCS	P4	LC1	LC1	P30	P4	P4	P4
1	LC1	LC1	LC1	LC1	LC1	LC1	LC1	LC1	LC1	LC1
Alpha	0.05	0.1	0.15	0.2	0.25	0.3	0.35	0.4	0.45	0.5

Gamma									
4	CH	CH	CH	CH	CH1	P4	P4	P4	P4
3	CH	CH	CH	CH	P4	P4	P4	P4	P4
2	LC4	CH	CH	CH	P4	P4	P4	P4	P4
1	LC1	LC1	LC1	LC1	LC1	S	S	S	S
Alpha	0.55	0.6	0.65	0.7	0.75	0.8	0.85	0.9	0.95

Interest elasticity = 1.0

Gamma										
4	CH	CH	CH	CH	CH	P5	P5	CH	LC1	P4
3	P26	CH	CH	PH	P11	P5	PH	P23	P13	P4
2	CH	CH	CH1	LC1	LC1	PH	LC1	PH	LC1	CH1
1	LC1	LC1	LC1	LC1	LC1	LC1	LC1	LC1	LC1	LC1
Alpha	0.05	0.1	0.15	0.2	0.25	0.3	0.35	0.4	0.45	0.5

Gamma									
4	P4	P4	P4	P8	CH	CH	CH	CH	P4
3	P4	P4	P4	P4	CH	CH	P4	P4	P4
2	P4	P4	P4	P4	P49	CH	CH	P4	P4
1	LC1	LC1	LC1	LC1	LC1	LC1	LC1	LC1	LC1
Alpha	0.55	0.6	0.65	0.7	0.75	0.8	0.85	0.9	0.95

LC = Limit cycle; Pi = period i; PH = period is high; CH = chaos.

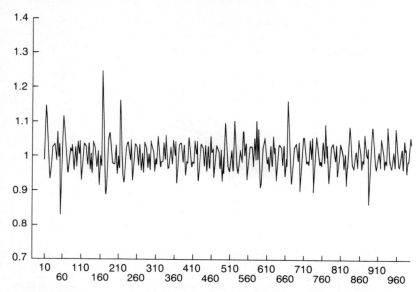

Figure 5.1 Simulated exchange rate of the model in the time domain (1000 iterations). Other parameters were $\alpha = 0.01$, inter.el = 0.1.

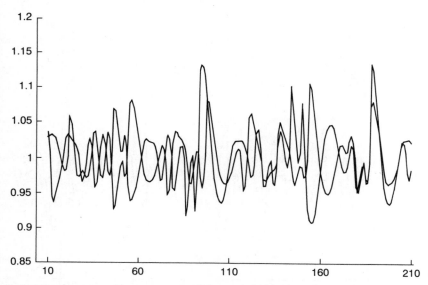

Figure 5.2 Sensitivity to initial conditions generated by different initial exchange rates (1 per cent difference). Other parameters were $\alpha = 0.01$, inter.el = 0.1.

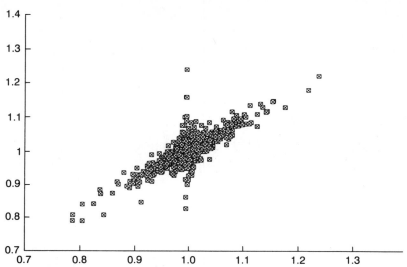

Figure 5.3 Phase diagram of the model in the $S_t - S_{t-1}$ space. Other parameters were $\alpha = 0.01$, inter.el $= 0.1$.

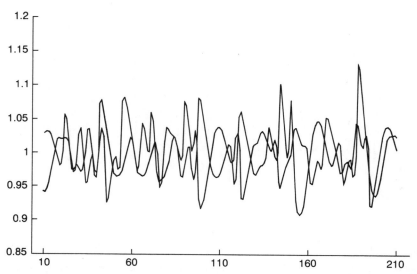

Figure 5.4 Sensitivity to initial conditions generated by a 1 percent difference in α; inter.el $= 0.1$.

short-term volatility around the equilibrium rate. There is no evidence that the exchange rate wanders away from the equilibrium value, as we observed in the model of chapter 3. In the monetary model of the present chapter, the exchange rate never stays on one side of the fundamental exchange rate for longer than a few periods. This feature of the dynamics of the exchange rate comes from the assumption that the monetary authorities rigidly fix the money stock. In such a policy regime the interest rate movements, which are substantial, quickly force the exchange rate back to its equilibrium value. The mechanism is as follows. When the exchange rate increases (a depreciation of the domestic currency) the price level tends to increase. This increases the demand for money, and therefore pushes the domestic interest rate upwards. The upward movement of the domestic interest rate leads to an instantaneous decline in the exchange rate (an appreciation of the domestic currency). In this regime of rigid monetary control where the authorities allow the interest rate to adjust freely, the exchange rate can never wander very far away from the equilibrium exchange rate, as perceived by the fundamentalists.

Things are quite different in other monetary regimes. We now introduce a monetary regime of interest-rate smoothing, and contrast the results with the regime of money supply targeting.

4 THE MODEL UNDER A REGIME OF INTEREST-RATE SMOOTHING

Interest-rate smoothing by the monetary authorities (a practice that is found in most, if not all, countries) can be formalized as follows:

$$\frac{M_{st}}{M_{s,t-1}} = \left(\frac{1 + r_t}{1 + r_{t-1}}\right)^{\theta} \tag{12}$$

This relation can be interpreted as follows. When the interest rate increases, the monetary authorities increase the domestic money stock. This in turn will tend to drive down the interest rate. The parameter θ measures the intensity with which the authorities perform this interest smoothing policy.

We simulated the model for different values of θ to test for

Table 5.2 Characterization of the asymptotic solution of the model in $\gamma-\alpha$ space

---

Theta = 100

Gamma

4	CH	CH	CH	CH	CH	CH	CH	CH	CH	CH
3	CH	CH	CH	CH	CH	P6	CH	CH	CH	CH
2	LC	CH	CH	CH	LC6	LC	LC	LC	P5	P10
1	P6	LC	LC	LC	LC	LC	LC	LC	LC	LC
Alpha	0.05	0.1	0.15	0.2	0.25	0.3	0.35	0.4	0.45	0.5

Gamma

4	P8	CH	P4	P4	P4	P4	P4	P4	P4	P4
3	CH	P4	P4	P4	P4	P4	P4	P4	P4	CH
2	LC	P9	LC	P4	P4	P4	P4	P4	P4	P4
1	LC	LC	LC	LC	LC	LC	LC	LC	LC	LC
Alpha	0.55	0.6	0.65	0.7	0.75	0.8	0.85	0.9	0.95	1

Theta = 10

Gamma

4	CH	CH	CH	CH	CH	CH	CH	CH	CH	P12
3	CH	CH	CH	CH	CH	P6	CH	P5	LC	CH
2	CH	CH	CH	CH	P6	LC	LC	LC	P4	LC
1	LC	LC	LC	LC	LC	LC	LC	LC	LC	LC
Alpha	0.05	0.1	0.15	0.2	0.25	0.3	0.35	0.4	0.45	0.5

Gamma

4	P4	P4	P4	P4	P4	P4	P4	CH	CH	CH
3	CH	P4	P4	P4	P4	P4	P4	CH	CH	CH
2	P14	P9	LC	P4	P4	P4	P4	P16	CH	CH
1	LC	LC	LC	LC	LC	LC	LC	LC	LC	LC
Alpha	0.55	0.6	0.65	0.7	0.75	0.8	0.85	0.9	0.95	1

Theta = 1

Gamma

4	CH	CH	CH	CH	CH	P10	LC	CH	CH	P4
3	CH	CH	CH	CH	PH	P8	LC	LC	P8	LC
2	LC	CH	P4	P11	LC	LC	LC	LC	P10	P10
1	LC	LC	LC	LC	LC	LC	LC	LC	LC	LC
Alpha	0.05	0.1	0.15	0.2	0.25	0.3	0.35	0.4	0.45	0.5

Gamma

4	P4	P4	P4	CH	CH	CH	CH	CH	CH	P4
3	P4	P4	P4	CH	CH	CH	CH	CH	P8	P8
2	P4	P4	P4	CH1	P8	CH	CH	CH	P4	P4
1	LC	LC	LC	LC	LC1	LC1	LC1	LC1	LC1	LC1
Alpha	0.55	0.6	0.65	0.7	0.75	0.8	0.85	0.9	0.95	1

For the meaning of the entries see table 5.1.

Table 5.3 Standard deviations (unconditional) of the interest rate, the exchange rate, and the money stock (in percent)

Interest rate (in % points)	Exchange rate		Money stock
	Period-to-period changes (%)	Levels around the mean (%)	
for $\theta = 0$: 0.7	2.3	3.1	0.0
for $\theta = 1$: 0.5	2.2	3.1	0.4
for $\theta = 10$: 0.2	1.9	3.3	1.8
for $\theta = 20$: 0.1	1.8	3.9	3.1

the existence of chaos. The results are shown in table 5.2, where we give solutions for three different values of θ (as before, we also vary the parameters α and γ). A striking result is that the range of parameter values for which chaos is obtained is drastically increased (compare table 5.2 with table 5.1). In addition, we now find chaos for relatively low extrapolation parameters of the chartists.

A second result of our model is that the degree of interest rate smoothing (the parameter θ) affects the variability of the exchange rate. In particular an increase in θ reduces not only the variability of the interest rate (which is not very surprising) but also the *short-term* variability of the exchange rate. We show this in table 5.3. It appears from this table that as the interest rate smoothing parameter increases, the standard deviation of the period-by-period changes in the exchange rate tends to decline. Note, however, that the standard deviation of the *level* of the exchange rate does not decline.

One way to interpret this result is as follows. The movements of the interest rate directly affect the spot exchange rate through the interest parity condition. Put differently, "noise" in interest rate creates noise in the spot exchange rate. Since chartists tend to extrapolate, they reinforce the noise in the exchange rate. Thus, by applying interest-rate smoothing, the authorities reduce the noise in both the interest rate and the exchange rate. This, of course, comes at a price, i.e. an increase in the noise in the money stock figures. Table 5.3 also shows the standard deviation around the mean of the money stock for different values of the interest-smoothing parameter. One observes that with increasing interest rate smoothing the variability of the money stock also increases. In addition, the long-run variability of the exchange rate (as measured by the standard deviation of the exchange rate relative to the mean) increases. This suggests that interest-rate smoothing enhances the long-run movements away from the fundamental exchange rate.

A third finding, which is related to the previous one, is that the nature of the exchange rate movements in this interest-rate smoothing model is quite different compared to the model without interest-rate smoothing. We show an example of this in figure 5.5, where we compare the time paths of the exchange rate for $\theta = 0$ and $\theta = 20$. We observe that the exchange rate has a tendency to exhibit relatively long cycles around the equilibrium value when interest-rate smoothing is applied ($\theta = 20$). In addition, it exhibits strong short-term movements around the longer-term cyclical movements.

The greater complexity of the dynamics of the exchange rate under interest rate smoothing suggests that the correlation dimension of this model (and thus the dimension of the attractor) is higher than in the model without interest rate smoothing. This is confirmed in figure 5.6, where we present estimates of the correlation dimensions of the two models. It can be seen that the correlation dimension of the model with interest-rate smoothing is approximately 3.3, whereas it is only 2.4 in the model of money supply targeting. Note also that the correlation dimensions obtained in the models of the present chapter are considerably larger than the correlation dimension of the model of chapter 4, which has a simpler structure.

Figure 5.7 presents the respective log–log plots of the power spectrum of the different models. The chaotic structure is again confirmed in the initial downward trend. Neither figure, moreover, displays large peaks (except the one at frequency zero). Therefore we suspect no real periodicity in the lower frequencies.

The greater complexity of the exchange rate dynamics of the models of this chapter, and in particular of the model with interest-rate smoothing, has the effect of generating time series of the exchange rate that come much closer to the "real life"

a

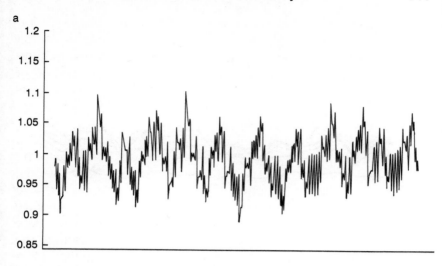

b

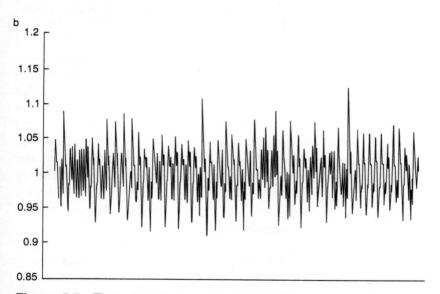

Figure 5.5 Time domain behavior for different degrees of interest-rate smoothing. (a) $\theta = 20$; (b) $\theta = 0$.

exchange rate movements. This is shown in figures 5.8 and 5.9, where we present real life exchange rates (the dollar/yen rate on a daily basis since 1986) and an exchange rate series as generated by our model (using a relatively high interest-rate

a

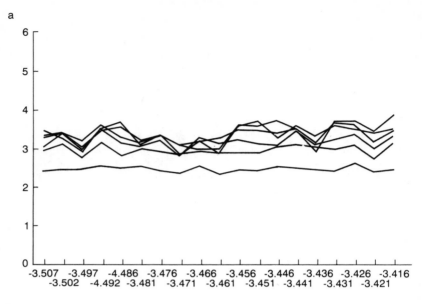

-3.507   -3.497   -4.486   -3.476   -3.466   -3.456   -3.446   -3.436   -3.426   -3.416
    -3.502   -4.492   -3.481   -3.471   -3.461   -3.451   -3.441   -3.431   -3.421

b

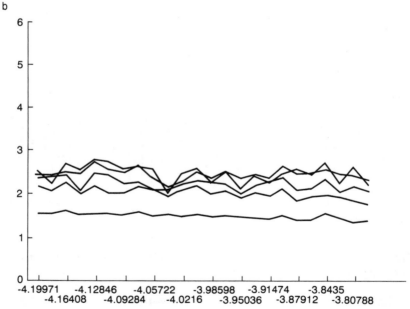

-4.19971   -4.12846   -4.05722   -3.98598   -3.91474   -3.8435
    -4.16408   -4.09284   -4.0216   -3.95036   -3.87912   -3.80788

Figure 5.6   Correlation dimension estimates for embedding 2 to 7.
(a) $\theta = 20$; (b) $\theta = 0$.

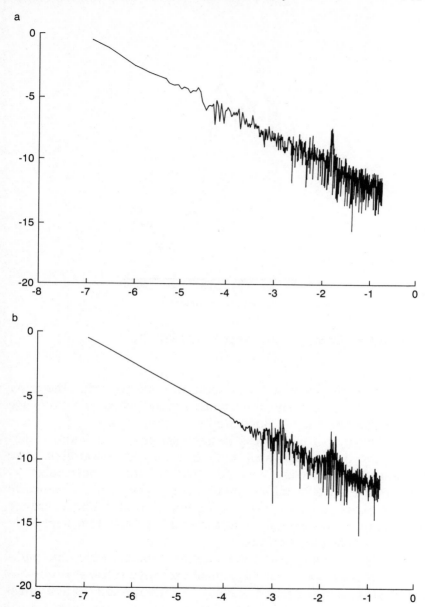

Figure 5.7 Log-log representation of the model. (a) $\theta = 20$; (b) $\theta = 0$.

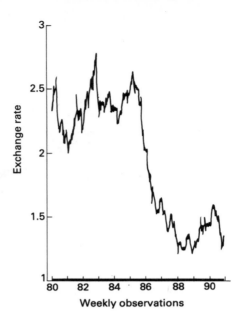

Figure 5.8   Dollar/yen exchange rate, 1987–91.

smoothing parameter). We observe in both cases that there are relatively long cyclical movements around which the exchange rate has a tendency to fluctuate in the short-run.

We have also performed tests of sensitivity to initial conditions on the model with high interest-rate smoothing. The results are shown in figure 5.9, and are quite spectacular. A small difference in initial conditions (a 2 percent difference in initial exchange rate) leads to a completely different exchange rate path, with long swings in the exchange rate that happen at very different time periods.

In the preceding discussion we have compared the time paths of the observed and the theoretical exchange rates. It is obvious that such a comparison cannot be interpreted as empirical evidence for our model. In section 6 we present more formal empirical evidence showing how the theoretical model is able to mimic some important features of actual exchange rate behavior.

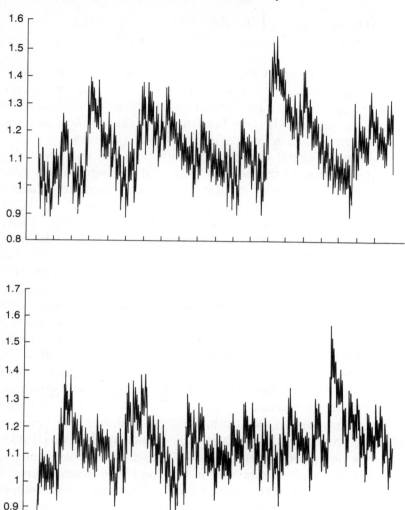

Figure 5.9 Sensitivity to initial conditions generated by different initial exchange rates. $\alpha = 0.1$, $\theta = 100$, inter.el = 1.0.

5 ADDITIONAL FEATURES OF THE MODEL WITH INTEREST-RATE SMOOTHING

In this section we study the sensitivity of our results to changes in the β parameter. As will be remembered, this parameter measures the degree of precision with which the fundamentalists are able to estimate the true fundamental value of the exchange rate. A high precision implies a high β, and vice versa.

In general we find that the β parameter does not affect the qualitative nature of the results. That is, if the model is chaotic, it remains so whatever the size of β. The β parameter does, however, affect the variability of the exchange rate. With increasing β, the variability of the exchange rate declines. Thus, if fundamentalists are very confident about the true underlying fundamental value of the exchange rate, the latter will not deviate very much from its fundamental value. We illustrate this feature in figure 5.10. This shows the time path of a chaotic solution for different values of β. It can be seen that the chaotic pattern is maintained for all these values of β. However, when β becomes very large, the movements of the exchange rate around the fundamental value become very small. This means that, as the confidence of the fundamentalists about their estimate of the true fundamental value increases, the size of the "misalignments" tends to decrease.

This result allows us to understand the behavior of the exchange rates within the European Monetary System (EMS). One striking empirical regularity is the fact that the movements of the EMS exchange rates within the band very much resemble the movements of exchange rates in a free float environment, except that the amplitude of these movements is much smaller. We illustrate this feature in figure 5.11, which shows the dollar/ Deutschmark rate and two intra-EMS exchange rates. It is striking to see that the structures of these movements are very much alike. The only apparent difference is that in the case of the dollar/Deutschmark, these movements occur in a band of approximately 30 percent, whereas in the case of the EMS exchange rates these bands are 12 and 4.5 percent.

This empirical regularity can be interpreted in the context of

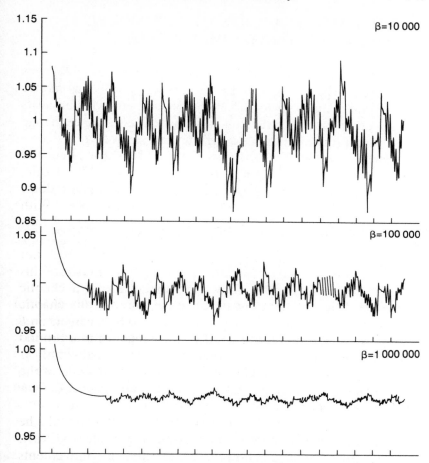

Figure 5.10 Effect of an increase in β for β = 10 000, 100 000, and 1 000 000. Other parameters were α = 0.1, θ = 20, inter.el = 1.0.

our model in the following way. The EMS has the effect of anchoring the expectations of speculators. If the system is credible, speculators will have no trouble believing that the parity rate is the fundamental rate. If this were not the case, they would expect a future realignment. In other words, for confidence in the fixity of the exchange rate to exist, it must be

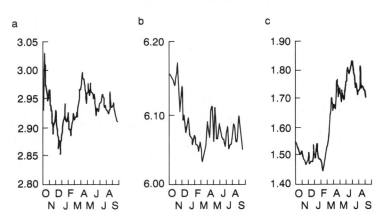

Figure 5.11 EMS and non-EMS nominal daily exchange rates, October 1990 to September 1991. (a) pound/Deutschmark; (b) French franc/Belgian franc; (c) dollar/Deutschmark.

the case that the parity rate is perceived as the true fundamental rate. This also implies that (in a credibly fixed exchange rate system) a deviation of the market exchange rate from that fundamental rate will quickly lead speculators to believe that a reversal in the future is likely. In the framework of the model of this chapter, this implies that β is large: fundamentalists can make a very precise estimate of the underlying fundamental exchange rate. Our model then shows that the movements of the exchange rate remain close to the fundamental rate.

These movemements, however, are chaotic in the same way as the movements of the free floating currencies are. We illustrate this in figure 5.12, which is a blow-up of the time series in the bottom part of figure 5.10. It appears that the structure of the dynamics is the same as in the top part of figure 5.10. The latter shows the simulations in which fundamentalists are much more uncertain about the true underlying fundamental exchange rate. These simulations can be considered as representing regimes of free floating exchange rates.

We have checked the similarity of the dynamics of these different regimes by performing tests of sensitivity to initial conditions, and by computing the correlation dimensions. We found that these different regimes have the same property

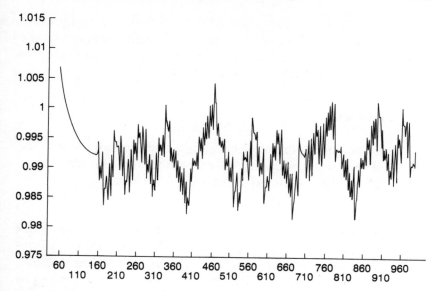

Figure 5.12 Time domain representation for the model. β = 1 000 000, $\alpha = 0.1$, inter.el = 1.0.

of sensitivity to initial conditions, and the same correlation dimensions.

6   SOME EMPIRICAL TESTS OF THE MODEL

The exchange markets have been subjected to considerable empirical analysis. Two results from that empirical literature stand out, and are not disputed. First, the time series of the exchange rates exhibits unit roots. Second, the forward premium (which is equal to the interest differential) is a biased predictor of future exchange rate movements. This has been documented in numerous empirical studies. (see, e.g. Fama, 1984; Takagi, 1988; McDonald and Taylor, 1990). See also the discussion in chapter 2.

In this section we analyze the simulated exchange rate and apply the same empirical tests as the ones applied to real life data. Thus we first study whether the simulated exchange rates exhibit unit roots. Second, we study the (un)biasedness of the forward premium (the interest differential) as a predictor of future (simulated) exchange rates in our model.

6.1 Unit roots

We subjected the simulated exchange rates to unit root tests. We used the model with interest-rate smoothing. In order to do so we applied the augmented Dickey–Fuller test.

$$S_t = a_1 S_{t-1} + rAR(1) \tag{13}$$

This equation was regressed on different exchange rate series assuming different θ parameters (interest smoothing parameters). The sample sizes were also varied. The Dickey–Fuller test then allows us to test for the existence of a unit root. The results are presented in table 5.4.

Our main finding is that we cannot reject the hypothesis that the exchange rates as generated by our model exhibit unit roots. It is good to remember here that the model is deterministic, and that it contains no stochastic disturbances. One can conclude that the exchange rates, as produced by our model, contain a feature which is universally found in real life exchange rates, i.e. a unit root. This can be considered as indirect empirical support for our model.

6.2 The forward premium as a predictor of future exchange rate movements

As indicated earlier, the empirical analysis of the exchange markets has led to the conclusion, which is now undisputed, that the forward premium is a biased predictor of future change in the exchange rate. That is, the forward premium predicts on average a future movement of the exchange rate in the wrong direction. This feature was most dramatic during the period 1980–5 when the dollar was continuously at a discount in the forward market and yet the dollar kept increasing in price.

In this section we test for unbiasedness of the forward

Table 5.4 Tests of unit roots in the simulated exchange rates with chaos

Sample size	a_1	r	DW	R^2	DF
$\theta = 20$					
100	0.998	0.28	1.73	0.63	−0.37
	(0.003)	(0.097)			
1000	0.999	0.29	1.72	0.69	−0.59
	(0.002)	(0.04)			
5000	0.999	0.31	1.71	0.69	−1.10
	(0.001)	(0.01)			
$\theta = 50$					
100	0.998	0.29	1.64	0.57	−0.41
	(0.003)	(0.10)			
1000	0.999	0.27	1.76	0.83	−0.57
	(0.002)	(0.04)			
5000	0.999	0.30	1.72	0.83	−1.22
	(0.001)	(0.01)			
$\theta = 100$					
100	0.997	0.25	1.76	0.91	−0.89
	(0.003)	(0.099)			
1000	0.999	0.31	1.70	0.87	−0.59
	(0.002)	(0.04)			
5000	0.999	0.30	1.71	0.89	−1.28
	(0.001)	(0.01)			

DW: Durbin–Watson. DF: Dickey–Fuller test statistic.

premium as generated by our model. If we find that our theoretical model produces the same biasedness result we have additional indirect support for the model.

Before we present the tests it is useful to look first at the time series as generated by our model. Figure 5.13 shows the simulated forward premium (interest differential) together with the simulated change in the exchange rate for different values of the interest-rate smoothing parameter. We have lagged the forward premium by one period, so that each datapoint has the realized and the predicted change in the exchange rate.

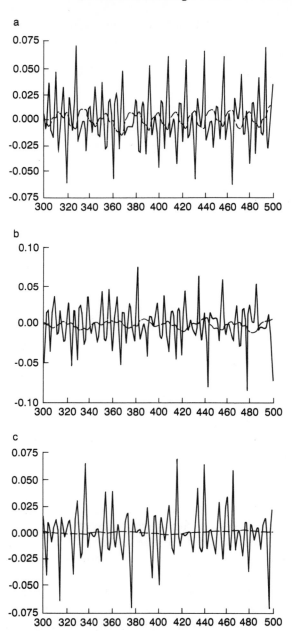

Figure 5.13 Forward premium and percentage change in exchange rate: simulations from the model. (a) $\theta = 0$; (b) $\theta = 10$; (c) $\theta = 20$.

We observe that the realized changes in the exchange rates are a multiple of the predicted ones (as measured by the forward premium). This feature of the movements of exchange rates has also been observed in reality. We illustrate this in figure 5.14, which shows the realized movements of the dollar/yen rate and the forward premium of the dollar (in the dollar/yen market). An implication of this empirical phenomenon is that the forward premium does not contain much useful information on future movements in the foreign exchange market. We find this in our model and in reality. Note that in our model this feature becomes more important as the intensity of interest-rate smoothing increases.

The bias of the forward premium as a predictor of the future exchange rate movements can be found econometrically as follows. One regresses the exchange rate change on the forward premium lagged one period:

$$D\ln S_t = a + b\, FP_{t-1} + u_t \tag{14}$$

where FP_{t-1} is the forward premium; it is also equal to the interest rate differential.

If the forward premium is an unbiased predictor b should be positive and significantly different from 0. Estimation of the econometric equation (14) using real life data shows, in most cases, that b is negative and significantly so. See Fama (1984) and De Grauwe (1989).

Our theoretical model is now capable of replicating these empirical results from "real life" exchange rate movements. We regressed equation (14) using the simulated numbers of our model. We present the results in table 5.5 for different values of the interest-rate smoothing parameter. The striking aspect of these results is that we systematically find the "wrong" negative value for b, indicating that, as in reality, the forward premium (the interest differential) in our model is a biased predictor of future exchange rate movements. This result is all the more striking in that we have assumed that open interest parity holds, i.e. there are no risk premia in the model that could explain these results. Put differently, the fact that the forward premium is a biased predictor of the future exchange rate movements can be explained without having to invoke the existence of risk

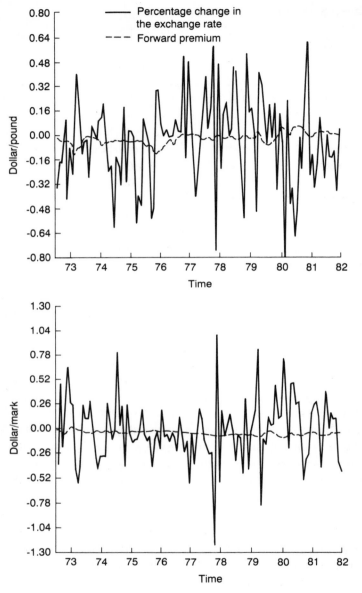

Figure 5.14   Forward premium and exchange rate changes for dollar/pound and dollar/Deutschmark (1973–1982).

Table 5.5 Estimates of equation (14)

	a	b	R^2	DW
for $\theta = 0$	0.0	−1.74	0.27	1.5
	(0.1)	(−19.2)		
for $\theta = 1$	0.0	−1.91	0.17	1.4
	(0.1)	(−14.1)		
for $\theta = 10$	−0.0	−2.20	0.04	1.3
	(−0.5)	(−6.4)		
for $\theta = 20$	0.0	−1.86	0.02	1.3
	(0.0)	(−4.23)		

premia (which up to now most researchers have been unable to detect).

How can one explain the result that a model without risk premia generates forward premia that are biased predictors of the future exchange rate changes? The explanation is as follows. An increase in the domestic interest rate leads to an instantaneous decline of the spot exchange rate (an appreciation of the domestic currency). To the extent that chartists extrapolate exchange rate movements, the increase in the interest rate can lead to expectations of future appreciations. If the chartists dominate the market, this extrapolative behavior will tend to be self-fulfilling, leading to actual future appreciations. Thus higher domestic interest rates will on average be associated with future appreciations of the domestic currency. Note again that this explanation does not rely on the existence of risk premia.

In this connection it is also important to realize that the interest parity condition imposed in the model hides the fact that there are implicit risk premia which chartists and fundamentalists face. This can be seen as follows. One can substitute the expectations of the chartists and the fundamentalists into the interest parity condition (3). This yields

$$(E_{ct}(S_{t+1})/S_t)^{mt}(E_{ft}(S_{t+1})/S_t)^{1-mt} = (1 + r_t)/(1 + r_{ft}) \qquad (15)$$

Since the interest differential equals the forward premium we can also rewrite this equation as follows:

$$(E_{ct}(S_{t+1})/S_t)^{mt}(E_{ft}(S_{t+1})/S_t)^{1-mt} = F_t/S_t \qquad (16)$$

where F_t is the forward exchange rate.

Market efficiency implies that the forward rate equals the market's expectation of the future exchange rate, $E_t(S_{t+1})$. However, it can now be seen from equation (16) that the chartists' and the fundamentalists' expectations will generally not be equal to the forward rate. For example, if chartists expect a future increase in the exchange rate, then we can derive from equation (16) that fundamentalists expect a future decline. As a result, we then must have that

$$E_{ct}(S_{t+1}) > F_t \qquad (17)$$

and

$$E_{ft}(S_{t+1}) < F_t \qquad (18)$$

Thus, chartists and fundamentalists will find that the forward rate does not reflect their expectations. They will therefore have an incentive to speculate further. That is, the chartists will buy forward (because they consider the forward rate to be cheap) and the fundamentalsits will sell forward (because they consider the forward rate to be expensive). In general, the inequalities (17) and (18) do not disappear. Therefore, it must be the case that the chartists and the fundamentalists consider further buying and selling to be too risky. Thus implicitly we have risk premia in our model. We assume, however, that these risk premia offset each other, and disappear at the level of the market. This is not an unreasonable assumption. In any trade there are two parties. The buyer who wants to take a risky position must find a seller, who will have to take a reverse and equally risky position. Both will have to be compensated by a risk premium, the sign of which will be different.

7 THE CHAOS MODEL WITH "NEWS"

As stressed in chapter 4, "news" also matters. In this section, therefore, we analyze the behavior of the model when stochastic shocks occur in one of the exogenous variables. We will limit

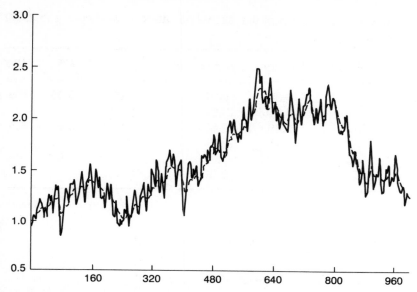

Figure 5.15 Exchange rate (——) and money stock (----), data-points 0–1000.

ourselves to an analysis of "news" in the domestic money stock. Most of the results discussed in this section carry through when disturbances occur in other exogenous variables.

We assume that the stochastic process driving the domestic money stock is a random walk, and we feed this random walk into the model with a parameter configuration that produces chaos. As an example, we present the exchange rate and the money stock in the time domain in figure 5.15. (We have assumed no interest-rate smoothing, so that the money stock is truly exogenous. The money stock is also the only exogenous variable that changes.)

As can be seen, over a time horizon of 1000 periods, the correlation between the exchange rate and the money stock (the fundamental) is quite close. A simple regression analysis confirms this:

Table 5.6 Regression of the exchange rate on the money stock (50 observations)

Sample period	Constant	Money stock	ρ	R^2	DW
900–950	0.00	0.97	0.83	0.85	0.9
	(0.0)	(3.6)	(12.9)		
950–1000	0.46	0.65	0.90	0.9	1.4
	(1.4)	(2.7)	(12.6)		
1000–1050	−0.12	1.07	0.91	0.93	1.2
	(−0.4)	(5.0)	(15.2)		

Constant	0.02
	(0.5)
Money stock	0.99
	(32.8)
ρ	0.91
	(70.3)
R^2	0.99
DW	1.3

From this we also find the theoretically expected value of the parameter of the money stock. This is equal to 1, as the theory predicts, i.e. a 1 percent increase in the money stock leads to a depreciation of the currency by 1 percent.

Suppose now that a researcher who wants to know the underlying structural relationship between the money stock and the exchange rate has at his disposal a much shorter sample period, say 50 periods. He then uses regression analysis to detect this relationship. How well will he do?

In table 5.6 we present the results of regressing the exchange rate on the money stock using small sample periods of 50 periods. A first thing to observe is the substantial variability of the coefficient of the money stock for these different sample periods. This has to do with the fact that the chaotic model produces a lot of endogenous noise. This can also be seen from figure 5.16, which shows the exchange rate and the money stocks during these small sample periods. One observes that,

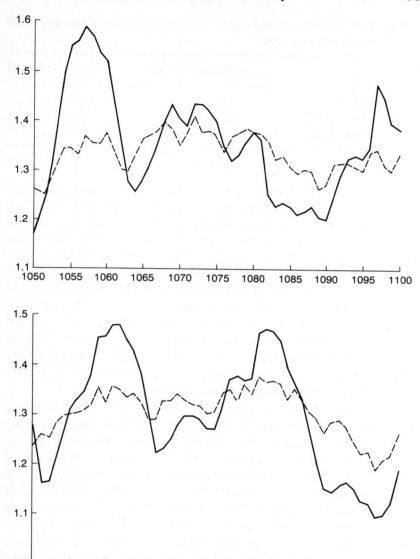

Figure 5.16 Exchange rate (——) and money stock (----), data-points 1000–1100.

Table 5.7 RMSEs of forecasts with structural models and with random walk (percentages)

	Structural model	Random walk
period 950–1000	7.9	4.2
period 1000–1050	9.2	3.9
period 1050–1100	11.6	4.4

although in the long run there is a relatively close fit between the exchange rate and the money stock, in the short run this relationship is weak. The variability of the exchange rate is much larger than that of the underlying money stock, and many of the long cyclical movements of the exchange rate are not explained by the movements of the money stock.

The next step in the analysis consisted of asking the question of how well a forecaster would fare if he used the estimated equations of table 5.7 to forecast the exchange rate out-of-sample. Would knowledge of the underlying stochastic process of the money stock allow him to make good forecasts? (Note that this was also the question Meese and Rogoff asked in their celebrated empirical study of the exchange rates.)

We answered this question by comparing the "out-of-sample" forecasts, using the regression models, with a simple random walk forecast. The latter forecasts next period's exchange rate to be equal to the current exchange rate. The results are presented in table 5.7, which shows the root mean squared errors (RMSEs) of these forecasts. We observe that the RMSEs of the simple random walk forecasts are much smaller that the forecasts based on the regression models. It should also be noted that the latter assume that the forecaster knows the value of the future exogenous variables exactly. Thus, even if the forecasters know the future value of the money stock, the use of a structural model leads to inferior forecasts compared to the random walk model, which does not use that information. This is also the result obtained by Meese and Rogoff in their analysis of the forecasting performance of structural models.

Our results have the following interpretation. The complex

dynamics of the chaotic model has the effect of obscuring the transmission of the exogenous money shocks to the exchange rate. It is as if the chaotic model works as a scrambling device, which erases the short-term influences of money shocks. As a result, the forecaster who estimates the effect of money shocks on the exchange rate using short sample periods faces the fact that the estimated coefficient is unstable and that the model does poorly as a predictive instrument.

This difficulty in the use of structural models to explain and to predict exchange rates has been widely observed in reality. Our model gives an explanation for this result. This explanation is not based on the possibility that the researcher uses the wrong structural model. In our analysis the regressions were based on the correct monetary model. The factor that obscures the relationship between the money stock and the exchange rate is the speculative dynamics, which introduces a complex (chaotic) exchange rate behaviour.

The difficulty encountered with forecasting based on structural models does not imply that exchange rates cannot be predicted. As was stressed in the previous chapters, one of the characteristics of chaotic models is that there is a (short) time horizon over which forecasting can be done in a useful way, even if the forecaster does not know the underlying structural model.

The possibility of short-term forecasting in an environment of chaotic exchange rate movements can be illustrated as follows. We used the same simulated exchange rate data as in the previous tables and figures. We then assumed a forecaster who computes a moving average model (with three lags). He estimates the coefficients of this model based on data for the sample period 1000–1050. The moving average model so obtained is:

$$S_t = 1.63S_{t-1} - 0.81S_{t-2} + 0.08S_{t-3} + 0.12$$

In the next step the forecaster uses this model to forecast the exchange rate (out of sample) during period 1050–1100. The result of this forecast is given in figure 5.17. Comparing this with figure 5.16, one observe that the forecasts are significantly better than those obtained using the structural model. In addition, the RMSE of this forecast, based on the moving average model, is

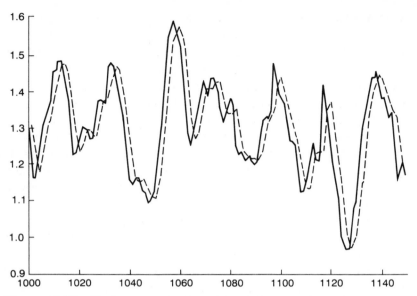

Figure 5.17 Exchange rate (———) and forecast based on moving average (----), $S_t = 1.63S_{t-1} - 0.81S_{t-2} + 0.08S_{t-3} + 0.12$.

3.6 percent, which is better than the random walk forecast (see table 5.7). Thus, the fact that the world is chaotic does not preclude to make short-term (one period ahead) forecasts that outperform the random walk forecasts. In a sense, this is not surprising. The exchange rate data generated by our chaotic model contain a structure that is not purely white noise.

The previous results are, in a very indirect way, corroborated by the facts. Short-term forecasting in the foreign exchange markets is now done almost exclusively using technical analysis. According to the empirical evidence collected by Allen and Taylor (1989) and by Schulmeister (1990) these forecasts are relatively succesful. In this sense our model mimics an aspect of reality, i.e. it generates an exchange rate dynamics which can be exploited to make forecasts. This cannot be said of the "news" model.

8 CONCLUSION

In this chapter the analysis of chapter 4 was extended. We developed a simple monetary model to which we attached the assumption that speculators use different information sets to forecast the future exchange rate. The main results of this model are the following.

First, the range of parameters for which we find chaotic behavior is drastically increased, when we assume that the monetary authorities follow policies of interest rate smoothing. Second, the realism of the exchange rate patterns generated by the model is significantly increased. In particular the time series of the exchange rates, generated by the model, exhibits long swings, which are also found in "real life" movements of the exchange rates. Third, a statistical analysis of the simulated exchange rates revealed some features that are also found in reality, i.e. exchange rates exhibit unit roots, and the forward premium is a biased predictor of future exchange rate changes. The latter result obtains despite the fact that our model does not assume risk premia.

Fourth, the confidence fundamentalists have in their estimate of the fundamental exchange rate does not affect the qualitative nature of the dynamics, i.e. when the solutions are chaotic they remain so whatever the precision is with which fundamentalists are able to estimate the underlying equilibrium exchange rate. We applied this result to interpret some empirical regularities found in the EMS.

Finally, the chaotic dynamics considerably obscures the effects of fundamental variables (like the money stock) on the exchange rate. We found that, at least over the short run, these fundamental variables have an unpredictable effect on the exchange rate. This makes it very difficult for the researcher to detect the influence of fundamental variables on the exchange rate or to use them for predictive purposes. All these phenomena have also been observed in reality.

NOTES

1 See e.g. Dornbusch (1976a,b), Frankel (1979).
2 In De Grauwe and Vansanten (1991) a different structure using the trade balance was specified, yielding chaotic results.
3 This steady state is found by setting $r_{ft} = 0$, $Y_t = 1$. In the steady state, $E_t S_{t+1}/S_t = 1$, and therefore (because of uncovered interest parity) $r_t = 0$ such that $P_t^* = M_{st}$ by the money market equilibrium condition.

6

Empirical Methods for Detecting and Describing Chaos

---

1 INTRODUCTION

In chapter 1 several concepts and definitions related to chaotic systems were introduced. We used these concepts to analyze the chaotic behavior of theoretical exchange rate models. In this chapter we will build on these concepts in order to determine whether a series of empirical data was generated by a chaotic system. There are several measures and indicators that can be applied; in particular, determination of the Liapunov exponents and estimation of the fractal dimension for a phase space collection of points will be useful. One of the most intriguing properties of a chaotic system is that a topological picture of the phase space trajectory can be reconstructed by analyzing just one component of the chaotic system. Such a reconstruction will be illustrated. This chapter will also provide a theoretical basis for evaluating the number of data required in order to estimate the correlation dimension.

Not directly related to the fractal dimension of a strange attractor is Hurst's rescaled range analysis. Hurst's rescaled range analysis allows us to see whether there are memory patterns in a series of data. Rescaled range analysis provides a direct framework to extend the notion of Brownian motion to fractal Brownian motion. While fractal Brownian motion does not directly result from an underlying chaotic process, it has certain fractal properties that justify a study in its own right.

2   RECONSTRUCTION OF A STRANGE ATTRACTOR IN PHASE SPACE

2.1   Introduction

The purpose of chaotic time series analysis is to determine whether an irregular and seemingly random set of datapoints resulted from a chaotic process. A set of discrete datapoints that represents values of a signal as a function of time (e.g. daily stock quotes) is called a *time series*. A chaotic time series has a phase space trajectory that evolves toward a *strange attractor*. Such a strange attractor is nothing but a phase space trajectory that stays on a fractal set. The strange attractor occupies just a small fraction of the available phase space. A strange attractor is a fractal, which can be characterized by a non-integer fractal dimension. *Chaotic time-series analysis* will allow us to find the dimension of this attractor. The higher the dimension, the more complex the underlying process that generated the time series will be.

A chaotic system can in principle be modeled by a number of coupled nonlinear first-order differential equations (or maps). The minimum number of differential equations to model the system is equal to the integer that *embeds* (i.e. is just larger than) the fractal dimension. The dimension of the phase space that spans this minimal number of differential equations required to model a chaotic system is called the *embedding dimension*. The embedding dimension will therefore always be larger than the fractal dimension of the strange attractor. Chaotic analysis will furthermore allow us to determine the Liapunov exponents. These Liapunov exponents can be used to estimate a measure for the timescale (or number of mapping steps) for which predictions could in principle be possible.

The most popular technique for a chaotic analysis of a time series is based on the *time delay method* (Packard et al., 1980; Takens, 1981). In this method a series of equally spaced data is considered: $x_1, x_2, x_3, x_4, \ldots x_N$, or

$$\{x_k = x(k \cdot \Delta t) \quad \text{for} \quad k = 1, \ldots, N\} \tag{1}$$

Takens showed that a topologically equivalent picture of the attractor in phase space can be constructed by the time delay method. Such a topological picture bears a reasonable resemblance to the original attractor, but certain directions have been stretched and deformed. The time delay method consists of choosing a proper delay time and reconstructing a set of n-dimensional vectors or n-tuples, where n is not known *a priori*. The components of the n-tuples form the directions of the new (topological equivalent) phase space in which the attractor will be reconstructed by plotting the points corresponding to the n-tuples in this new phase space.

2.2 Generating n-tuples for attractor reconstruction

The first step for reconstructing the attractor of a time series of N datapoints requires the construction of a set of n-tuples of successive data at different times according to

$$\vec{x}_1 = \{x_1, x_{1+\tau}, x_{1+2\cdot\tau}, \ldots, x_{1+(n-1),\tau}\}$$
$$\vec{x}_2 = \{x_{1+\tau}, x_{1+2\cdot\tau}, x_{1+3\cdot\tau}, \ldots, x_{1+n,\tau}\} \tag{2}$$
$$\vec{x}_3 = \{x_{2+\tau}, x_{1+3\cdot\tau}, x_{1+4\cdot\tau}, \ldots, x_{1+(n+1)\cdot\tau}\}$$
$$\ldots$$
$$\vec{x}_M = \{x_{N-(n-1)\cdot\tau}, x_{N-(n-2)\cdot\tau}, \ldots, x_N\}$$

n is the maximal dimension of the vector space being considered. Note that the n-tuples are elements of an n-dimensional (vector) space. τ is the delay time. This delay time has to be chosen to be large enough to remove all correlation between the data.

If the embedding dimension of the attractor is D_A, Takens has shown that it is sufficient to consider a space of dimension $(2D_A + 1)$ to recover the attractor. For an intuitive explanation of why this dimension is $(2D_A + 1)$ and not just D_A we consider the narrow Möbius band of figure 6.1. A Möbius band can be created by taping a narrow strip of paper together at its ends, after just twisting the strip of paper once. Even when the topological dimension of a narrow Möbius band is 1, the twist forces us to use a three dimensional space to embed such a Möbius band structure.

When dealing with a time series of data one would of course not know *a priori* whether there was a strange attractor at all,

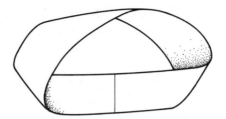

Figure 6.1 A narrow Möbius band, with topological dimension equal to 1, requires a three-dimensional space for its embedding.

nor what the dimension of the embedding space of such an attractor would be.

2.3 Choosing the delay time

A second step for reconstructing the attractor in phase space involves the choice of the proper delay time, τ, between the successive datapoints. Almost any choice for τ would work well for reconstructing the attractor. Choosing too small a delay time, however, would cause $x(t)$ and $x(t + \tau)$ to become almost indistinguishable. This implies that the reconstruction of the attractor in the $x(t) - x(t + \tau)$ projection would be concentrated along the main diagonal of this projection. Several authors suggest choosing τ such that the data are not correlated anymore. In order to select τ one would therefore look at the *autocorrelation function*, $\psi(\tau)$, of the time series. The autocorrelation function is defined as

$$\psi(\tau) = \frac{\dfrac{1}{N} \sum_{k=1}^{N} [x(t_k + \tau) - \bar{x}] [x(t_k) - \bar{x}]}{\dfrac{1}{N} \sum_{k=1}^{N} [x(t_k) - \bar{x}]^2}$$

where the average is given by

$$\bar{x} = \frac{1}{N} \sum_{k=1}^{N} x(t_k)$$

Often the e-folding time of the decay of the autocorrelation function or the first zero of the autocorrelation function will be used as delay times.

2.4 Reconstruction of the attractor

Once the proper delay time has been determined, and the n-tuples have been generated, the reconstruction of a topological picture of the attractor (if there is one) is straightforward. One would consider here as the phase space the vector space of the n-tuples, and just plot the points corresponding to the n-tuples in this vector space.

One of the main difficulties in following this procedure relates to the fact that the dimension of the phase space that embeds the attractor is not known *a priori*. In order to deal with this uncertainty, one would go ahead and apply Takens's reconstruction technique assuming various dimensions for the phase space (n-tuples). Once the dimension of the phase space is high enough to embed the attractor, the topological reconstruction of the attractor will not change further for larger dimensions of the phase space. The dimension of the phase space that is just large enough to contain the attractor is called the *embedding dimension*.

The reconstruction of an attractor will be illustrated for the Lorenz system. We know that the Lorenz attractor is embedded in a three-dimensional phase space. The n-tuples in this case are vectors with three elements. In order to reconstruct the attractor, 10000 points for the X component of the Lorenz system were generated numerically (figure 6.2a). These points span a period of 20 seconds, and the time between successive points was chosen to be extremely small, so that there is a large amount of autocorrelation between neighboring points in this time series. We will test the hypothesis that a faithful reconstruction of the attractor results by choosing a time delay that avoids correlation between the components of the n-tuples. The autocorrelation function is calculated for the data, and plotted as a function of the delay time in figure 6.2b, which shows that about 180 points have to be skipped in order to avoid correlation between the components of the n-tuples.

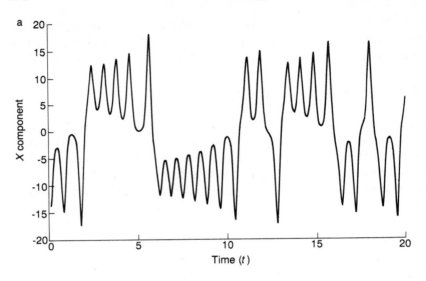

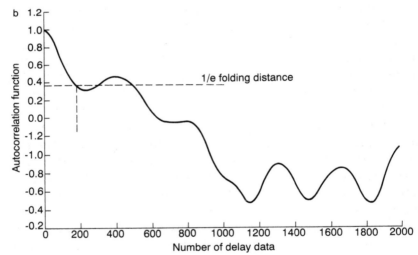

Figure 6.2 Datapoints for the Lorenz attractor. (a) First 10 000 points for the X component of the Lorenz system ($t = 0-20$ seconds); (b) autocorrelation function for 10 000 points of the X component of the Lorenz attractor ($t = 0-20$ seconds).

Table 6.1 lists the first 100 datapoints for the X component of the Lorenz attractor and the first ten 3-tuples that were constructed from these data, by skipping ten datapoints. The process for generating n-tuples by skipping 180 datapoints would be applied in a similar fashion.

The reconstruction of the Lorenz attractor from the X component of the data is illustrated for 3-tuples that were obtained by skipping 5, 10, 20, and 50 datapoints (figure 6.3). It turns out that a faithful topological reconstruction of the attractor can be obtained with far shorter delay shifts than are necessary to avoid autocorrelation. One notices that too short a delay time causes the 3-tuples to be strongly correlated so that the recovered attractor is concentrated along the main diagonal. Long delay times, for which there is little correlation between the n-tuples, will give a rather diffused attractor structure: the successive points in phase space will switch from one wing of the "butterfly" to the other in the Lorenz attractor. Connecting successive points in phase space by a line segment will no longer give a faithful picture of the attractor. The longer delay time might also cause us to run out of data for a finite time series before enough points were plotted to obtain a good covering of the attractor. The optimal choice of delay should avoid information redundancy, while preserving enough information for a reliable attractor recovery. When the delay time is large enough so that the n-tuples are not correlated, just plotting the points in phase space will provide a nice ergodic covering of the attractor (figure 6.4). However, in that case one cannot expect to be able to recover the attractor by connecting successive points in phase space by line segments. The distribution of the points themselves will serve here as a picture for the recovered attractor.

The topology of the Lorenz attractor does not allow a good illustration of this principle, because the Lorenz attractor almost densely covers a two-dimensional $X–Z$ or $Y–Z$ projection of the phase space. Figure 6.4 shows the points in phase space corresponding to a delay of 180 datapoints. It is clear from figures 6.3 and 6.4 that, as far as recovering the attractor is concerned, the time delay is not very critical, as long as the delay time is large enough to avoid the reconstructed attractor being concentrated along the main diagonal. If there is sufficient

Table 6.1 Construction 3-tuples for the X component of the Lorenz attractor

Data

−11.085	−11.182	−11.280	−11.376	−11.472	−11.567	−11.661	−11.754	−11.846	−11.937
−12.026	−12.115	−12.202	−12.288	−12.372	−12.454	−12.535	−12.614	−12.691	−12.766
−12.839	−12.910	−12.979	−13.045	−13.110	−13.171	−13.230	−13.287	−13.341	−13.392
−13.440	−13.485	−13.527	−13.567	−13.603	−13.636	−13.665	−13.692	−13.715	−13.735
−13.751	−13.764	−13.773	−13.779	−13.781	−13.780	−13.775	−13.767	−13.754	−13.739
−13.719	−13.696	−13.670	−13.639	−13.606	−13.568	−13.528	−13.483	−13.435	−13.384
−13.330	−13.272	−13.211	−13.147	−13.079	−13.009	−12.935	−12.859	−12.780	−12.698
−12.613	−12.526	−12.436	−12.344	−12.249	−12.152	−12.053	−11.952	−11.849	−11.744
−11.637	−11.529	−11.419	−11.307	−11.195	−11.080	−10.965	−10.849	−10.731	−10.613
−10.494	−10.374	−10.253	−10.132	−10.011	−9.889	−9.767	−9.644	−9.522	−9.400
−9.277	−9.155	−9.033	−8.911	−8.789	−8.668	−8.547	−8.427	−8.308	−8.189
−8.070	−7.953	−7.836	−7.720	−7.605	−7.491	−7.378	−7.266	−7.156	−7.046
−6.937	−6.829	−6.723	−6.618	−6.514	−6.411	−6.310	−6.210	−6.111	−6.014
−5.918	−5.823	−5.730	−5.638	−5.548	−5.459	−5.371	−5.285	−5.200	−5.117
−5.035	−4.955	−4.876	−4.798	−4.722	−4.647	−4.574	−4.502	−4.432	−4.363
−4.295	−4.229	−4.164	−4.101	−4.038	−3.978	−3.918	−3.860	−3.804	−3.748

-3.694	-3.642	-3.590	-3.540	-3.491	-3.443	-3.397	-3.352	-3.308	-3.265
-3.223	-3.183	-3.144	-3.105	-3.068	-3.033	-2.998	-2.964	-2.931	-2.900
-2.869	-2.840	-2.811	-2.784	-2.758	-2.732	-2.708	-2.684	-2.662	-2.640
-2.619	-2.600	-2.581	-2.563	-2.546	-2.530	-2.514	-2.500	-2.486	-2.473
-2.461	-2.450	-2.440	-2.430	-2.421	-2.413	-2.406	-2.399	-2.394	-2.388
-2.384	-2.381	-2.378	-2.376	-2.374	-2.374	-2.374	-2.374	-2.376	-2.378

3-tuples

-11.085	-12.115	-12.979
-12.115	-12.979	-13.567
-12.979	-13.567	-13.781
-13.567	-13.781	-13.568
-13.781	-13.568	-12.935
-13.568	-12.935	-11.952
-12.935	-11.952	-10.731
-11.952	-10.731	-9.400
-10.731	-9.400	-8.070
-9.400	-8.070	-6.829

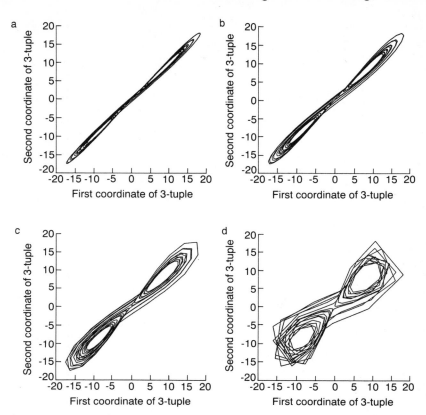

Figure 6.3 Reconstruction of the Lorenz attractor by skipping 5 (a), 10 (b), 20 (c), and 50 (d) datapoints.

correlation between the *n*-tuples a topological picture of the time trajectory in phase space can be reconstructed by connecting successive points by line segments.

A proper choice of delay time, which avoids all correlation, is generally not needed for recovering the attractor. However, avoiding correlation between the components of the *n*-tuples will be necessary for an accurate fractal dimension estimate of the attractor.

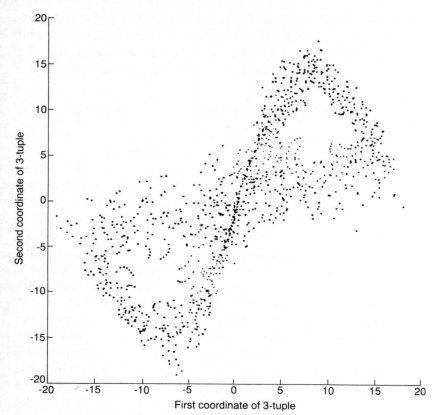

Figure 6.4 Reconstruction of the Lorenz attractor in phase space by skipping 180 datapoints.

3 ESTIMATING THE FRACTAL DIMENSION OF A PHASE SPACE RECONSTRUCTION

3.1 The two-point correlation function

The fractal dimension of the attractor can be estimated by centering a hypersphere on a point in hyperspace or phase space. Letting the radius of the hypersphere grow until all points are enclosed and keeping track of the number of datapoints that are enclosed by the hypersphere as a function of the hypersphere radius, R, on a log–log scale will yield the fractal dimension. In practice one would center hypersheres on several different points and take the average. If we call $N(R)$ the number of pairs of two points, with distance smaller than R (or $|\vec{x}_i - \vec{x}_j| \le R$), we have that

$$N(R) \equiv \{\text{number of pairs with } |\vec{x}_i - \vec{x}_j| \le R\} \propto R^v, \qquad (5)$$

where v is the correlation exponent. There is one problem, however. We do not yet know what the dimension of the phase space is. In other words, we do not know *a priori* how many components there are in the vectors cited above, which makes the calculation of the distance between two vectors not feasible yet. In order to overcome this problem, one would just assume a dimension for the phase space (or assume an n for the n-tuples). The analysis is carried out for various assumed dimensions of the phase space and the fractal dimension is plotted as a function of the assumed dimension of the phase space. By following this procedure and looking at such a plot, it can be noticed that the correlation exponent initially increases with increasing dimension of the phase space, but eventually saturates. It is this saturated value that is the (fractal) correlation dimension. Once the fractal dimension does not increase with increasing dimension of the vector space or phase space, we know we have taken sufficient components for constructing the n-tuples.

An orderly way to proceed with this algorithm requires the evaluation of the *two-point correlation function* or *correlation integral*, on the set of M vectors for various values of R, and for various embeddings of the vector space. The two-point correlation function is defined as:

$$C(R) = \frac{1}{M \cdot (M - 1)} \sum_{i=1}^{M} \sum_{j<>i}^{M} \theta\left[R - d\left(\vec{x}_i - \vec{x}_j\right)\right] \qquad (6)$$

where

$$\begin{cases} \theta = 1 & \text{if} \quad d(\vec{x}_i - \vec{x}_j) < R \\ \theta = 0 & \text{if} \quad d(\vec{x}_i - \vec{x}_j) \ge R \end{cases} \qquad (7)$$

In the above expression $d(\vec{x}_i - \vec{x}_j)$ represents the distance between two n-dimensional vectors. Several different measures for the distance between two vectors can be defined. Intuitively we are the most familiar with the *Euclidean distance*. In our analysis a different measure for the distance between two vectors was used: the *Takens norm*. The use of this alternative measure for the distance between two vectors speeds up the computing time for estimating the fractal dimension. It will provide the same value for the fractal dimension as the results based on the Euclidean distance. For the time being just think of the distance between two vectors as being a Euclidean distance (the interested reader can consult the next section for a definition of the Takens norm).

3.2 The influence of the norm on dimension estimates

We are normally familiar with the Euclidean norm for measuring the distance between two vectors. In this metric the distance between two vectors (e.g. containing two elements), $\vec{a}(x_1, y_1)$ and $\vec{b}(x_2, y_2)$, would be (figure 6.5a):

$$\text{norm}_E = \sqrt{(x_1^2 - x_2^2) + (y_1^2 - y_2^2)} \tag{8}$$

We used in our analysis the Takens norm as a measure for the distance or norm between two vectors. This metric leads to a more elegantly nested program for estimating fractal dimensions, resulting in considerable savings in computing time. It was proven by Brock (1986) that the calculation of the fractal dimension is independent of the norm of the vector space.

An example of a non-Euclidean norm for measuring the distance between two vectors is the *Manhattan norm* (figure 6.5b). The Manhattan norm is based on the checkerboard street map layout of the island of Manhattan in New York City. For a person walking the streets of Manhattan, the distance between two skyscrapers, at locations (x_1, y_1) and (x_2, y_2), would be

$$\text{norm}_M = \|x_1 - x_2\| + \|y_1 - y_2\| \tag{9}$$

The extension of the Euclidean norm and the Manhattan norm to higher dimensional spaces (i.e. larger than 2) is straightforward.

A completely different type of norm for measuring how close

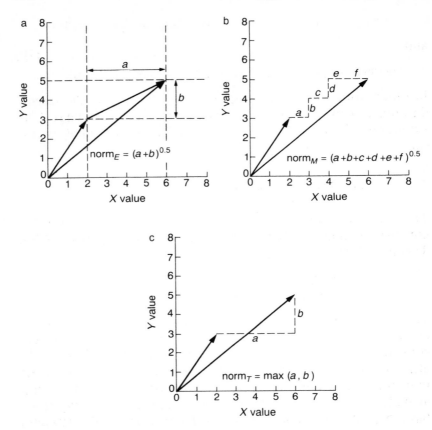

Figure 6.5 Illustration of the Euclidean norm (a), the Manhattan norm (b), and the Takens norm (c) as a measure for the distance between two vectors in a plane. The Euclidean norm is the difference between the two vectors. The Manhattan norm is the sum of the dashed line elements. The Takens norm is the larger of the vertical or horizontal dashed lines.

two vectors are to each other is the Takens norm (figure 6.5c). This norm is not as easy to understand as the Euclidean norm. Consider two vectors in a two-dimensional space: $\vec{a}(x_1, y_1)$ and $\vec{b}(x_2, y_2)$. The Takens norm for a two-dimensional vector space is defined as

$$\text{norm}_T = \|x_1 - x_2\| \quad \text{if} \quad \|x_1 - x_2\| > \|y_1 - y_2\|$$

and

$$\text{norm}_T = \|y_1 - y_2\| \quad \text{if} \quad \|x_1 - x_2\| < \|y_1 - y_2\| \tag{10}$$

In other words, the Takens norm for two vectors is the largest difference between any two equivalent vector coordinates. The extension of the Takens norm to higher-dimensional vector spaces is self-evident from this definition.

3.3 The correlation dimension

The correlation exponent, v, can now be determined from the correlation function. It has been shown (Packard et al., 1980; Takens, 1981) that:

$$v = \lim_{R \to 0} \frac{\partial \log[C(R)]}{\partial \log(R)} \tag{11}$$

The correlation exponent depends on the dimension of the embedding vector space of n-tuples. The correlation exponent converges to the (fractal) correlation dimension, D_C, of the attractor when the dimension of the embedding space is larger than the fractal dimension of the attractor. To be correct one actually should say that the dimension of the embedding space has to be taken maximally 2 times the dimension of the attractor + 1. The procedure for determining the correlation dimension from the correlation function yields accurate results under the following conditions:

- there are many n-tuple data vectors;
- the analysis applies for R going to zero;
- the analysis requires sufficiently high embeddings of the vector space of n-tuples.

Due to the presence of noise in the data and the limited number of data available one will usually follow a slightly different approach in practice. It is postulated (Grassberger, 1986) that the correlation function scales as:

$$C(R) \simeq \lim_{R \to 0} \lim_{n \to \infty} r^{D_c} e^{-nK_2\tau} \tag{12}$$

where

n = dimension of the n-tuple space;
K_2 = lower bound for the Kolmogorov or K-entropy;
D_C = correlation dimension;
τ = time delay.[1]

The correlation dimension can now be estimated from the slope of the linear part of the log $[C(R)]$ versus $\log(R)$ curve according to

$$D_C = \lim_{R \to 0} \frac{\partial \log |C(R)|}{\partial \log(R)} \tag{13}$$

Keep in mind here that this procedure is valid only in the limit of an infinite number of datapoints and R going to zero. For a finite number of datapoints, and in the presence of noise in the data, a practical lower limit value for τ will be set, causing an inherent error in the estimate of the correlation dimension. Note that the above formula will also allow us to estimate the Kolmogorov entropy, which can be used to estimate over how many time steps the signal can be predicted with a certain accuracy.

Schuster (1989) gives an additional formula for estimating the Kolmogorov entropy, which is very similar to the estimate of the correlation function and can be carried out in the same program:

$$K = \lim_{R \to 0} \lim_{n \to \infty} \frac{1}{n} \frac{1}{N} \sum_i \log \left\{ \frac{1}{N} \sum_j \theta \left[R - \sqrt{\sum_{m=0}^{n-1} (\vec{x}_{i+m} - \vec{x}_{j+m})^2} \right] \right\} \tag{14}$$

In practice the slope of the $\log[C(R)]$ versus $\log R$ curve is estimated assuming various embeddings. When the value for this slope no longer changes with embeddings (or increasing dimensions of the vector space of n-tuples considered) it is assumed that the correlation dimension defined by the above formula has converged to its correct value.

In summary, the procedure for recovering the attractor from a time series, and the estimate of the dimension of the attractor, is based on the following procedure:

1   Collect a sufficiently long series of equally spaced data in time.

2 Determine the delay time by checking the autocorrelation function.
3 Generate n-tuples (we usually take an embedding $D_E = 11$).
4 Determine the correlation function for various values of R and various embeddings (up to $D_E = 12$ in our case), and plot $\log[C(R)]$ as a function of $\log(R)$.
5 The correlation dimension is the slope of $\log[C(R)]$ versus $\log(R)$ curve.

3.4 Estimating the fractal dimension of the Lorenz attractor

This section will illustrate how the fractal dimension of the Lorenz attractor can be determined by estimating the correlation dimension. It is proper to mention here that the correlation dimension is strictly speaking not equal to the Hausdorff dimension, but is in fact a lower estimate for the Hausdorff dimension (Schuster, 1989).

The correlation dimension for various embeddings was calculated for the Lorenz attractor with the procedure described in this chapter. Six thousand 12-tuples were generated from the X component of the Lorenz system. The time delay was chosen as the $1/e$ time of the autocorrelation function. Figure 6.6a shows the correlation integral versus the radius, R, of the hyperspheres on a log–log scale for various dimensions, n, of the n-tuples. The upper curve in figure 6.6a corresponds to dimension $n = 2$, while the lower curve was obtained assuming $n = 11$. We can distinguish three regions in each one of the 10 curves of figure 6.6a with increasing values for increasing R:

1 For small values of $\log(R)$ the curves are not very straight yet. This can be for a variety of reasons. In this case we do not have good enough statistics (i.e. not enough points for estimating the correlation integral) in this region.
2 The region with radii varying between 0.5 and 10.0 seems to be quite linear. This is the region that will be explored for estimating the fractal dimension as the slope of the log of the correlation integral versus the logarithm of R.
3 When the radius of the hypershers keeps growing, it eventually becomes as large as the size of the attractor itself.

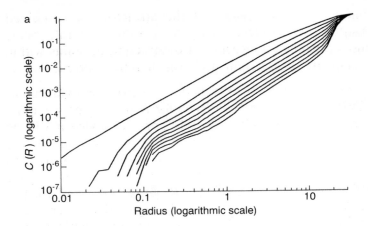

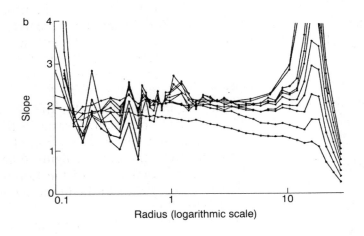

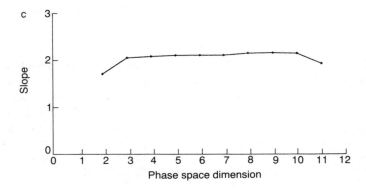

In that case all the points of the attractor are contained within the hypersphere. The correlation integral, being nothing other than a measure of the fraction of points within a hypersphere of a certain size, will therefore saturate to 1.

Figure 6.6b shows the instantaneous slope of the logarithm of the correlation integral versus $\log(R)$ for R ranging between 0.1 and 30, and n ranging from 2 to 11. For the novice it will be hard to estimate from this plot what the proper value of the correlation dimension will be. Notice how the curves tend to coincide with each other when the dimension of the phase space (n-tuples) grows for the region with R between 0.5 and 10. For smaller values of R the plot shows a zig-zag tendency. This sawtooth type of structure is a consequence of too fine a bin spacing on the one hand, and poor statistics in this region on the other hand. Selecting a larger bin spacing for calculating the correlation integral would yield smoother curves, but only with hindsight will it be known what the proper bin spacing has be to. Figure 6.6b lets us conclude that the correlation dimension for the linear region (radius between 0.5 and 10) is about 2.

Figure 6.6c provides the least squares estimate for the slope of the curve of the logarithm of the correlation integral in the linear region as a function of the dimension, n, of the n-tuples. This slope was evaluated directly from the data of figure 6.6a. From figure 6.6c we estimate that the dimension of the Lorenz attractor is 2.05. This value is frequently cited in the literature as the fractal dimension of the Lorenz attractor.

The log of the correlation function of the time delay method applied to a chaotic data series is illustrated again in figure 6.7. In this figure the embedding dimension goes up to 6. Figure 6.7b

Figure 6.6 Estimating the fractal dimension of a time series. (a) Logarithm of the correlation integral versus $\log(R)$ for the Lorenz attractor: 5000 n-tuples with properly chosen time delays were utilized. (b) Determining the fractal dimension of the Lorenz attractor as the instantaneous slope of $\log[C(R)]$ versus $\log(R)$ for various choices of the dimension n of the n-tuples. (c) Fractal dimension of the Lorenz attractor as the least mean squares slope in the linear region of (a). The linear region was taken for R between 0.5 and 10.

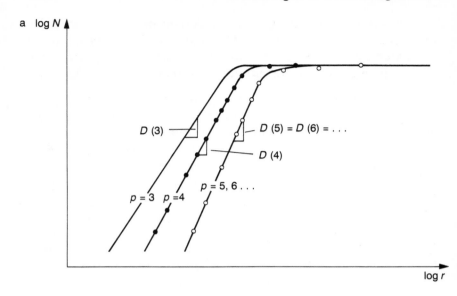

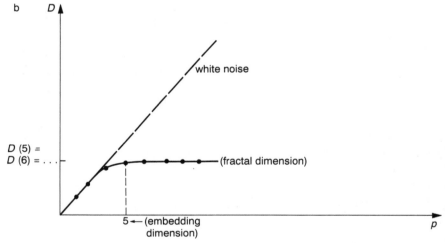

Figure 6.7 Illustration of the time delay method for estimating the correlation dimension. (a) The number of points within a hypersphere of a certain radius versus the radius of the hypersphere on a log-log scale. In (b) it can be seen that the fractal dimension is nothing other than the saturated value for the slope of the log$N(R)$ versus log(R) curves when the dimension of the hyperspace (or the value for n in the n-tuples) increases. Note also that for white noise no such saturation can be noticed, i.e. white noise is not fractal.

provides a plot of the correlation dimension as a function of the dimension of the vector space. The correlation dimension estimated in figure 6.7b saturates for an embedding dimension of 5. This means that the embedding dimension of the attractor is 5. The slopes of the correlation plots in figure 6.7a remain constant for small values of R. Figure 6.7a implies that the topology of the attractor under consideration here is a rather simple one, and the slope of the log of the correlation function saturates for an embedding dimension equal to 5. Figure 6.7b shows what the embedding dimension would be for white noise. For white noise there is no saturation of the slope of the log of the correlation function. One could argue that the fractal dimension for the attractor is infinite in that case. This merely indicates that there is no strange attractor in the sense that we defined it before: there is no stretching and folding, and the attractor occupies all the available phase space. In this case no phenomena such as sensitivity to the initial conditions would be noticed.

For the limited number of data typically available for economic indicators only low-dimensional attractors can be recovered at best. Furthermore, we did not even address the issue of non-stationary data series. An article by Grassberger (1986) provides some warning for avoiding common mistakes in estimating the dimension of a time series when only a limited number of datapoints is available. The literature cites various different estimates for the number of required datapoints for recovering a strange attractor of a given dimension. Several authors come to the conclusion that at least 5000 uncorrelated datapoints would be required to recover an attractor of dimension 6 (Smith, 1988).

If, for instance, the attractor is embedded in a six-dimensional space, this would imply that about 5000 thirteen-tuples would be necessary to be able to realize that there is an chaotic process that governs the evolution of the data series. In other words we can say here that in order to discover that there is a strange attractor with fractal dimension between five and six at least 5000 thirteen-dimensional vectors, with uncorrelated components, have to be considered to recover the attractor. For economic data, it is usually hard to find so many relevant datapoints. It obviously does not make any sense to study the gross national product of a society in such a framework, and even if these data were available or could be estimated (e.g. for Egypt), the different economic structures would defy requirements of stationarity. For exchange rate data, on the other hand, where records for very small time periods do exist, the huge data requirements might not pose any objection *per se*.

Generally there will be far fewer *n*-tuples than there are datapoints for this kind of analysis. This is easy to comprehend when we think of the fact that datapoints were diluted (table 6.1) by skipping data within the delay period in order to avoid correlation. Several authors (e.g. Frank et al., 1990) propose the introduction of a second delay time for identifying the time interval between the first component of successive vectors in the reconstruction. One would do more here than just making the *n*-tuples overlap with each other. While this technique would provide more *n*-tuples, and ultimately would give more precise results, we decided to abstain from such methods in order to avoid the risk of artificially introducing additional correlations in the data. For certain examples we have found that Frank's proposed method with a second delay time could introduce artificial low-dimensional attractors, even when measures to exclude any correlations where taken.

3.5   Setting bounds on predictability for a chaotic time series

Once it has been established that a time series is chaotic, the concept of chaos implies that short-term predictions could be possible. Such predictions could be based on collecting a long history of data, and looking at the evolution of exactly those data that are close to the datapoint for which predictions are being made. One would now employ any statistical averaging technique for forecasting. Note, however, that because of the sensitivity to the initial conditions, only short-term predictions are possible. One of the key questions that will be addressed in this section is exactly how long such a short term is.

The number of mapping steps, N_{MAP}, for which a series can be predicted was given in chapter 1 as a function of the precision, δ, and the Kolmogorov entropy or K entropy as

$$N_{MAP} = \frac{1}{K} \log \frac{1}{\delta} \tag{15}$$

Notice that a lower bound for the Kolmogorov entropy can be calculated directly from one of the formulas in section 3.3. This estimate for the lower bound of the Kolmogorov entropy is based on the scaling of the correlation function. Grassberger and Procaccia (1983) postulated that the correlation function scales as

$$C(R) \simeq \lim_{R \to 0} \lim_{n \to \infty} R^{D_C} e^{-nK_2\tau} \tag{16}$$

where K_2 is a lower bound estimate for the Kolmogorov entropy, and n is the dimension of the phase space considered. Taking the logarithm on both sides yields:

$$\log C(R) = D_C \log(R) - nK_2\tau \tag{17}$$

We can hereby directly estimate a lower bound for the Kolmogorov entropy from the $\log[C(R)]$ versus $\log(R)$ curves. We therefore would calculate the correlation dimension for two embedding dimensions of the phase space, n_1 and n_2, at some value for R and calculate K_2 from

$$K_2 = \frac{\log[C(R)_{n_1}] - \log[C(R)_{n_2}]}{n_2 - n_1} \tag{18}$$

It is assumed here that the proper time delay was already included in the n-tuple construction so that τ equals unity in this case. For the analysis of the Lorenz attractor the above formula yields $K_2 \simeq 0.60$ as a lower bound for the Kolmogorov entropy (figure 6.6a). We now could estimate the number of time steps, N_{MAP}, for which prediction of the Lorenz attractor would in principle be possible starting from an initial state located with a precision of 10 percent. Such an estimate (chapter 1) would yield

$$N_{MAP} = \frac{1}{0.60} \log \frac{1}{0.10} = 1.67 \tag{19}$$

For our data set for the Lorenz attractor we would conclude that we can predict values for the Lorenz attractor about two steps ahead with a 10 percent accuracy. One could actually interpret our result here as an experimental verification for the expressions relating the Kolmogorov entropy to time prediction.

3.6 Reconstruction of the Hénon attractor with the time delay method

The time delay method was utilized to reconstruct the Hénon attractor, following a procedure similar to the reconstruction of the Lorenz attractor. We chose the Hénon map

$$\begin{cases} X_{t+1} = 1 + Y_t - aX^2t \\ Y_{t+1} = bX_t \end{cases} \tag{20}$$

with $a = 1.4$ and $b = 0.3$. Figure 6.8a shows the X component for 100 datapoints of this map. It is our objective to reconstruct a topological picture of the Hénon map using X data only. Five thousand datapoints for the X component of the Hénon map were generated. The data are not autocorrelated, so that the time series of data can be used directly without any data skipping for sufficient time delays. Figure 6.8b shows the next X component as a function of the previous X component for the Hénon attractor, and gives a faithful topological reconstruction for the Hénon map. Two thousand datapoints were plotted in figure 6.8b.

The correlation function was calculated for various dimensions of the phase space in figure 6.9a. The instantaneous slope of $\log[C(R)]$ versus $\log(R)$ is estimated in figure 6.9b. From figure 6.9b it can be seen that the slopes saturate for higher embedding dimensions and remain more or less constant in a wide range for R. We could estimate from figure 6.9b the correlation dimension by eye, which would yield a correlation dimension of about 1.2 for the Hénon attractor. A quadratic curve fitting for the slopes of the curves of figure 6.9a in the linear region is summarized in figure 6.9c. From this figure we would conclude that the correlation dimension is about 1.23. Schuster reports 1.261 for this dimension. It is not clear why this dimension is underestimated in our analysis by about 3 percent.

Estimating a lower bound for the Kolmogorov entropy yields $K_2 = 0.394$ (figure 6.9a). This is slightly higher than the estimate

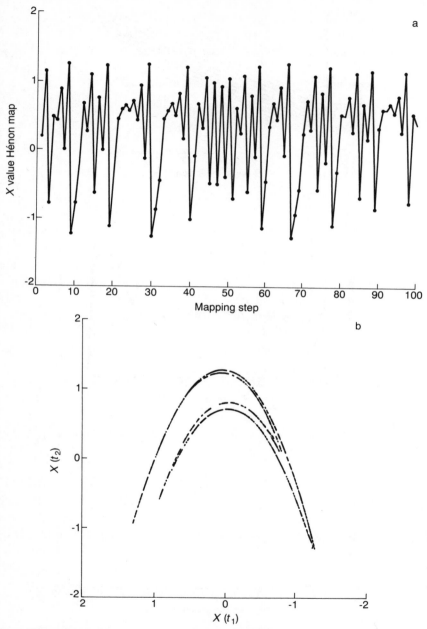

Figure 6.8 Reconstruction of the Hénon attractor with the time delay method. (a) One hundred successive mappings for the *X* component of the Hénon attractor; (b) reconstruction of the Hénon attractor with the time-delay method.

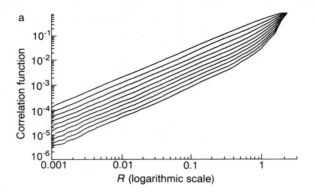

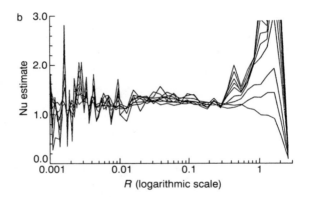

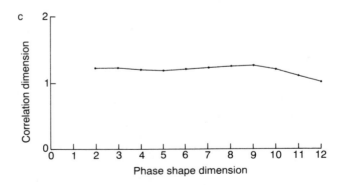

of 0.325 reported by Grassberger and Procaccia (1983). From this value for the Kolmogorov entropy we can estimate the number of mapping steps for which prediction is possible. For a precision of 10 percent for which the initial state is located, we could calculate (eqn 19) that we can predict six time steps ahead.

4 ON THE INTRINSIC LIMITS FOR DIMENSION CALCULATIONS

4.1 Introduction

The number of datapoints required in a time series to recover a strange attractor can be quite large. Usually we have only a limited number of data available for economic variables: it is obviously meaningless to speak of 5000 datapoints for the gross national product of a country. In this section we will shed more light on the number of datapoints that would be required to estimate the fractal dimension of an attractor that was recovered with the time delay method.

Several authors have commented on the number of datapoints required to recover an attractor of the time series (Gershenfeld, 1988; Grassberger, 1986; Smith, 1988). It is commonly mentioned that in order to recover an attractor of dimension d the number of datapoints required, N, scales as

$$N = 10^{ad} \tag{21}$$

Figure 6.9 Estimating the fractal dimension of the Hénon attractor. (a) Correlation functions versus R on a log-log scale for various dimension of the supporting phase space. (b) Estimate of the correlation dimension of the Hénon attractor as the instantaneous slope of $\partial \log[C(R)]/\partial \log(R)$ for various dimensions of the phase space. (c) Estimate of the correlation dimension of the Hénon attractor as a function of the dimension of the supporting phase space. The slopes of (a) were determined by a quadratic curve fit through the datapoints.

where α is the number of decades for which a correlation function with a constant slope on a log–log scale is desired.

This formula can easily be derived following Gershenfeld. In his analysis he considers the number of points needed from a white noise model. It is assumed here that N points are uniformly distributed in a multidimensional box of side L in a d-dimensional space. Such a box is called a *d-dimensional hypercube*. The upper limit value for R, R_{max}, in the evaluation of the correlation integral, $C(R)$, is the size of the box itself, L, so that

$$R_{max} \simeq L \tag{22}$$

The minimum value for R, R_{min}, is the nearest-neighbor distance between the points. If the points are uniformly distributed in a d-dimensional hypercube with side L this distance equals

$$R_{min} = \frac{L}{N^{1/d}} \tag{23}$$

We could easily verify this expression for a two- or three-dimensional space (figure 6.10). For evaluating the correlation dimension over several decades, say α decades, that number of decades equals

$$\alpha = \log_{10}\left(\frac{R_{max}}{R_{min}}\right) \tag{24}$$

Substituting for R_{max} and R_{min} yields

$$\alpha = \frac{1}{d}\log_{10}N \tag{25}$$

Rearranging this formula yields equation (21).

For fitting the correlation function over one or two decades (α is 1 or 2) for an embedding dimension of 3 the required number of datapoints (for estimating this dimension) ranges from a thousand to a million. Of course, in principle we could estimate the dimension even when the correlation function has a constant slope for just a tiny fraction of a decade. This would require far fewer datapoints. The trick for this kind of analysis when trying to determine the dimension of a strange attractor is just deciding in which (tiny) region $\log[C(R)]$ versus $\log(R)$

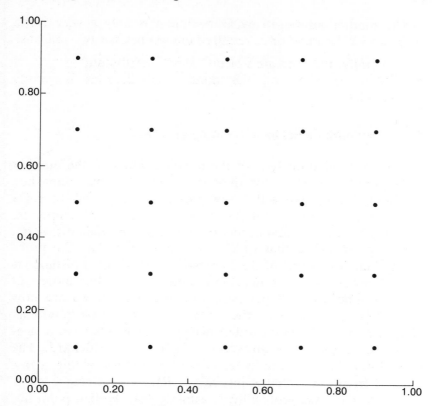

Figure 6.10 Nearest neighbor distance for N points in a two-dimensional square with side L. There are on average $N^{1/2}$ points for the X coordinate. The average distance between two points if they are equally distributed is $L/\sqrt{N}$. For example, for the 25 points equally distributed in the figure, and with $L = 1$, it is obvious that the average distance between neighboring points is 0.2. This fits the formula. The extension to three or more dimensions is straightforward.

would be linear. It is therefore not clear exactly how many datapoints are really required to estimate the fractal dimension. If we could determine with certainty that the $\log[C(R)]$ versus $\log(R)$ curve was linear, we could actually get by with relatively few datapoints.

The method proposed by Gershenfeld is only a very crude estimate for the number of required datapoints, for two reasons:

- generally, the data are not uniformly distributed;
- the requirement on the number of decades is purely artificial.

4.2   The Smith model for estimating data needs

A more revealing analysis of the intrinsic limits on the number of required datapoints for dimension estimates was published by Smith (1988). We will follow part of his approach to get a more realistic estimate for the number of required datapoints. Looking back at the definition of the correlation function, $C(R)$, it is easy to realize that $C(R)$ is nothing other than the probability that two points of the hyperspace are within a distance R of each other. Considering again a randomly distributed data set in an d-dimensional hyperspace with unit length, we are now interested in estimating the probability that two randomly chosen points are within a distance P of each other. In a one-dimensional space the answer would be straightforward. The probability that two randomly chosen points are within a distance R from each other is just $R(2 - R)$.

To calculate this probability, assuming that the first point lies at a random place in the unit interval, there will be a region with width $2R$ (a region R to the left of the first point and a region R to the right) around this point for which the second point would fall within a distance R from the first point. However, just setting $2R$ for the probability that the points are within R from each other is an overestimate. If the first point is near one of the two edges of the unit interval, we could not measure R in both directions. We therefore have to deduct from the original probability $2R$ the correction term $R/2 \times 2R$. In this correction term $R/2$ represents the average distance from an edge for which the probability $2R$ is not valid anymore, and $2R$ is the probability that the first point is within R from one of the two edges. If x is the coordinate of the first point on the unit interval, and y the coordinate of the second point, we now have that

$$P(|x - y| < R) = R(2 - R) \tag{26}$$

The probability that the distance between two points, chosen at random in the unit interval, is smaller than one is obviously equal to one. The probability that this distance is zero has to be equal to zero. We can verify from the formula above that these two conditions are indeed satisfied.

The method used in the previous paragraph can be extended to higher-dimensional spaces. Consider now a d-dimensional hyperspace with the Takens norm (i.e. the Takens norm is less than R if each of the distances in any coordinate is less than R). Because for randomly chosen points all the dimensions set an independent condition for the Takens norm, the probability that all of the d coordinates fall within R from each other is $[R(2 - R)]^d$. The correlation function being this probability therefore equals

$$C(R) = [R(2 - R)]^d \qquad (27)$$

so that

$$\log[C(R)] = d[\log(R) + \log(2 - R)] \qquad (28)$$

The correlation exponent v is defined as

$$v = \frac{\partial \log[C(R)]}{\partial \log(R)} \qquad (29)$$

so that

$$\frac{\partial \log[C(R)]}{\partial \log(R)} = d + d \frac{\partial \log(2 - R)}{\partial \log(R)} \qquad (30)$$

which yields, after evaluating the second term

$$v(R) = d\left[1 - \frac{R}{2 - R}\right] \qquad (31)$$

If the value of the correlation exponent saturates with increasing dimension of the vector space we call the saturated value the correlation dimension. The correlation function and the correlation exponent as the instant slope of the correlation function on a log–log scale are plotted in figure 6.11 for various embeddings of the phase space. Notice that the x-axis represents the logarithm of the distance between two points. Because the slope of the correlation function increases with the embedding

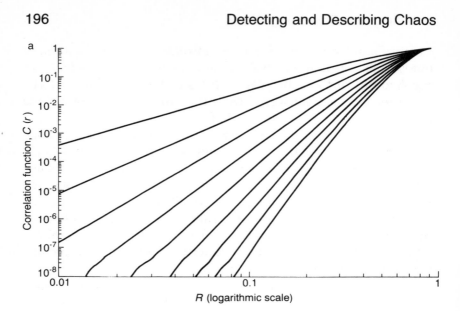

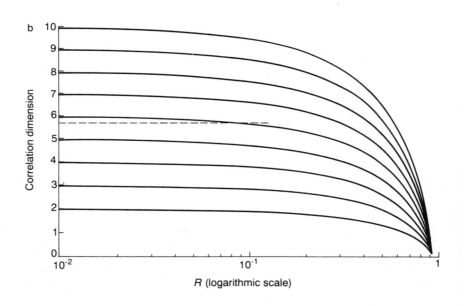

dimension without saturation, the resulting embedding dimension for this system will be infinity. This is to be expected for a collection of random points. Notice that the value of the correlation function decreases when the dimension of the embedding space increases and that the correlation function decreases for increasing values of R. For small values of R the correlation exponent approximates the dimension of the vector space of the n-tuples (figure 6.11b).

From the expression for the correlation function above, an estimate can be made of the number of datapoints that are required to calculate the correlation dimension to a certain accuracy. Assuming that we tolerate a certain error range for estimating the correlation dimension, a *quality factor* Q can be defined as $(1 -$ relative error). For instance, if an error of 5 percent is tolerated, the quality factor would be equal to 0.95. From the plot in figure 6.12b the maximum distance R_{max} could be determined, where R_{max} is such that when R is less than R_{max} our estimate is within the specified error range. For the random collection of datapoints the estimate of the correlation exponent will keep increasing with increasing dimension of the phase space without saturation. If a relative error of $(1 - Q)$ is tolerated, an estimate of the value R_{max} for which dimension estimates fall within the specified tolerance could be obtained from

$$v(R_{max}) = Q \times d \tag{32}$$

Figure 6.11 Smith model for determining the number of data to evaluate the correlation dimension of a chaotic time series. (a) Correlation function versus R on a log-log scale for the Smith model. The points are randomly distributed in hyperspace. (b) Correlation dimension, $v(R)$ as the slope of the correlation function in a log-log plot for various embeddings of the phase space. Note that the correlation dimension could be evaluated theoretically as

$$v(R) = d\left[1 - \frac{R}{2 - R}\right].$$

R_{max} is estimated for an embedding dimension of 6 and a quality factor of 0.95.

Figure 6.11b illustrates that for a phase space dimension $d = 6$, and $Q = 0.95$, R_{max} would be roughly equal to 0.1. An explicit expression for this maximum distance can now be obtained by combining the previous two formulas, leading to:

$$d\left[1 - \frac{R_{max}}{2 - R_{max}}\right] = Q \times d \tag{33}$$

so that

$$R_{max} = 2\left[\frac{1 - Q}{2 - Q}\right] \tag{34}$$

For estimating the correlation dimension, one would generally desire an extended region for R, where the correlation dimension remains more or less constant. Because R_{max} is fixed for a specified quality factor, the region for a constant correlation dimension ranges from R_{min} to R_{max}, where R_{min} remains to be determined. R_{min} can be related to R_{max} by specifying a measure S for the *range* or *confidence interval* according to

$$S = \frac{R_{max}}{R_{min}} \tag{35}$$

S obviously has to exceed unity, and it is generally desirable that S spans a decade or more (i.e. $S \geq 10$).

We could now calculate the minimum distance R_{min} by replacing R_{max} by $S \times R_{min}$ in the previous formula, leading to

$$S \times R_{min} = 2\left[\frac{1 - Q}{2 - Q}\right] \tag{36}$$

In order to be able to determine the minimal resolution, R_{min}, in a d-dimensional hyperspace we need at least a number of points, N_{min}, determined by (figure 6.12):

$$N_{min} = \frac{1}{R_{min}{}^d} \tag{37}$$

or, combining the previous two formulas,

$$N_{min} = \left[\frac{S(2 - Q)}{2(1 - Q)}\right]^d \tag{38}$$

Assuming $Q = 0.8$ and $S = 10$ yields

$$N_{min} = \left[\frac{10 \times 1.2}{2 \times 0.2}\right]^d = 30^d \tag{39}$$

A more elaborate interpretation of the above formula for the number of required datapoints is presented in figure 6.12a. In this figure the minimum number of required datapoints (normalized over S^d) is plotted versus the dimension of the embedding space for various quality factors Q ($Q = 0.75$, 0.80, 0.85, 0.90, and 0.95), according to

$$\frac{N_{min}}{S^d} = \left[\frac{(2 - Q)}{2(1 - Q)}\right]^d \tag{40}$$

Values obtained from figure 6.12a have to be multiplied by S^d to give general results. Figure 6.12b allows us to estimate the required number of datapoints for a confidence interval of one decade ($S = 10$) for various quality factors.

Note that the above procedure provides only a crude estimate for the minimum number of datapoints required to estimate the fractal dimension of an attractor with a certain quality factor Q. This is the case because the Smith model assumes a uniform distribution of datapoints. When the data result from a chaotic series the points will of course not be uniformly distributed any more. A strange attractor will only occupy a small fraction of the available phase space, so that there will be more points within small distances from each other. The Smith analysis therefore overestimates the required number of datapoints. Note also that reducing the confidence interval (e.g. from one decade to a factor of 2.72) has a dramatic impact on the required number of data.

The above formula with $S = 10$ (one decade) and $Q = 0.8$ requires a minimal number of datapoints corresponding with the values of table 6.2 and depends on the dimension of the phase space considered.

4.3 More analysis illustrating fractal dimension estimates

So far we have illustrated the time delay method for recovering the Hénon attractor and the Lorenz attractor and estimated

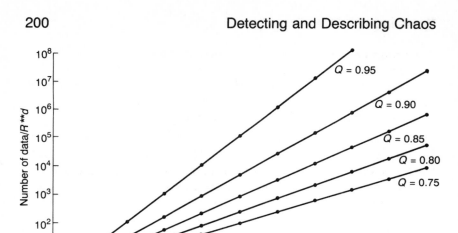

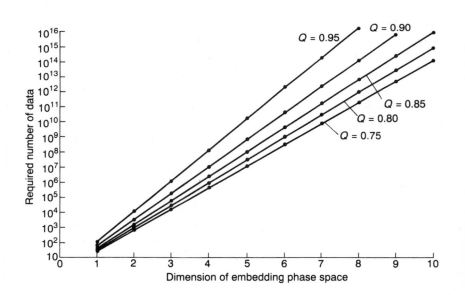

Table 6.2 Minimal number of datapoints for estimating the fractal dimension from the Smith model ($S = 10$, $Q = 0.8$)

Fractal dimension	Required no. of datapoints
2	900
3	27 000
4	810 000
5	24 300 000

their fractal dimension. We used about 5000 uncorrelated points for estimating the correlation dimension and illustrated that the methods introduced in this chapter seem to work well. In this section the correlation dimension is estimated for Gaussian noise and a quasiperiodic 4-torus. The correlation dimension determined from phase space reconstruction of Gaussian noise is infinity, and the dimension for a quasiperiodic 4-torus should be exactly equal to 4. The correlation dimensions for Gaussian noise and a 4-torus are obviously higher than those for the Lorenz or the Hénon attractor. According to the previous section on data requirements for dimension estimates, higher fractal dimensions require more datapoints to estimate the fractal dimension to the same accuracy. In this section we will verify whether we still could estimate the fractal dimension of Gaussian noise and the fractal dimension of a 4-torus with just 5000 datapoints.

Figure 6.12 Required number of datapoints from the Smith model. (a) Minimum number of required datapoints (normalized by S^d) versus the dimension of the embedding space for various quality factors Q, according to

$$\frac{N_{min}}{S^d} = \left[\frac{(2 - Q)}{2(1 - Q)} \right]^d.$$

These results have to be multiplied by S^d to obtain the actual data requirements. (b) Number of datapoints required for a one decade confidence interval versus dimension of embedding space.

The datapoints, distribution function, and Fourier spectrum for Gaussian noise were analyzed in chapter 1. Figure 6.13a shows the correlation functions versus the radius of the hypersphere for Gaussian noise on a log–log scale for various assumptions of the dimensionality of the vector space of the n-tuples (2 through 11). Five thousand datapoints were used to obtain this figure. Figure 6.13b shows the instantaneous slope of figure 6.13a. Figure 6.13c estimates the slopes of the straight part of the curves of figure 6.13a by a least squares method. Figure 6.13b shows that at low values for the hypersphere radius the slope of the logarithm of the correlation function versus the logarithm of the radius of the hypersphere tends to be equal to the dimension of the vector space itself. These curves are relatively smooth for up to a six-dimensional embedding. The dimension of the space of n-tuples varies from 2 to 11, and one cannot observe a saturation for the slope of figure 6.13a with increasing embeddings. However, estimating what the average slope should be for the linear part of the curves in figure 6.13a is not easy from figure 6.13b. Figure 6.13c shows a least squares fit of the linear parts of the curves in figure 6.13a. Even when there seems to be a tendency for slightly underestimating the slopes, figure 6.13c generally correctly interprets the values of these slopes and matches the theoretical model, which concludes that the value of the slopes for Gaussian noise equals the dimension of the embedding vector space. Figure 6.13b illustrates that a confidence interval of factor two is sufficient here for accurate dimension estimates and that the requirements set by the Smith model are extremely conservative for this case.

Figure 1.26 shows the datapoints, relative distribution function, and Fourier power spectrum for the quasi-periodic signal generated by

Figure 6.13 Estimating the correlation dimension for Gaussian noise. (a) Log[$C(R)$] versus log(R), embedding dimension from 2 (top) to 11 (bottom). (b) Instantaneous slope of log[$C(R)$] versus log(R), embedding dimension from 2 (bottom) to 11 (top). (c) Least mean squares estimate of the correlation dimension versus dimension of n-tuples.

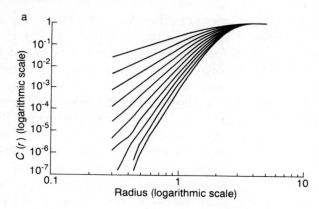

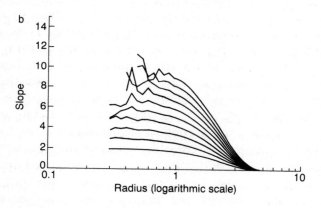

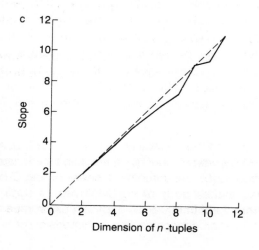

$$f(t) = \cos\left(\frac{2\pi}{18} t\right) + \cos\left(\frac{2\sqrt{11}\pi}{18} t\right) + \cos\left(\frac{2\sqrt{3}\pi}{18} t\right)$$
$$+ \cos\left(\frac{\sqrt{2}\pi}{18} t\right) \tag{41}$$

This same quasi-periodic signal was also studied by Gotfried Mayer-Kress (1987). Figure 6.14a shows the correlation function versus the radius of the hypersphere for several embedding dimensions of the vector space (or phase space) of n-tuples. The dimension of the phase space, n, ranges from 2 to 11, where $n = 2$ corresponds with the lower curve. The curves in figure 6.14a are plotted on a log–log scale. The limit value of the slope of the curves for higher embeddings and the radius of the hypersphere going to zero should correspond with the correlation dimension. Figure 6.14b shows the instantaneous slope of the curves of figure 6.14a. It is not easy to conclude from this figure what the correct value for the fractal dimension should be. The curves tend to saturate and remain constant for R ranging from 0.7 to 2. The fractal dimension estimated from figure 6.14b would be around 4. We used 5000 points in our analysis, and we note that the region for a constant slope ranges over a factor that is roughly equal to e. According to the Smith model (figure 6.12), at least 10 000 datapoints would be required for a 25 percent accuracy (quality factor of $Q = 0.75$). It looks that, for the quasi-periodic 4-torus, we can more or less confirm the estimates for data needs from the Smith model. We actually seem to need fewer datapoints than the Smith model would predict. Figure 6.14c yields the estimate for the slopes of the linear part of the curves of figure 6.14a, based on a least mean squares estimate, for various values of the dimension of the embedding vector space. The correlation dimension tends to saturate to about 4, for an embedding dimension of 7, but

Figure 6.14 Estimating the correlation dimension for a quasiperiodic 4-torus. (a) Log[$C(R)$] versus log(R), embedding dimension from 2 (top) to 11 (bottom). (b) Instantaneous slope of log[$C(R)$] versus log(R), embedding dimension from 2 (bottom) to 11 (top). (c) Least mean squares estimate of the correlation dimension versus dimension of n-tuples.

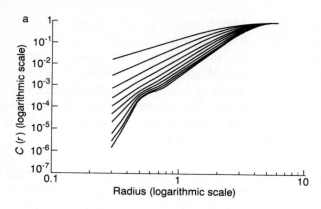

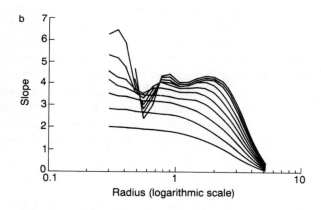

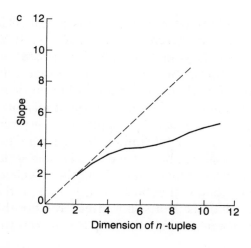

steadily increases with increasing values for the embedding vector space. It is hard to provide a fair value for the fractal dimension from figure 6.14c (especially if one knows that the correct value is four). Regardless of which fitting criterion is used, there would be a tendency to overestimate the fractal dimension of the 4-torus. We would estimate this dimension to be about 4.25. The obtained accuracy seems to be better than the bounds predicted by the Smith model.

In the examples for estimating the fractal dimensions for a 4-torus and Gaussian noise, we concluded that the Smith model is probably a conservative bound for estimating data requirements. We noticed that for determining a correlation dimension equal to 4 from 5000 datapoints skill and experience are required, just to recognize the fractal signature. The fractal dimension estimate alone does not allow us to distinguish the quasi-periodic signal, which is not chaotic, from a chaotic signal. A Fourier analysis would clear up this ambiguity, however. We will generally analyze at most 5000 datapoints for economic indicators in this book. Based on the results from this section, we already have some indication that it might be difficult to identify correctly a chaotic time series with correlation dimensions higher than 5.

5 RESCALED RANGE ANALYSIS OR *R/S* ANALYSIS

Rescaled range analysis or *R/S* analysis is a statistical method used to evaluate the occurrence of rare events. It is an ideal statistical tool for analyzing (geo)physical processes such as earthquakes and floods. Because rescaled range analysis was invented to come up with a statistical description of rare events this technique should also be one of the tools of choice to describe stock market crashes. The application of rescaled range analysis does not have to be limited to just rare events, and rescaled range analysis can be applied to any time series of data. The result of rescaled range analysis is the *Hurst coefficient*, which is a measure for the bias or trend in a time series. Rescaled range analysis bears no direct relationship to the correlation dimension of a phase space reconstruction but is essential to generalize the concept of *Brownian motion*. Brownian motion cannot be characterized by a low-order strange attractor, and is therefore not chaotic. A reconstruction of Brownian motion in phase space would lead to an attractor with an infinite correlation dimension. However, Brownian motion has certain fractal properties. It is just these (let us call them non-chaos related) fractal properties that can be related to the so-called Hurst coefficient.

Rescaled range analysis was first introduced by the British scientist Harold Edwin Hurst (1880–1978), who was studying the flood patterns of the Nile. H. E. Hurst introduced this new statistical analysis method with the purpose of designing reservoirs. Hurst was a maverick and realized the necessity for the High Dam and reservoir at Aswan. Mandelbrot rediscovered the work of Hurst and deserves the credit for putting rescaled range analysis in a more general framework. Mandelbrot (1983) describes Hurst's method and provides a brief historical background on the life of Hurst. Other excellent references for rescaled range analysis can be found in Feder (1989) and Peters (1991). We will just provide a brief tutorial on rescaled range analysis, and refer the interested reader to the literature for a more lengthy expose.

An easy way to introduce Hurst analysis relates to the problem of designing a reservoir that is filled by a river, and that will provide a steady flow of water to a city. The question is to choose the height of the dam such that the reservoir will never overflow or be empty (figure 6.15). The river annually brings an amount of water in the reservoir, which we will note as $\xi(t)$. Let us assume that we could forecast the annual river flow rate during the coming τ number of years, and that a regulated volume of water, $\langle \xi \rangle_\tau$, will be released to the city each year. This regulated volume to be discharged is just the average or mean river flow into the reservoir, where the average is taken over τ years:

$$\langle \xi \rangle_\tau = \frac{1}{\tau} \sum_{t=1}^{\tau} \xi(t) \tag{42}$$

Of course, it would take drastic hindsight to know the appropriate $\langle \xi \rangle_\tau$. The actual annual flow into the lake will

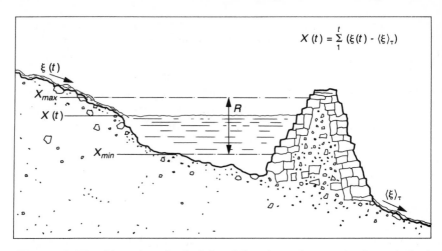

Figure 6.15 Choosing the height of the dam of a reservoir such that the reservoir will never overflow or be empty (after Feder, 1989).

evidently deviate from the average flow. If the flow of the river is lower than the average annual flow during a particular year, we will borrow from the supply of the reservoir to provide the city with the promised amount $\langle \xi \rangle_\tau$. If the flow of the river is larger than the average annual flow, the excess amount will be saved in the reservoir. On average this scheme would work out nicely, provided we chose the right height for the dam of the reservoir, and provided that we accumulated enough water initially to accommodate future borrowing. If the water level in the reservoir started out at a level L, the actual level of the lake with respect to L, $X(t, \tau)$, will indicate the *accumulated departure from the mean* of the the flow of river water into the reservoir according to

$$X(t, \tau) = \sum_{t=1}^{\tau} [\xi(i) - \langle \xi \rangle_\tau] \tag{43}$$

Note that $X(t, \tau)$ is also a function of τ. The actual values for such a problem applied to data for Lake Albert are shown in figure 6.16. The difference between the maximum and the

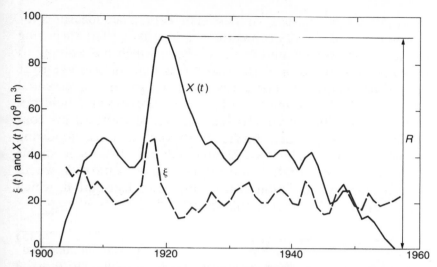

Figure 6.16 Illustration of rescaled range analysis for data from Lake Albert: annual discharge, $X(t)$, and accumulated departures from the mean discharge, $Y(t)$. The range is indicated by R (after Hurst et al., 1965).

minimum of the accumulated departure from the mean is the range, R:

$$R(\tau) = \max_{0 \le t \le \tau} X(t, \tau) - \min_{0 \le t \le \tau} X(t, \tau) \qquad (44)$$

The range corresponds to the fluctuation of the water level of the reservoir. A good choice for the height of the dam of the reservoir is therefore nothing other than the range. The range depends on the time period considered, and can only increase with increasing τ. For a Gaussian distribution the range will eventually level off to some asymptotic value with increasing τ.

The only lucrative element in this analysis is that, for a finite number of observations for the river flow, the range and the average discharge will depend on the number of observations. There is nothing surprising so far about this kind of analysis. Assuming that the average river flow has a Gaussian distribution we could design the dam, and estimate confidence measures for failure (i.e. running dry or overflowing the dam). The surprising element that Hurst found in his analysis, which has nothing to do with the method of analysis so far, is that the average river flow is *not* Gaussian. For a real dam design, this is essential information! The assumption of a wrong distribution could put you at odds with nature. To see how Hurst came to his conclusion, let us proceed further with our analysis, following Hurst's approach. Hurst considered not just the range in his analysis, but concentrated on the dimensionless ratio R/S, where S is the standard deviation of the underlying distribution, which can be estimated from a set of observed datapoints as

$$S = \sqrt{\frac{1}{\tau} \sum_{t=1}^{\tau} [\xi(t) - \langle \xi \rangle_\tau]^2} \tag{45}$$

Hurst observed experimentally that for many natural phenomena R/S follows an empirical relationship which can be described as

$$R/S \sim \left(\frac{\tau}{2}\right)^H \tag{46}$$

where H is defined as the *Hurst coefficient*. For many of his observations, ranging from tree rings to river discharges and lake levels, Hurst found that the exponent H is more or less symmetrically distributed around $H = 0.73$. His findings are summarized in Table 6.3.

For independent records with a finite variance it was shown that the ratio R/S should become asymptotically proportional to $\sqrt{\tau}$ according to

$$R/S = \sqrt{\frac{\pi\tau}{2}} \tag{47}$$

This relationship can be proven quite easily for a Gaussian distribution function. It is obvious from Hurst's experimentation that many natural phenomena do not adhere to Gaussian statistics. While this is an important finding, Hurst's conclusion might not be all that surprising. Why should nature follow Gaussian statistics in the first place? What is interesting in Hurst's study, however, is that the Hurst coefficient is more or less the same for all natural phenomena. Nature definitely wants to adhere to certain statistical laws and these laws are clearly not of the Gaussian type. There are several interpretations for Hurst's statistics. We refer the reader to the appropriate literature (Peters, 1991). Let us just point out here that a Hurst coefficient different from 0.5 can be interpreted as a *bias* or *memory* effect. It refers in a sense to the biblical picture of seven dry years after seven prosperous years. A Hurst coefficient larger than 0.5 indicates a memory effect, where there is a bias to enforce the current trend. This tendency is called *persistence*. A Hurst coefficient less than 0.5 indicates a negative bias that tends to oppose the ongoing trend; this is called *anti-persistence*.

The concept of Brownian motion has been extended by Mandelbrot to fractal Brownian motion (fBm). Such fBm adheres to Hurst's statistics (Peitgen and Saupe, 1988). There is a correlation between the Hurst coefficient and certain fractal measures. Let us point out here that fractal dimensions can be associated with Brownian motion. Brownian motion is not exactly a self-similar process but a *self-affine* process. In such a self-affine process the time scale and the record scale have to be scaled by different parameters to generate a similar picture when rescaling the process. The interpretation of the fractal dimension is more complicated for self-affine processes (Feder, 1989). The various fractal dimensions that were introduced earlier (box counting, correlation and Hausdorff dimension) will not be equivalent for self-affine fractals, and estimating the Hausdorff dimension can become quite challenging in such a case. Let us point out here that the concept of chaos bears no direct relationship with Hurst statistics, and that the two concepts have to be studied independently and have their own merits. For the X data of the Lorenz attractor we found a Hurst coefficient of 0.7 (figure 6.17a, 10000 data). (The change in slope in figure 6.17a confirms the periodic tendency of the X component of the Lorenz attractor.) This Hurst coefficient is sensitive to the number of data considered. For the Hénon attractor, on the other hand, we calculated a Hurst coefficient of about 0.4, indicating anti-persistency (figure 6.17b). This Hurst coefficient was calculated for 10000 datapoints and did not

Table 6.3 Hurst coefficient for natural phenomena

Phenomenon	Range of N years	Number of phenomena	Sets	H Mean	H Std devn	H Range	Coeff. of auto-correlation
River discharges	10–100	39	94	0.72	0.091	0.50–0.94	
Roda gauge	80–1080	1	66	0.77	0.055	0.58–0.86	0.025 ± 0.26 $n = 15$
River and lake levels	44–176	4	13	0.71	0.082	0.59–0.85	0.07 ± 0.08 $n = 65$
Rainfall	24–211	39	173	0.70	0.088	0.46–0.91	
Varves							
Lake Saki	50–2000	1	114	0.69	0.064	0.56–0.87	-0.07 ± 0.11 $n = 39$
Moen and Tamaskaming	50–1200	2	90	0.77	0.094	0.50–0.95	
Corintos and Haileybury	50–650	2	54	0.77	0.098	0.51–0.91	

Temperatures	29–60	18	120	0.68	0.087	0.46–0.92
Pressures	29–96	8	28	0.63	0.070	0.51–0.76
Sunspot numbers	38–190	1	15	0.75	0.056	0.65–0.85
Tree rings and spruce index	50–900	5	105	0.79	0.076	0.56–0.94
Totals and means of sections						
Water statistics		83	346	0.72	0.08	0.46–0.94
Varves		5	258	0.74	0.09	0.50–0.95
Metereology and trees		32	268	0.72	0.08	0.46–0.94
Grand total and means	10–2000	120	872	0.726	0.082	0.46–0.95

Source: Hurst et al. (1965)

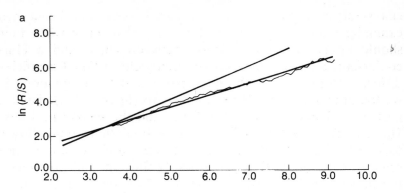

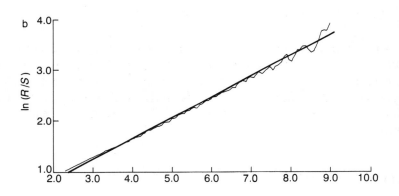

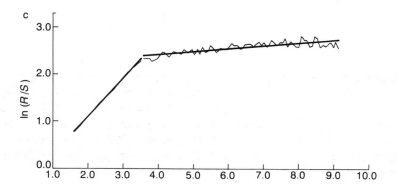

change significantly when we considered fewer data. From these examples we could generalize by saying that, even when there should be no direct correlation between chaos and a Hurst coefficient, a chaotic time series often yields a Hurst coefficient different from 0.5. For the quasi-periodic data of equation (41) we found two different Hurst coefficients (figure 6.17c). The first part has a Hurst coefficient of 0.813 and the second part has a Hurst coefficient of 0.0635. A closer examination would allow us to divide this second straight line into three separate linear regions, each with a different Hurst coefficient. The crossings of the linear regions would correspond to the different periods of the quasi-periodic signal.

6   CONCLUSION

In this chapter we have discussed methods for detecting chaos in observed data. Apart from gaining additional insights into the nature of chaotic motion, this discussion allows us to test the hypothesis that the observed exchange rates are driven by chaotic motion. These empirical tests are performed in the next chapter.

NOTE

1 The time delay is equal to unity if we construct a new series based on the appropriate delay time.

Figure 6.17   Estimating the Hurst coefficient, H, from the slope of R/S plotted against datapoint number on a log-log scale. (a) Lorenz attractor, 10 000 datapoints with step 0.3s, estimated $H = 0.707$. The change in slope at datapoint 33 (exp. 3.5) indicates a periodic tendency. (b) Hénon attractor, estimated $H = 0.405$. (c) Quasiperiodic signal (4-torus, eqn 41), $H = 0.813$ for the lower part and 0.0635 for the upper part.

7

On Detecting Chaos in Exchange Rate Data

1 INTRODUCTION

In this chapter we apply some of the techniques described in chapter 6 to detect chaos in the observed exchange rate data. We will use the time delay method as developed by Takens (see chapter 6). The experimental techniques for identifying chaos have been developed in the domain of mathematical physics and require a large amount of data (say 20000 datapoints). To obtain such a large amount of data is typically impossible in empirical economics. However, in financial markets we come closer to the required amount of data so as to be able to use the experimental techniques in a useful way.

2 EMPIRICAL ANALYSIS OF EXCHANGE RATES

Daily exchange rates for US dollars per Deutschmark, dollars per pound sterling and dollars per yen were obtained from Reuters for the period from January 4, 1971 through December 30, 1990. Looking at the autocorrelation function for these data series it becomes obvious that the proper time delays for applying the time delay method would leave us with too few n-tuples to proceed. Daily returns were utilized, rather than the actual exchange rates, in order to obtain sufficient datapoints. The *daily returns* were calculated according to

$$\text{return}(t) = 100.0[\log(S_t) - \log(S_{t-1})]$$

Table 7.1 Guide to figures 7.1 to 7.12

Figure	Currency	Period	Brief commentary
7.1	Deutschmark/dollar	1971–2	not conclusive
7.2	Deutschmark/dollar	1973–81	non-chaotic
7.3	Deutschmark/dollar	1982–90	random walk
7.4	Deutschmark/dollar	1973–90	not conclusive
7.5	Pound sterling/dollar	1971–2	speculative $D \approx 1.5$
7.6	Pound sterling/dollar	1973–81	chaotic, $D \approx 2$
7.7	Pound sterling/dollar	1982–90	random walk
7.8	Pound sterling/dollar	1973–90	chaotic, $D \approx 2$
7.9	Japanese yen/dollar	1971–2	chaotic, $D \approx 0.8$
7.10	Japanese yen/dollar	1973–81	not conclusive
7.11	Japanese yen/dollar	1982–90	random walk
7.12	Japanese yen/dollar	1973–90	possibly chaotic, $D \approx 2.2$

where S_t is the exchange rate at time t, and S_{t-1} the exchange rate on the previous day. Note that the scaling factor (100) does not influence any conclusions about the presence or dimensionality of a possible attractor. Daily returns can now be used for the time delay method because there is no autocorrelation between the daily returns.

For each of the exchange rates, four different time periods were analyzed with the time delay method: 1971–2, 1973–81, 1982–90, and 1972–90. The time period 1971–2 was isolated from the overall data series because the exchange rates during this time frame were mainly fixed and did not become true floating rates until February 1973. The periods 1973–81 and 1982–90 were selected for our study in order to have roughly the same number of data (about 2250) for both time periods. About 500 twelve-tuples were constructed for the period 1971–2, 2250 for the periods 1973–81 and 1982–90, and 4500 for the period 1973–90. The correlation function and the instantaneous slope of the logarithm of the correlation function versus the logarithm of the separation were determined with the methods described earlier. The results from our analysis are shown in figures 7.1 to 7.12. Part a of each figure shows the correlation function of the returns versus the distance measure R on a log–log scale for embeddings ranging from 2 to 11. Part b of each figure shows the instantaneous slope of the natural logarithm of the correlation function versus the logarithm of R, as a function of the distance measure R (and all for embeddings ranging from 2 to 11). Table 7.1 summarizes the contents of figures 7.1 to 7.12.

The return maps did not show any pronounced visual evidence for the presence of a strange attractor and are therefore not reproduced here. However, the visual lack of a strange attractor should not lead to the conclusion that there is no chaos in these exchange rate returns: it is conceivable that the inherent noisy characteristics of daily exchange rates would mask the visual presence of a strange attractor if such an attractor were present here. We did abstain from any filtering methods to avoid introducing artificial correlations between the data. Some return maps were clearly different from those produced by Gaussian noise, but – to put it mildly – the presence of a strange attractor was not at all obvious.

2.1   Analysis of the mark/dollar returns

Figure 7.1 shows the time delay method applied to returns of the German mark/dollar for the years 1971 and 1972. From figure 7.1b three distinct regimes can be noticed:

1   For small distance measures ($R < 0.04$) there is a noisy fluctuating regime due to statistical fluctuations (because of the limited number of data in this regime). Noise would mask any indications of chaos in this regime.

2   A second regime in figure 7.1b ($0.04 < R < 0.1$) shows a weak saturation tendency for the correlation dimension at a more or less constant value ($D = 4$). This behavior could indicate chaos. The correlation dimension in that case is about 4. The saturation effects are not entirely obvious and there are insufficient data to be conclusive about whether figure 7.1b manifests chaos.

3   In a third regime the instantaneous slope decreases monotonously with increasing values for the separation, R. No pronounced saturation effects can be observed.

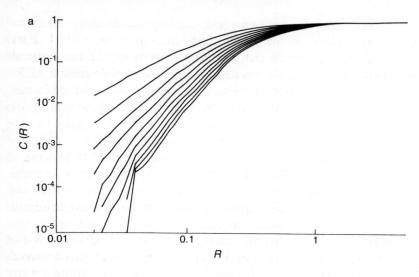

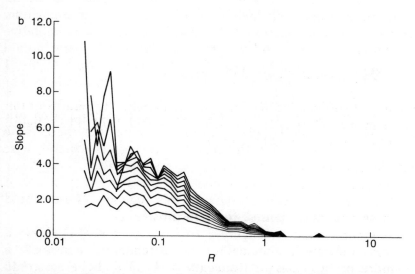

Figure 7.1 Time delay analysis for Deutschmark/US dollar returns, 1971–2. (a) $C(R)$ versus R on a log-log scale for embedding from 2 (top) to 11 (bottom). (b) Instantaneous slope of (a) for embedding dimensions from 2 (bottom) to 11 (top).

Figure 7.2 shows the time delay method applied to returns of the mark/dollar for the years 1973–81. There is no indication of any saturation for the instantaneous slope of the logarithm of the correlation function versus the logarithm of R (figure 7.2a). Figure 7.2b has some tendency to show horizontal plateaus. Mainly because of the lack of saturation and a qualitative agreement with similar curves for Brownian motion returns (see next section), this regime is labeled "non-chaotic".

Figure 7.3 shows the time delay method applied to returns of the mark/dollar for the years 1982–90. These figures are similar to the results from Brownian motion (random walk) returns. We will therefore label this regime as "random walk", to distinguish it from a possibly chaotic regime.

Figure 7.4 shows the time delay method applied to returns of the mark/dollar for the period 1973–90. While these curves show a horizontal plateau for the instantaneous slope of the correlation function around $D = 5$, the saturation of the instantaneous slope with higher embeddings seems to occur only in a very small region about $R = 0.4$. Because of the qualitative similarity of figure 7.4b with non-stationary Brownian motion (see figure 7.1b) and the lack of chaos for the periods 1973–81 and 1982–90, we label these results as being "not conclusive" for any evidence of chaos.

To summarize the results from a time delay method or chaotic analysis of the mark/dollar returns, we state that there is no conclusive evidence for the manifestation of chaos for these exchange rates.

2.2 Analysis of the pound/dollar returns

Figure 7.5 shows the time delay method applied to returns of the pound sterling/dollar for the years 1971 and 1972. Figure 7.5b has some similarity to figure 7.1b. Notice in addition the small region with a more or less constant slope which tends to saturate to the value 1.5 with increasing embeddings about $R = 0.2$. Interpreting this as a sign of chaos is highly speculative at best.

Figure 7.6 shows the time delay method applied to returns of the pound/dollar for the years 1973 and 1981. Figure 7.6b shows

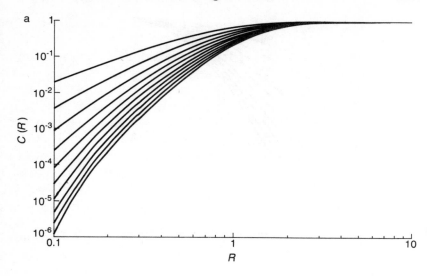

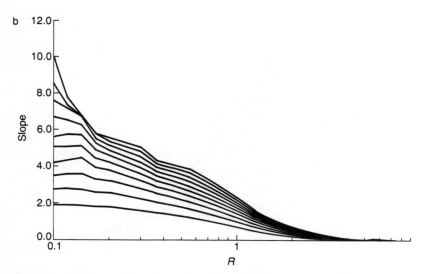

Figure 7.2 Time delay analysis for Deutschmark/US dollar returns, 1973–81. (a) $C(R)$ versus R on a log-log scale for embedding dimensions from 2 (top) to 11 (bottom). (b) Instantaneous slope of (a) for embedding dimensions from 2 (bottom) to 11 (top).

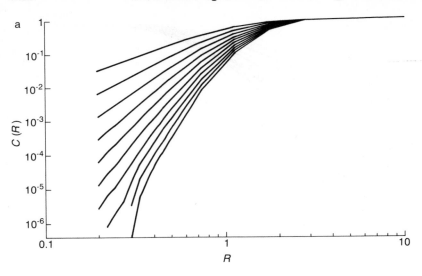

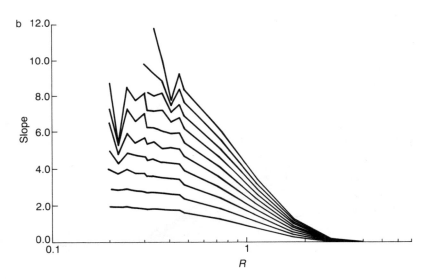

Figure 7.3 Time delay analysis for Deutschmark/US dollar returns, 1982–90. (a) $C(R)$ versus R on a log-log scale for embedding dimensions from 2 (top) to 11 (bottom). (b) Instantaneous slope of (a) for embedding dimensions from 2 (bottom) to 11 (top).

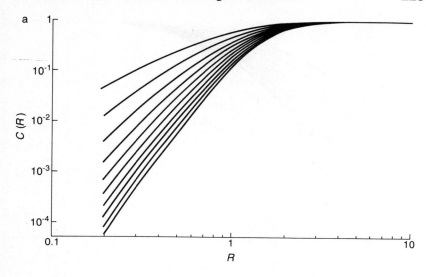

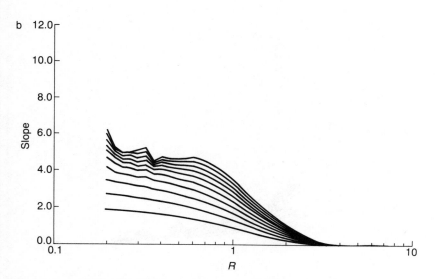

Figure 7.4 Time delay analysis for Deutschmark/US dollar returns, 1973–90. (a) $C(R)$ versus R on a log-log scale for embedding dimensions from 2 (top) to 11 (bottom). (b) Instantaneous slope of (a) for embedding dimensions from 2 (bottom) to 11 (top).

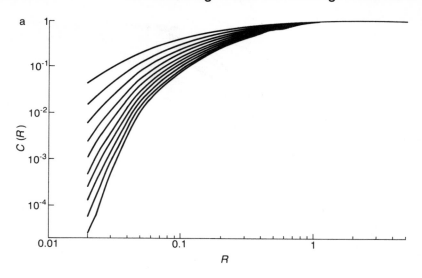

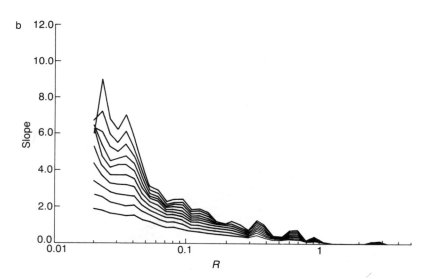

Figure 7.5 Time delay analysis for pound sterling/US dollar returns, 1971–2. (a) $C(R)$ versus R on a log-log scale for embedding dimensions from 2 (top) to 11 (bottom). (b) Instantaneous slope of (a) for embedding dimensions from 2 (bottom) to 11 (top).

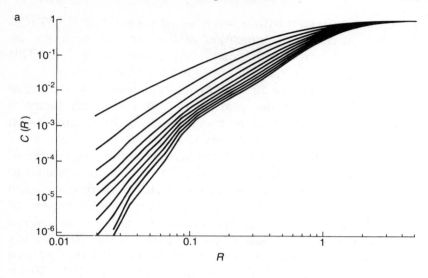

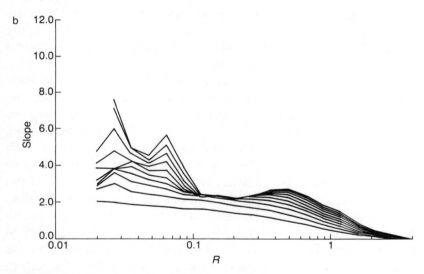

Figure 7.6 Time delay analysis for pound sterling/US dollar returns, 1973–81. (a) $C(R)$ versus R on a log-log scale for embedding dimensions from 2 (top) to 11 (bottom). (b) Instantaneous slope of (a) for embedding dimensions from 2 (bottom) to 11 (top).

a pronounced region with constant slope ($D \simeq 2$) for $0.1 < R < 0.3$. This might be an indication of the presence of a low dimensional attractor with fractal dimension around 2. This regime is labeled as "chaotic" with a dimension of about 2.

Figure 7.7 shows the time delay method applied to returns of the pound/dollar for the years 1982 and 1990. This figure is similar to the results from the random walk or Brownian motion returns, and this regime is clearly not chaotic.

Figure 7.8 shows the time delay method applied to returns of the pound/dollar for the period 1973–90. This figure is similar to figure 7.6, and we label this regime as chaotic with correlation dimension close to 2. Note here that the chaotic regime of 1973–81 (figure 7.6b) is dominant for determining the overall shape of figure 7.8b, even when the period 1981–90 is clearly not chaotic. This phenomenon leads to the observation that when chaos seems to be present during the period 1973–90 for the returns of the pound/dollar, this chaotic regime might only be prevalent during a relatively modest time span, and actually not be present at all for the major part of the period ranging from 1973 to 1990. Identifying exactly where the chaotic regime begins and ends is not that easy.

The reason why the part with the lowest dimensional attractor will dominate the behavior of the entire data series in the correlation domain (such as in figure 7.8) becomes clear when we consider the definition of the correlation function again (see chapter 2). The Heavyside function, defined previously, will only contribute to the correlation function when the distance between two n-tuples is smaller than a certain measure R. If the data set is subject to larger fluctuations (such would be the case for the data of the period 1981–90, which shows larger fluctuations than the period 1982–90), and if only a small number of the data are characterized by smaller fluctuations as well (as would be the case for the data during 1973–81), then the nature of the definition of $C(r)$ is such that the smaller fluctuations would be the dominant factor for determining the behavior in the correlation domain.

As a conclusion we could state that the results of a chaotic analysis of the returns calculated from daily exchange rates for the pound/dollar reveals the possibility of a chaotic regime somewhere during the period 1973–81.

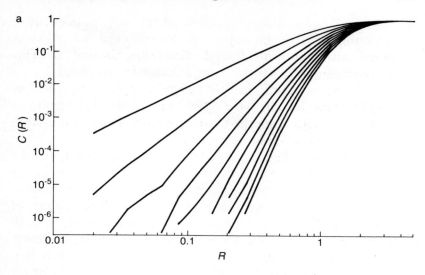

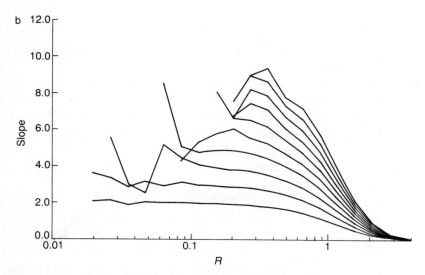

Figure 7.7 Time delay analysis for pound sterling/US dollar returns, 1982–90. (a) $C(R)$ versus R on a log-log scale for embedding dimensions from 2 (top) to 11 (bottom). (b) Instantaneous slope of (a) for embedding dimensions from 2 (bottom) to 11 (top).

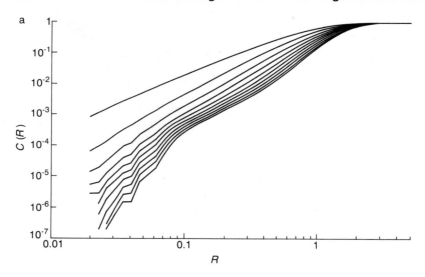

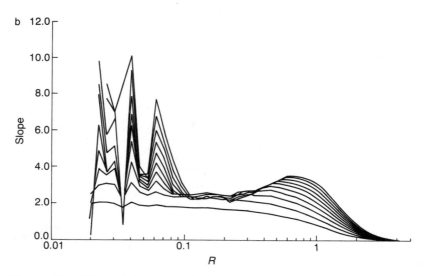

Figure 7.8 Time delay analysis for pound sterling/US dollar returns, 1973–90. (a) $C(R)$ versus R on a log-log scale for embedding dimensions from 2 (top) to 11 (bottom). (b) Instantaneous slope of (a) for embedding dimensions from 2 (bottom) to 11 (top).

2.3 Analysis of the yen/dollar returns

Figure 7.9 shows the time delay method applied to returns of the Japanese yen/dollar for the years 1971 and 1972. Figure 7.9a is qualitatively very different from similar figures for the Deutschmark (figure 7.1b) and the pound (figure 7.5b). The more or less constant slope during the entire range, and the pronounced saturation effects with increasing embeddings, strongly suggest that this is a chaotic regime with $D \simeq 0.8$.

Figure 7.10, which results from yen/dollar data during 1973–81, shows a constant region for the slope of the correlation function (on a log–log scale) around $R = 0.5$. There is no distinguished saturation region with increasing embedding of the vector space. The speculation of a chaotic regime here is not evident. We therefore label this regime as "non-chaotic"'. It is possible that there might be a chaotic period somewhere between 1973 and 1981, but in that case there are not enough data to make a strong case.

Figure 7.11 shows trends (yen/dollar for 1982–90) similar to corresponding figures for the mark (figure 7.3) and the pound (figure 7.7), and is labeled as a "random walk" regime, because of its similarity with returns from Brownian motion.

Figure 7.12 (yen/dollar for 1973–90) shows some similarities to figure 7.9. There is an extensive region with constant slope for the correlation function, and this time the curves saturate with higher embeddings. We therefore label this regime as chaotic with a correlation dimension $D \simeq 2.2$.

To summarize our results from a time delay method analysis for the yen/dollar returns we note that 1971–2 is very likely a chaotic regime. The overall shape of the slope of the correlation function for the period 1973–90 suggests chaos, but no convincing support for this conclusion can be drawn from the analysis of the 1973–81 and 1982–90 series.

3 FURTHER EMPIRICAL ANALYSIS OF EXCHANGE RATE FLUCTUATIONS

To put the conclusions from the previous paragraph in the proper perspective we shall also look at the time series, distribution

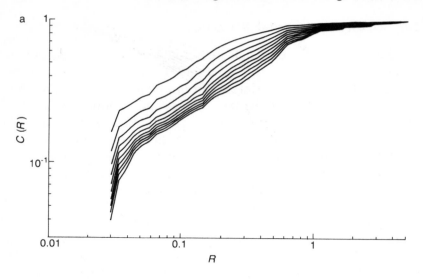

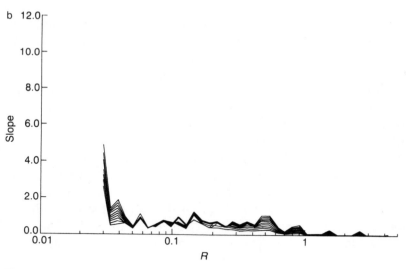

Figure 7.9 Time delay analysis for Japanese yen/US dollar returns, 1971–2. (a) $C(R)$ versus R on a log-log scale for embedding dimensions from 2 (top) to 11 (bottom). (b) Instantaneous slope of (a) for embedding dimensions from 2 (bottom) to 11 (top).

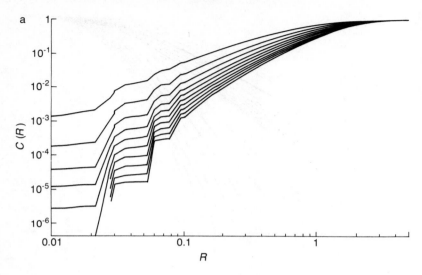

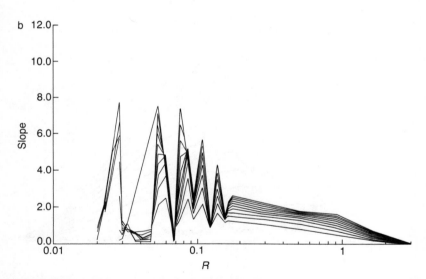

Figure 7.10 Time delay analysis for Japanese yen/US dollar returns, 1973–81. (a) $C(R)$ versus R on a log-log scale for embedding dimensions from 2 (top) to 11 (bottom). (b) Instantaneous slope of (a) for embedding dimensions from 2 (bottom) to 11 (top).

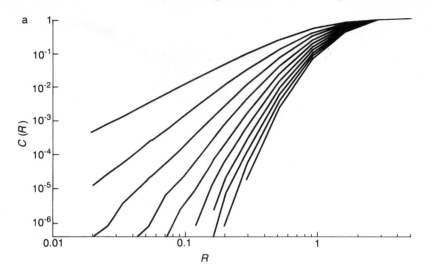

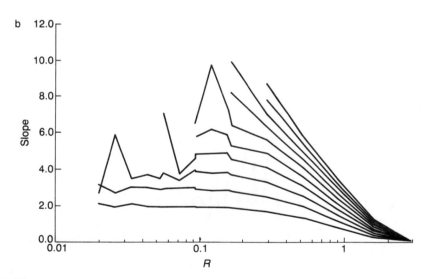

Figure 7.11   Time delay analysis for Japanese yen/US dollar returns, 1982–90. (a) $C(R)$ versus R on a log-log scale for embedding dimensions from 2 (top) to 11 (bottom). (b) Instantaneous slope of (a) for embedding dimensions from 2 (bottom) to 11 (top).

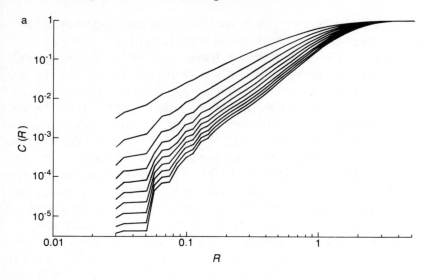

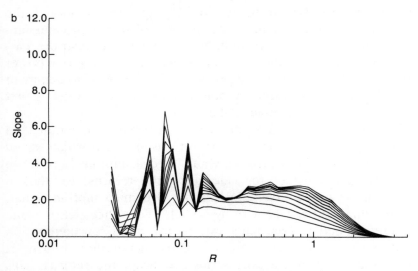

Figure 7.12 Time delay analysis for Japanese yen/US dollar returns, 1973–90. (a) $C(R)$ versus R on a log-log scale for embedding dimensions from 2 (top) to 11 (bottom). (b) Instantaneous slope of (a) for embedding dimensions from 2 (bottom) to 11 (top).

functions and Fourier power spectra of the exchange rate returns and compare them with random walk returns.

Figure 7.13a shows the exchange rate data for the pound/dollar for the period 1973–81 in cents per pound. There are about 2250 datapoints available during this period and the horizontal axis labels the datum number rather than the time. Figure 7.13b shows the distribution function for the exchange rates corresponding to figure 7.13a. Figure 7.13c shows the Fourier power spectrum for the same data. Figure 7.14 represents the actual returns for the pound, the distribution function for the returns, and the power spectrum for the returns. The mark and the yen data show very similar figures for the equivalents of figures 7.13 and 7.14 and are therefore not reproduced here.

We now compare figures 7.13 and 7.14 with figures 7.15 and 7.16, which present a random walk process (Brownian motion) drawn from a Gaussian distribution. It can be seen that figure 7.13a resembles figure 7.15a and is typical for a Brownian motion or random walk type of fluctuation. Figure 7.13b shows that the distribution of the exchange rate (pound/dollar) is non-Gaussian. The Fourier power spectrum in figure 7.13c has a linear decreasing trend on a log–log scale very much like the Fourier power spectrum of the random walk process. This leads us to comment that the time and frequency behavior of exchange rates is first order similar to Brownian motion.

Figure 7.16 shows the time series, distribution function, and Fourier power spectrum for the returns of a Brownian signal with increments drawn from a Gaussian distribution. In order to avoid negative values for calculating the returns, we took a value of 60 as the first point for the Brownian motion signal. Comparing figures 7.14 with figure 7.16, we notice clearly some differences between exchange rate returns and Brownian motion returns. The time series for the Brownian motion returns is more regular than the time series for the pound returns. This observation is supported when we compare the distribution function for Brownian motion returns with the distribution function for the pound returns. While the distribution function for the random walk returns has a Gaussian shape (because the increments were drawn from a Gaussian distribution), the distribution function for the pound returns is obviously too peaked to be

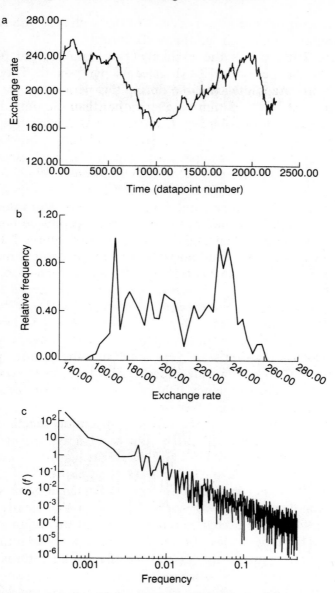

Figure 7.13 Analysis of the pound sterling/US dollar exchange rate, 1973–81. (a) Time series (US cents per pound); (b) distribution function; (c) Fourier power spectrum.

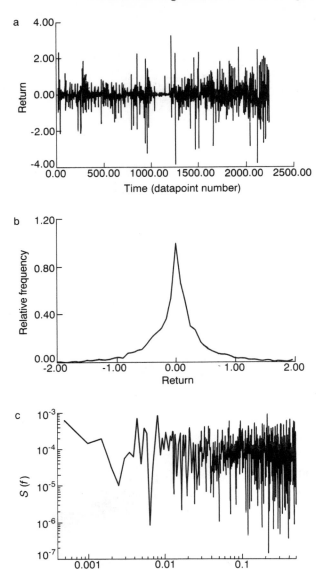

Figure 7.14 Analysis of the pound sterling/US dollar returns, 1973–81. (a) Time series (US cents per pound); (b) distribution function; (c) Fourier power spectrum.

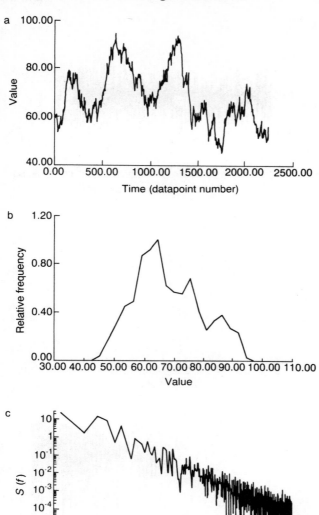

Figure 7.15 Analysis of Brownian motion with increments drawn from a Gaussian distribution. (a) Time series; (b) distribution function; (c) Fourier power spectrum.

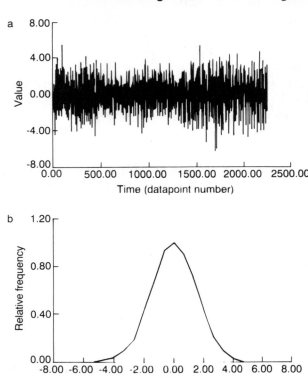

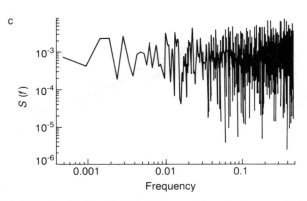

Figure 7.16 Analysis of Brownian motion returns with increments drawn from a Gaussian distribution. (a) Time series; (b) distribution function; (c) Fourier power spectrum.

Gaussian. One could say that, to first approximation, figure 7.14b represents a fat-tailed Gaussian distribution where large fluctuations are more frequent than would be the case in a normal Gaussian distribution. Some experimenting leads to the observation that a Student t distribution with two degrees of freedom more closely resembles figure 7.14b.

The power spectra of figures 7.14c and 7.16c are flat (compared to figures 7.13c and 7.15c), and represent a broadband power spectrum. The peaked symmetrical distribution for pound returns is definitely different from the distribution functions for chaotic signals we encountered earlier in the first few chapters. But this is not a criterion to reject chaos *per se*. So far, the distinction between a random walk and exchange rate fluctuations is mainly reflected in the shape of the distribution function of the returns.

Figure 7.17 shows the correlation function versus the separation measure on a log–log scale (figure 7.17a), and the instantaneous slope of that figure versus R for various embedding dimensions for random walk returns (figure 7.17b). This figure is similar to the correlation function and instantaneous slope for Gaussian noise encountered earlier. We took 2250 datapoints for preparing the plots of figure 7.17 (the same number as in the time series for the exchange rates). Notice that we do not quite reach the dimension of the embedding space here. In order to do so more data would be required. Figure 7.17b for the random walk returns is very different from figure 7.6b for the pound returns. This is a second distinction between exchange rate data and Brownian motion.

So far we have shown that exchange rate fluctuations look similar to a random walk signal but tend to have sharper distribution functions for their returns. The correlation domain plots for exchange rate returns can look similar to correlation domain plots for random walk returns, or non-stationary Brownian motion returns, but the exchange rates can show very different correlation plots, which is indicative of a chaotic signal as well (figures 7.6b, 7.8b, 7.9b, and 7.12b).

An entirely different viewpoint on the fractal nature of exchange rate data can be obtained by looking at the Hurst coefficient obtained from a rescaled range analysis or R/S analysis.

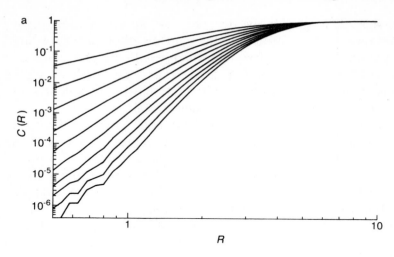

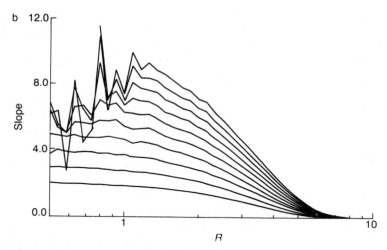

Figure 7.17 Time delay analysis for Brownian motion returns. (a) $C(R)$ versus R on a log-log scale for embedding dimensions from 2 (top) to 11 (bottom). (b) Instantaneous slope of (a) for embedding dimensions from 2 (bottom) to 11 (top).

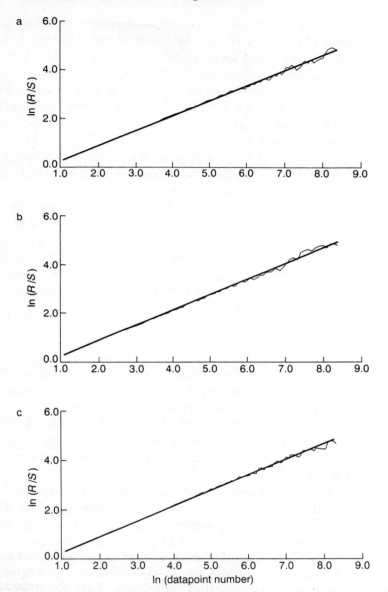

Figure 7.18 Estimating the Hurst coefficient, H (the slope), from returns. (a) Deutschmark/US dollar, estimated $H = 0.620$. (b) Pound sterling/US dollar, estimated $H = 0.634$. (c) Japanese yen/US dollar, estimated $H = 0.620$.

An *R/S* analysis for the mark, pound, and yen yields about one for all three of them. A Hurst coefficient of unity indicates that an upward or downward trend is more likely to continue in the future than to reverse. This information is not surprising in view of the strong correlation between values for a random walk. It is more relevant to look at the Hurst coefficients for the returns (figure 7.18). Looking at the daily returns between 1973 and 1990 we found Hurst coefficients of 0.63 (± 1.2 percent), 0.62 (± 2.4 percent), and 0.60 ($\pm$ 2.9 percent) for the mark, pound, and yen respectively. This indicates that there is some correlation between the returns, and that trends from the past in the returns are more likely to continue in the future. Although there is no mathematical requirement (as far as we are aware of), a Hurst coefficient significantly different from 0.5 often goes hand-in-hand with the presence of a strange attractor. If anything, the results from a rescaled range analysis provide some support to there being a chaotic structure in the exchange rate returns.

4 CONCLUSION

In this chapter we have presented empirical evidence on the existence of chaos in some major exchange markets. Our results are mixed. There are some indications for the occurrence of chaos in the yen/dollar and pound/dollar markets. We did not find evidence of chaotic behaviour in the mark/dollar market. Thus, although we find some evidence for chaos, it cannot be said that it is conclusive.

There are several possible reasons for the lack of conclusive evidence of the existence of chaos. The most important one has to do with the fact that the number of datapoints we used still falls short of the amount required to employ usefully the statistical techniques. A second reason is that noise masks chaos, making the detection of the latter very difficult. In order to improve on the statistical analysis of chaos it will, therefore, be necessary to use more powerful noise-filtering techniques that do not introduce artifacts in the time series.

In the next chapter we complete the empirical analysis by

analysing the exchange rate data for nonlinearities. Finding evidence for nonlinearities in the data is important, because the existence of nonlinearities is necessary for the process to be chaotic (although not sufficient).

8

Evidence of Nonlinearities in Foreign Exchange Rates

1 INTRODUCTION

The purpose of this chapter is to show that there is in fact a nonlinear mechanism that drives the observed exchange rate. More precisely we will use two different nonlinearity tests, namely the BDS test and the Hinich–Patterson test (HP test). The strength of these tests is that they are non-parametric. The drawback is that, if we find nonlinearities, this does not prove that the underlying structure is chaotic. Other nonlinear structures could also lead to observed nonlinearities. Thus, passing the BDS and HP tests is a necessary condition for chaos, not a sufficient one.

2 RETURNS AND NONLINEARITY

For good understanding, we will define exactly what is meant by a nonlinear system. In fact there is no generally used definition in the literature that allows us to employ the following definition, based on the Wold decomposition.

Definition: A system $X_t = h(\Omega_t, \alpha)$ is called a nonlinear system if it is not possible to regenerate X_t by one linear model:

$$X_t = \sum_{i=0}^{\infty} \gamma_i \varepsilon_{t-i} \text{ and } \varepsilon \text{ is white noise and}$$

$$\{\gamma_i\} \sum_{t=0}^{\infty} \text{ is such that } \sum_{t=0}^{\infty} |\gamma_t| < \infty \tag{1}$$

The definition of nonlinearity stems from the negation of linearity. This leaves a lot of other possibilities open for a so-called nonlinear system.

The tests will be performed on the returns of the data. This is done to conform with the literature and to allow comparison with other studies in this domain. The choice of level or of return will not affect the results of the test. If the system is nonlinear, then this structure will show up in the levels as well as in the returns. This preservation of nonlinearity when passed through linear filters was proven by Brock (1986) in the so-called residual theorem. This allows us to make the data stationary, which is a prerequisite for the Hinich–Patterson tests.

3 NON-PARAMETRIC NONLINEARITY TESTS

In this section we discuss the above mentioned nonlinearity test. We selected two different tests because of their complementarity. First we will discuss the BDS statistic, and second the HP statistic. Because of the importance of the tests, the statistical background will be provided as well.

3.1 The BDS statistic

Brock et al. (1987) proposed this test. The test is based on the concepts of chaos theory and more specifically the correlation function (see chapter 6).

The BDS test looks at the dispersion of the points in a number of spaces with dimension going from 2 to n. This dispersion will be either in line or at odds with the assumption of white noise. The BDS test then amounts to a test of the difference between the dispersion of the observed data in these consecutive spaces with the dispersion that a white noise process (i.i.d.) would generate in these same spaces.

White noise (i.i.d.) processes produce the following correlation function when the embedding dimension is n:

$$C(R, 1)^n \tag{2}$$

where R is the radius (see chapter 6). This expression says that the correlation integral of a white noise process with embedding dimension n can be written as the nth power of the correlation dimension with embedding dimension 1.

The BDS statistics is then defined as:

$$\text{BDS} = \frac{C(R,n) - C(R,1)^n}{\sigma^2[C(R,n) - C(R,1)^n]} \rightarrow N(0,1) \tag{3}$$

We reject white noise (i.i.d.) when BDS exceeds in absolute value the chosen critical value. This will occur if the dispersion of the points over the consecutive spaces is not in line with the expected dispersion under white noise.

One of the problems in applying the BDS procedure is the proper choice of R. Choosing an R too small will yield totally unreliable results while the choice of a very large R will reduce the number of observations very drastically. However, Hsieh and Le Baron (1988a,b) performed a lot of simulations. According to their results the "best" choice of R is between 0.5 and 1.5 times the standard deviation.

Finally, it must be stressed that this test does not conform with the definition of nonlinearity as posited above. In fact the conditional mean of linear systems differs across time such that the identicality assumption is violated. Therefore the BDS test will also correctly reject i.i.d. in the case of linearity. We will apply this test, however, because of its power against nonlinear alternatives. The complementarity of the other test makes sure that we can discriminate between linearity and nonlinearity.

3.2   The HP statistic

One of the earliest types of nonlinearity test is those based on the bispectrum theory. Two tests were proposed by Subba Rao and Gabr (1980) and Hinich (1982). The approaches differ, however. While Subba Rao and Gabr use the symmetry properties, Hinich exploits the asymptotic properties of the bispectrum estimator. Because of its importance we will discuss not only the test statistic but also the theory of the bispectrum serving as its base. Let $\{X_t\}_{t=0}^{\infty}$ be a third order stationary process with zero mean. The third order cumulant (bicovariance function) of this process is defined in (4):

$$C_{xxx}(\tau_1, \tau_2, \tau_3) = E(X\tau_1 X\tau_2 X\tau_3)$$

$$\tau_1, \tau_2, \tau_3 = 0, \pm 1, \pm 2, \ldots \tag{4}$$

This function is also known as the bicovariance function. If the series is third order stationary we can look at this function in the frequency domain. This frequency decomposition is called the bispectrum of X. Formally we can define the bispectrum as in (5):

$$B(\omega_i, \omega_j, \omega_k) =$$

$$\frac{\iiint C_{xxx}(\tau_1, \tau_2, \tau_3)\exp - (i(\omega_1\tau_1 + \omega_2\tau_2 + \omega_3\tau_3)d\tau_1 d\tau_2 d\tau_3}{\delta(\omega_1 + \omega_2 + \omega_3)} \tag{5}$$

where $\delta(\ )$ is the delta Dirca function.[1]

Without loss of generality we can set $\tau_1 = 0$. It can be shown that for a univariate process the frequency space over which the bispectrum must be computed reduces to the D described in (6)

$$D = \{(\omega_1, \omega_2) \mid 0 \leq \omega_1 \leq \pi/2, \omega_2 \leq \omega_1, 2\omega_1 + \omega_2 \leq 2\pi\} \tag{6}$$

This set is in fact triangular, as will be shown when we present some of the estimation results.

The adequateness of the bispectrum for the detection of non-linear structure stems from the following property. Let $\{X_t\}_{t=0}^{\infty}$ be a linear zero mean, third order stationary process. Then

$$|BS(\omega_i, \omega_j)|^2 = \frac{\mu_3^2}{\sigma_\varepsilon^6} S(\omega_i)S(\omega_j)S(\omega_i + \omega_j) \quad \forall(\omega_i, \omega_j)\varepsilon D \tag{7}$$

where $S(\omega_i)$ is the power spectrum of the series at frequency ω_i.

This property implies that all linear systems have a totally flat bispectrum. Whether or not the bispectrum has nonzero value depends on the stochastic characteristics of the innovations. If the distribution of the innovations is symmetric then the bispectrum is zero all over D. In the other case the bispectrum takes a positive value. The test for linearity becomes evident; if we can show that the bispectrum is not flat, then we have shown that the process is nonlinear in the sense of the above definition.

It can be shown that the bispectrum is consistently estimated by (8):

$$\hat{B}(w_i, w_j) = \frac{1}{N^2} \sum_{j=(m-1)M}^{Nm-1} \sum_{k=(n-1)M}^{Mn-1} F(j, k)$$

$$F(j, k) = X(j)X(k) \, X^*(j + k)$$

$$X(j) = \sum_{T=0}^{N-1} x_t \exp\left(-\frac{2\pi j t}{N}\right) \tag{8}$$

The m, and n are defined such that (ω_i, ω_j) is in D. Hinich proved the asymptotic normality of this estimator.

This asymptotic result is used by Hinich in the construction of his test statistic. In fact the frequency decomposition has turned a difficult stochastic problem into a standard one. Hinich (1982) proposes the statistic presented in (9):

$$T = \sum_m \sum_n |\hat{B}S(\omega_i, \omega_j)|^2 \sim \chi^2(2p, \lambda_{m,n}) \tag{9}$$

$$\lambda_{m,n} = 2 \left(\frac{N}{m^2}\right)^{-1} \frac{|B(\omega_1, \omega_2)|^2}{S_x(\omega_1)S_x(\omega_2)S_x(\omega_1 + \omega_2)}$$

$$\hat{B}S(\omega_i, \omega_j) = \frac{|\hat{B}(\omega_i, \omega_j)|^2}{\hat{S}_t(\omega_i)\hat{S}_t(\omega_j)\hat{S}_t(\omega_i + \omega_j)}$$

The T value presents the test statistic and is distributed as a non-central chi-squared with centrality parameter $\lambda_{m,n}$. For symmetrical distributions this distribution becomes a central chisquared distribution such that statistical inferences are straightforward. A value of T exceeding the critical chi-squared value implies a rejection of linearity and symmetry of the series.

In the actual implementation of the test the T statistic is approximated by its equivalent standard normal statistic. We call this statistic Z_1. However, this test will fail to discriminate between nonlinear and linear systems with skewed innovations. Therefore a complementary statistic was proposed by Hinich. Consider the 80 percent sample quartile $\xi_{0.8}$ of the estimates $BS(\omega_i, \omega_j)$.

Hinich shows that

$$Z_2 = \frac{\hat{\xi}_{0.8} - \xi_{0.8}}{\sigma^2 \xi} \sim N(0, 1)$$

The real 80 percent quartile under the hypothesis of one single non-central chi-squared distribution is $\xi_{0.8}$. This value can be computed by the use of the estimated non-centrality parameter.[2] Ashley and Patterson (1989) and Ashley et al. (1986) conducted simulations. Their conclusions are that this test statistic has a lot of power against some classes of nonlinear models (e.g. bilinear, SETAR). However, some classes of models will not be detected. The best known class is the GARCH class. Therefore a rejection of nonlinearity is decisive.

4 EVIDENCE OF NONLINEARITIES IN FOREIGN EXCHANGE RATES

In this section the above-mentioned tests are applied to six foreign exchange rates (more specifically the DM/$, ¥/$, £/$, £/DM, £/¥ and ¥/DM). We will not restrict ourselves to one single frequency. Instead we go through the whole spectrum from daily up to monthly data. The value added to our research compared to that of others is that first of all it employs more than one test statistic.[3] Second, we analyze different frequencies. Most important, however, is the use of complementary statistics. This allows us to get a better idea about what causes the BDS to reject the null (if it rejects it at all). This has not been done in previous studies.

The data set consists of three original exchange rate series, namely the Deutschmark, the pound and the yen against the dollar. The exchange rate data are daily closing rates from January 1, 1971 to December 30, 1990. The remaining three series were calculated using triangular arbitrage.

We will concentrate on two issues. First we test whether the return data are identically and independently distributed (i.i.d.). Since this test rejects any serial correlation, the acceptance of the null hypothesis implies the rejection of nonlinearity. Second, if i.i.d.-ness is rejected we test whether or not the cause of this rejection was a linear generating mechanism. This step is tested by the bispectral test. Rejection of the null hypothesis is an indication of a nonlinear structure in the data.

The entire data set (1971–90) is first analyzed according to the above steps. Second, we split the sample period into

Table 8.1   BDS test performed on daily exchange rate returns

				Embedding dimension					
	2	3	4	5	6	7	8	9	10
Period January 1, 1971 to December 30, 1990									
DM/$	12.5	18.6	24.3	29.9	36.7	44.9	55.2	68.9	86.4
¥/$	17.4	22.0	26.9	31.7	37.2	43.5	51.3	61.5	74.4
£/$	17.6	23.5	29.3	35.6	43.7	53.4	65.4	80.5	100.7
£/DM	13.6	18.5	23.4	28.5	34.9	42.8	52.5	65.3	82.3
¥/£	15.5	20.6	25.6	30.9	38.0	47.0	58.4	73.5	93.8
¥/DM	17.9	22.5	26.6	30.3	34.7	40.0	46.0	53.1	61.9
Period 1974–80									
DM/$	8.0	11.7	15.4	18.8	22.6	26.7	31.4	37.3	44.2
¥/$	12.8	15.3	18.3	21.0	24.2	27.6	31.7	36.9	43.3
£/$	14.3	17.18	20.38	23.64	27.9	32.6	37.9	44.6	53.6
£/DM	6.3	8.1	9.6	10.9	12.1	13.3	14.4	15.5	16.5
¥/£	9.7	11.2	12.5	13.8	15.3	17.2	19.2	21.8	24.6
¥/DM	9.9	12.5	15.3	17.8	20.3	23.2	26.3	29.9	34.6
Period 1980–90									
DM/$	2.24	4.5	6.5	7.8	9.2	10.0	11.6	13.4	15.3
¥/$	7.0	8.7	10.5	11.7	13.1	14.4	15.8	17.8	20.0
£/$	4.4	5.5	6.5	7.3	8.7	9.8	10.7	11.5	12.3
£/DM	3.9	4.6	5.3	5.8	6.5	7.2	7.7	8.4	9.0
¥/£	4.6	5.7	6.5	6.9	7.7	8.5	9.3	10.3	11.7
¥/DM	9.7	12.4	14.2	15.9	18.3	20.1	3.5	26.7	30.4

subsamples (the 1970s and the 1980s) to check whether our results change over the two sample periods.

We start the analysis with the daily return data. The results of the BDS test are presented in table 8.1. I.i.d.-ness is rejected for all sample periods at any standard level of significance. These results are in line with those of Hsieh (1989). Qualitatively, however, there is a difference between the first and the second subsamples. As can be seen, the values of the BDS test are much higher in the 1970s than in the 1980s.

In order to discriminate between linear and nonlinear struc-

Table 8.2 Bispectral tests on daily exchange rate returns

Z_i	DM/$	¥/$	£/$	£/DM	¥/£	¥/DM
Period January 1, 1971 to December 30, 1990						
Z_1	17.5	20.9	33.1	12.0	13.8	30.8
Z_2	5.2	4.2	7.5	6.1	8.5	9.9
Period January 1, 1974 to December 3, 1979						
Z_1	44.8	41.1	32.1	24.11	22.1	35.3
Z_2	8.2	7.6	7.2	5.0	6.8	10.1
Period January 1, 1980 to December 30, 1990						
Z_1	11.5	10.1	20.0	7.8	7.2	30.2
Z_2	9.3	7.1	6.8	5.6	5.0	9.4

tures we applied the HP test. The results are presented in Table 8.2. As discussed in the previous section, the HP statistic consists of two tests. The first one is called the "Gaussianity" test. It tests for the existence of a linear and symmetric structure. The result is given by Z_1, which is distributed as a standard normal. The second test checks for linear structure with skewed innovations. The test results are presented by Z_2 which has the same degrees of freedom as Z_1.

The results of the HP test clearly reject linearity as the generating principle. This result holds for the standard levels of significance. Moreover, we do not find strong differences between the first and second subsamples. Note that this result rejects the results of the symmetric GARCH(1, 1) class for daily exchange rate returns.

We now turn to the analysis of weekly returns. The BDS results in table 8.3 again indicate the non i.i.d.-ness of the data. The dichotomy between the 1970s and the 1980s (the latter numbers are smaller) remains. Note, however, that i.i.d.-ness is also rejected within each subperiod at all standard levels, except for the yen/pound-rate, which seems to be i.i.d. in the 1980s.

The bispectral estimates (see figure 8.1 and table 8.4) reject linearity for all exchange rates in all sample periods (except for the yen/pound during 1980–90). The subdivision of this period

Table 8.3 BDS test performed on weekly exchange rate returns

	Embedding dimension								
	2	3	4	5	6	7	8	9	10
Period January 1, 1971 to December 30, 1990									
DM/$	8.0	11.9	15.3	18.8	22.8	28.0	34.7	44.0	55.8
¥/$	8.5	12.1	14.8	17.5	20.5	23.9	28.2	33.4	39.5
£/$	7.2	10.3	12.3	14.5	17.2	20.3	24.7	29.8	35.3
£/DM	6.5	8.9	10.5	12.5	14.8	17.7	21.5	26.3	32.2
¥/£	5.3	7.5	9.3	11.5	13.9	16.9	20.7	25.4	31.5
¥/DM	8.2	10.3	12.7	14.5	15.9	17.4	19.1	20.9	23.1
Period January 1, 1974 to December 30, 1974									
DM/$	6.1	9.6	11.6	13.7	15.7	18.2	21.4	25.0	29.4
¥/$	4.9	6.6	8.2	9.6	10.8	11.8	12.8	13.8	14.8
£/$	5.1	7.0	9.2	9.4	11.0	12.7	14.5	16.2	17.9
£/DM	2.9	3.9	3.5	3.3	3.1	3.6	2.9	3.0	2.9
¥/£	3.7	4.1	4.4	5.0	5.5	6.1	6.6	7.1	7.5
¥/DM	6.0	6.9	7.5	8.1	8.1	8.1	8.3	8.6	8.9
Period January 1, 1980 to December 30, 1990									
DM/$	1.41	3.2	4.7	6.1	7.2	7.8	8.6	9.1	9.3
¥/$	3.8	5.4	6.5	7.3	7.9	8.5	9.2	9.8	10.3
£/$	2.0	3.0	3.6	3.9	4.1	4.1	4.2	4.5	4.6
£/DM	2.4	3.2	3.5	3.7	3.8	4.2	4.6	4.9	5.2
¥/£	1.2	1.7	1.7	1.8	1.6	1.5	1.5	1.4	1.2
¥/DM	5.1	6.1	7.9	9.3	10.5	11.6	12.5	13.3	14.0

does not show the same dichotomy as the BDS test. Note again the rejection of the symmetric GARCH model. It is fair to conclude that the weekly returns display a similar nonlinear dependence to the daily returns.

Finally we analyze the monthly exchange rate returns. We have 240 non-overlapping monthly returns. This number is at the limit of reliability for the two test statistics. The BDS statistic (table 8.5) reports non i.i.d.-ness for all exchange rates at standard levels of significance. The other test (table 8.6) gives a more diversified picture of the structure. We reject linearity for

Table 8.4 Bispectral tests on weekly exchange rate returns

Z_i	DM/$	¥/$	£/$	£/DM	¥/£	¥/DM
Period January 1, 1971 to December 30, 1990						
Z_1	4.1	9.2	14.0	5.9	4.9	6.0
Z_2	4.9	3.2	3.7	4.9	3.3	3.1
Period January 1, 1974 to December 30, 1979						
Z_1	14.1	11.5	7.4	1.94	5.0	8.0
Z_2	4.0	2.8	1.5	3.4	2.64	1.8
Period January 1, 1980 to December 30, 1990						
Z_1	3.0	5.9	12.6	2.3	2.51	4.0
Z_2	2.6	3.2	6.1	1.83	1.5	4.6

Table 8.5 BDS test performed on monthly exchange rate returns

Period January 1, 1971 to December 30, 1990								
DM/$	3.6	4.2	4.7	5.7	7.3	9.0	11.2	14.5	18.9
¥/$	−0.9	0.7	1.2	1.6	2.17	2.44	3.0	3.4	4.8
£/$	2.2	2.3	2.3	3.1	3.4	3.7	3.9	4.7	5.3
£/DM	1.8	1.3	1.6	2.1	2.7	3.6	4.7	6.1	8.0
¥/£	0.6	0.7	1.1	1.8	2.4	2.8	3.9	5.3	7.4
¥/DM	4.2	4.6	5.5	6.5	7.8	8.9	10.0	11.1	12.6

the three exchange rates against the dollar. For the other exchange rates we were unable to reject linearity.

The conclusion of these tests is that some exchange rates no longer have nonlinear properties at the monthly frequency. This could be due to the fact that the number of non-overlapping data in these monthly tests is at the limit of acceptability. Nonlinear structures, in general, require a lot of data to leave their fingerprints in the bispectrum. It should also be remembered that if the HP test cannot reject the null hypothesis, this does not imply the acceptance of linearity.

Table 8.6   Bispectral estimates of monthly exchange rate returns

Period January 1, 1971 to December 30, 1990					
DM/$	¥/$	£/$	£/DM	¥/£	¥/DM
Z_1 2.7	1.5	2.0	0.23	+0.35	0.26
Z_2 5.0	2.4	2.1	−0.1	0.8	−0.14

5   CONCLUSION

In this chapter we discussed the nonlinear characteristics of exchange rate returns. We used two different and complementary statistics, i.e. the BDS test and the HP test. Within the framework of a stationary sequence these tests are sufficient to detect nonlinearity.

These tests were applied to six exchange rate returns at different frequencies. The results that emerged were very clear. At high frequencies (daily and weekly) we could not reject the existence of nonlinear structures for any of the exchange rates. At lower frequency (monthly) we had to reject nonlinearity in only one case, the pound/yen exchange rate.

To conclude, we found nonlinearities to abound in exchange rate returns. Therefore the subject of nonlinearity is no longer a *fait d'hiver* at the margin, but is of real importance for the understanding of the foreign exchange markets.

As stressed in the Introduction, the existence of nonlinearities in the exchange rate returns does not prove that chaos exists. Other nonlinear structures than chaotic ones could be driving the exchange rates. However, our theoretical analysis in the first part of this book has shown that under plausible assumptions, chaotic movements can emerge from simple exchange rate models. In other words, we have some theoretical reason to believe that exchange rates can behave in a chaotic manner.

These theoretical insights, together with the empirical evidence of this chapter and chapter 7, can give some credibility to the view that chaotic processes are important in the foreign exchange markets.

NOTES

1 This delta Dirac function is necessary to get the same results if you do a double Fourier transform on the bicovariance function or if you do the Fourier transform on the series itself and thereafter construct the bicovariance function.
2 For more details the reader is referred to Hinich (1981), Hinich and Patterson (1986), Ashley and Patterson (1989).
3 Most of the papers on nonlinearity use the BDS test statistic. A good example of this approach to daily exchange rates is Hsieh (1989).

9

Conclusion

The rational expectations paradigm has thoroughly permeated economic theory. The intellectual attraction of this paradigm is very great. The reason is simple. It extends the rationality hypothesis to the psychological domain of how economic agents process and use information. In so doing, it makes assumptions about how economic agents form expectations consistent with the economic model used by the researcher, instead of introducing *ad hoc* assumptions about the formation of expectations.

The trouble with this paradigm is that the empirical evidence rejecting the rational expectations assumption has a tendency to accumulate. This negative empirical evidence is especially striking in the field of foreign exchange markets. However, this has not prevented researchers from continuing to use rational expectations models. The main reason seems to be that no alternative modelling approach has as yet emerged.

In this book we have attempted to provide such an alternative modelling approach. We have presented theoretical models that use concepts of chaos theory. In so doing, we have abandoned the rational expectations assumption, taking the view that a significant number of economic agents (whom we called chartists) do not use all relevant information to forecast the future. An essential feature of our modelling approach was that there are two classes of economic agents, the chartists and the fundamentalists, the relative importance of which is determined by market conditions.

This modelling approach allowed us to show that chaotic behavior of the exchange rate emerges with rather plausible parameter values of the underlying model. This model generates exchange rate movements that appear to be random, although the underlying structure is deterministic. One of the interesting implications of the model is that it generates a complex dynamics of exchange rate movements without having to rely on exogenous movements in the fundamental variables driving the exchange rate.

We also showed that the chaotic foreign exchange market model is capable of mimicking some important stylized facts observed in the foreign exchange market (for example, the bias of the forward premium as a forecast of future exchange rate changes). The model also made clear that in a chaotic environment there is scope for short-term forecasting based on the past behavior of the exchange rates, and illustrated the inherent difficulties of forecasting based on "fundamental" information. Thus, in a sense the model rationalizes what one observes, i.e. that the predominant method of forecasting is based on the analysis of trends and patterns of past foreign exchange rate movements. This phenomenon surely cannot be explained by the rational expectations models.

A large part of the book analyzed statistical methods to detect chaos in exchange rate data. Since there is no unique definition of chaos, there is also no unique statistical method to detect chaos. We contrasted the different methods, and applied them to the foreign exchange rates of a number of major currencies during the period 1971–90. We found some, albeit weak, evidence of chaotic behavior of the dollar/yen and the dollar/sterling rates, but none for the dollar/Deutschmark rate. We also found significant evidence of nonlinearities in the exchange rate returns.

The empirical analysis presented in this book can certainly not be considered as conclusive evidence for the existence of chaos in the foreign exchange market. It would therefore be premature to claim that we have found an alternative model for the rational expectations model of the foreign exchange rate. Nevertheless, the evidence presented in this book convinces us that it is worthwhile to continue to do research in order to detect whether chaotic models are useful devices to understand the foreign exchange markets.

References

Adler, M. and Lehman, B. (1983) On the econometric testing of rationality-market efficiency. *Review of Economics and Statistics*, 63, 318–23.

Allen, P. R. and Kenen, P. B. (1978) *The Balance of Payments, Exchange Rates and Economic Policy*. Athens: CEPR.

Allen, P. R. and Tayler, S. (1989) Charts, noise and fundamentals: a study of the London foreign exchange market. CEPR Discussion Paper no. 341.

Ashley, R. A. and Patterson, D. M. (1989) Linear versus non-linear macroeconomics: a statistical test. *International Economic Review*, 30, 685–704.

Ashley, R. A., Patterson, D. M. and Henich, M. J. (1986) A diagnostic check for non-linear social dependence in time series fitting errors. *Journal of Time Series*, 7 (3), 165–78.

Bachus, D. (1984) Empirical models of exchange rates: seperating the wheat from the chaff. *Canadian Journal of Economics*, 17 (4), 824–46.

Baillie, R. T. and Bollerslev, T. (1989) Common stochastic trends in a system of exchange rates. *Journal of Finance*, 44 (1), 167–81.

Ballie, R. T. and McMahon, P. C. (1989) *The Foreign Exchange Market Theory and Econometric Evidence*. Cambridge: Cambridge University Press.

Baillie, R. T. and Selover, D. D. (1987) Cointegration and models of exchange rate determination. *International Journal of Forecasting*, 3, 43–52.

Baker, G. L. and Gollub, J. P. (1990) *Chaotic Dynamics: an Introduction*. Cambridge: Cambridge University Press.

Barnsley, M. (1988) *Fractals Everywhere*. New York: Academic Press.

Bilson, J. (1978a) The monetary approach to the exchange rates. Some empirical evidence. *IMF Staff Papers*, 25, 48–75.

Bilson, J. (1978b) Rational expectations and the exchange rate. In J. A. Frankel and M. G. Johnson (eds), *The Economics of Exchange Rates*. Reading, MA: Addison-Wesley.

Bilson, J. (1979a) The Deutsche-mark–dollar rate: a monetary analysis. In K. Brunner and A. H. Meltzer (eds), *Policies for Employment Prices and Exchange Rates*. Amsterdam: North-Holland.

Bilson, J. (1979b) Recent developments in monetary models of exchange rate determination. *IMF Staff Papers*, 2, 201–23.

Boothe, P. and Glassman, P. (1987) The statistical distribution of exchange rates: empirical evidence and economic implications. *Journal of International Economics*, 2, 297–319

Branson, W. H. (1969) The minimum covered interest differential needed for international arbitrage activity. *Journal of Political Economy*, 77, 1028–35.

Branson, W. H. (1975) Comment on Whitman. *Brookings Papers on Economic Activity*, 4, 537–41.

Branson, W. H. (1977) Asset markets and relative prices in exchange rate determination. Institute for International Economic Studies Paper no. 96.

Brillinger, D. (1975) *Time Series, Data Analysis and Theory*. New York: Holt, Rinehart and Winston.

Brock, W. (1986) Distinguishing random and deterministic systems: an expanded version. *Journal of Economic Theory*, 90, 168–95.

Brock, W. A., Dechert, W. D. and Scheinkman, J. A. (1987) A test for independence based on the correlation dimension. SSRJ Working Paper no. 8762, Department of Economics, University of Wisconsin-Madison.

Caudill, M. (1989–1992) Various articles about neural networks. *AI Expert*, various issues.

Corbae, D. and Ouliaris, S. (1986) Robust test for unit roots in the foreign exchange rate market. *Economic Letters*, 22, 375–80.

Cutler, D. M., Poterba, J. M. and Summers, L. H. (1989a) Speculative dynamics. NBER Working Paper no. 2441.

Cutler, D. M., Poterba, J. M. and Summers, L. H. (1989b) Speculative dynamics: the role of feedback traders. NBER Working Paper no. 2442.

De Grauwe, P. (1989) On the nature of risk in the foreign exchange markets: evidence from the dollar and the EMS markets. Discussion paper no. 352, CEPR, London.

De Grauwe, P. and Vansanten, K. (1991) Speculative dynamics and chaos in the FX markets. In R. O'Brien and S. Hewin (eds), *Finance and International Economy*, 4th edn. Oxford: Oxford University Press.

De Long, J., Bradford, B., Schleiffer, A., Summers, L. and Waldman, R. (1990a) Noise trader risk in financial markets. *Journal of Political Economy*, 98, 703–38.

De Long, J., Bradford, B., Schleiffer, A., Summers, L. and Waldman, R. (1990b) Positive feedback investment strategies and destabilizing rational speculation. *Journal of Finance*, 45, 115–30.

Dickey, D. A. and Fuller, W. A. (1979) Distribution of the estimates for autoregressive time series with a unit root. *Journal of the American Statistical Association*, 74, 427–32.

Dickey, D. A. and Fuller, W. A. (1981) Likelihood ratio statistics for autoregressive time series with a unit root. *Econometrica*, 49, 1057–72.

Dornbusch, R. (1976a) Expectations and exchange rate dynamics. *Journal of Political Economy*, 84, 1161–76.

Dornbusch, R. (1976b) Exchange rate expectations and monetary policy. *Journal of International Economics*, 6, 231–44.

Dornbusch, R. and Fisher, S. (1980) Exchange rates and the current account. *American Economic Review*, 70 (5), 960–71.

Driksell, R. A. and Sheffrin, S. M. (1981) On the mark: comment. *American Economic Review*, 71 (5), 1058–74.

Engle, R. and Granger, C. (1987) Cointegration and error correction. *Econometrica*, 55, 251–76.

Falconer, K. (1990) *Fractal Geometry: Mathematical Foundations and Applications*. New York: John Wiley and Sons.

Fama, E. (1984) Forward and spot exchange rates. *Journal of Monetary Economics*, 14, 319–38.

Farmer, D. and Sidorowich, J. (1988) Exploiting chaos to predict the future and reduce noise. In Y. S. Lee (ed.), *Evolution, Learning and Cognition*. Singapore: World Scientific.

Farmer, J. D. (1982) Information dimension and the probabilistic structure of chaos. *Zeitschrift für Naturforschung*, 37a, 1304.

Feigenbaum, M. J. (1978) Quantitative universality for a class of nonlinear transformations. *Journal of Statistical Physics*, 19, 25.

Feder, J. (1989) *Fractals*. New York: Plenum Press.

Feigenbaum, M. J. (1980) Universal behavior in nonlinear systems. *Los Alamos Science*, Summer, 4–27.

Flannery, B. P., Press, W. H., Teukolsky, S. A. and Vetterling, W. T. (1985) *Numerical Recipes: the Art of Scientific Computing*. Cambridge: Cambridge University Press.

Frame, M. (1992) *An Introduction to Fractals and Chaos*. New York: McGraw-Hill.

Frank, G. W., Lookman, T. and Nerenberg, M. A. H. (1990) Recovering the attractor: a review of chaotic time-series analysis. *Canadian Journal of Physics*, 68, 711–18.

Frankel, F. A. (1979) On the mark: a theory of floating exchange rates based on real interest rate differentials. *American Economic Review*, 69, 601–22.

Frankel, F. A. (1984) Tests of monetary and portfolio balance models. In J. F. Bilson and R. C. Martson (eds), *Exchange Rate Theory and Practice*. Chicago: University of Chicago Press.

Frankel, F. A. and Froot, K. A. (1987) Using survey data to test propositions regarding exchange rate expectations. *American Economic Review*, 77, 133–53.

Frankel, F. A. and Froot, K. A. (1988) Chartists, fundamentalists and the demand for dollars. *Greek Economic Review*, 10, 49–102.

Frankel, J. A. (1976) A monetary approach to the exchange rate: doctrinal aspects and empirical evidence. *Scandinavian Journal of Economics*, 78 (2), 200–24.

Froot, K. A. and Ito, T. (1989) On the consistency of short run and long run exchange rate expectations. *Journal of International Money and Finance*, 8, 487–510.

Froot, K. A. and Frankel, F. A. (1990) Exchange rate techniques, survey data and implications for the foreign exchange market. IMF Working Paper 90143.

Gershenfeld, N. (1988) An experimentalist's introduction to the observation of dynamical systems. In Hao Bai-Lin (ed.), *Directions in Chaos Volume 2*. Singapore: World Scientific.

Geo (1990) Special issue: Chaos und Kreativität. 5 July.

Gleick, J. (1987) *Chaos: Making a New Science*. New York: Viking Press.

Goodhart, C. (1989) News and the foreign exchange market. London School of Economics Financial Markets Group Discussion Paper no. 71.

Grassberger, P. (1986) Do climatic attractors exist? *Nature*, 323, 609–12.

Grassberger, P. and Procaccia, I. (1983) Estimation of the Kolmogorov entropy from a chaotic signal. *Physics Review A: General Physics*, 28, 2591.

Hacche, G. and Towned, J. (1983) Some problems in exchange rate modeling: the case of sterling. *Zeitschrift für National Ekonomie*, 3, 127–62.

Haynes, S. E. and Stone, J. A. (1981) On the mark: comment. *American Economic Review*, 71 (5), 1060–7.

Hecht-Nielsen, R. (1990) *Neurocomputing*. Reading, MA: Addison-Wesley.

Hénon, M. (1976) A two dimensional mapping with a strange attractor. *Communications in Mathematical Physics*, 130, 69–77.

Hinich, M. J. (1982) Testing for Gaussianity and linearity of a stationary sequence. *Journal of Time Series*, 3 (3), 169–76.

Hinich, M. J. and Patterson, D. M. (1985) Evidence of non-linearity in daily stock returns. *Journal of Business and Economic Statistics*, 3 (1), 69–77.

Hofstadter, D. (1979) *Gödel, Escher, Bach: an Eternal Golden Braid.* New York: Vintage Books.

Hooper, P. and Morton, J. (1982) Fluctuations of the dollar: a model of nominal and real exchange rate determination. *Journal of International Money and Finance*, 1 (1), 39–56.

Hsieh, D. A. (1989) Testing for non-linear dependence in daily foreign exchange rates. *Journal of Business*, 62 (3), 25–43.

Hsieh, D. A. and Le Baron, B. (1988a) Finite sample properties of the BDS-statistic I: distribution under the null hypothesis. Mimeo, Graduate School of Business, University of Chicago, and Department of Economics, University of Wisconsin.

Hsieh, D. A. and Le Baron, B. (1988b) Finite sample properties of the BDS-statistic II: distribution under the alternative hypothesis. Mimeo, Graduate School of Business, University of Chicago, and Department of Economics, University of Wisconsin.

Hurst, H. E. (1955) Methods of using long-term storage in reservoirs. *Proceedings of the Institution of Civil Engineers*, part I, 519–77.

Hurst, H. E., Black, R. P. and Simaika, Y. M. (1965) *Long Term Storage: an Experimental Study.* London: Constable.

Isard, P. (1980) Expected and unexpected changes in exchange rates: the role of relative price levels, balance of payment factors, interest rates and risk. International Finance Discussion Papers no. 156.

Ito, T. (1990) Foreign exchange rate expectations. *American Economic Review*, 80, 434–43.

Kaplan, J. and Yorke, J. (1979) Period three implies chaos. In H. O. Peitgen and H. O. Walther (eds), *Functional Differential Equations and Approximations of Fixed Points.* Berlin: Springer-Verlag.

Lapedes, A. S. and Farber, R. M. (1986) Nonlinear signal processing using neural networks: prediction and system modelling. Los Alamos preprint LA-UR-87-2662.

Levich, R. M. (1979) On the efficiency of foreign exchange. In R. Dornbusch and J. Frenkel (eds), *International Economic Policy, Theory and Evidence.* Baltimore, MD: Johns Hopkins University Press.

Lorenz, E. N. (1963) Deterministic nonperiodic flow. *Journal of the*

Atmospheric Sciences, 20, 130–41.

McDonald, R. (1989) *Floating Exchange Rates: Theories and Evidence*. London: Unwin Hyman.

McDonald, R. and Taylor, M. D. (1989) Foreign exchange market efficiency and co-integration: some evidence of the recent float. *Economics Letters*, 29 (1), 63–8.

McKinnon, R. I. and Oates, W. R. (1966) The implications of international economic integration for monetary, fiscal and exchange rate policy. Princeton Studies in International Finance no. 16.

Mandelbrot, B. (1983) *The Fractal Geometry of Nature*. New York: Freeman.

Mayer-Kress, G. (1987) Applications of dimension algorithms to experimental analysis. In Hao Bai-Lin (ed.), *Directions in Chaos Volume 1*. Singapore: World Scientific.

Meese, R. A. and Rogoff, K. (1983) Empirical exchange rate models of the seventies: do they fit out of sample? *Journal of International Economics*, 14, 3–24.

Meese, R. A. and Rogoff, K. (1984) The out of sample failure of empirical exchange rate models. In J. A. Frenkel (ed.), *Exchange Rates and International Macroeconomics*. Chicago: NBER.

Meese, R. A. and Singleton, K. J. (1982) On unit roots and the empirical modeling of exchange rates. *Journal of Finance*, 37 (4), 1029–35.

Minford, P. and Peel, D. A. (1983) *Rational Expectations and the New Macroeconomics*. Oxford: Martin Robertson.

Muller, B. and Reinhardt, J. (1990) *Neural Networks: an Introduction*. Berlin: Springer-Verlag.

Mussa, M. (1976) The exchange rate, the balance of payments and monetary policy union: a regime of controlled float. *Scandinavian Journal of Economics*, 78, 229–48.

Mussa, M. (1979) Our recent experience with fixed and flexible exchange rates. *Carnegie Rochester Supplement*, 3, 1–50.

Mussa, M. (1991) Exchange rates in theory and in reality. Essays in International Finance no. 179, IFS, Princeton University.

Packard, N., Crutchfield, J. P., Farmer, J. D. and Shaw, R. S. (1980) Geometry from a time series. *Physical Review Letters*, 45, 712.

Peitgen, H. O. and Saupe, D. (eds) (1988) *The Science of Fractal Images*. Berlin: Springer-Verlag.

Pesaran, M. (1988) Formation of inflation expectations in British manufacturing industries. *Economic Journal*, 95, 948–75.

Peters, E. E. (1989) Fractal structure in the capital markets. *Financial Analysis Journal*, July/August, 32–7.

Peters, E. E. (1991) *Chaos and Order in the Capital Markets: a New View of Cycles, Prices, and Market Volatility*. New York: John Wiley and Sons.

Phillips, P. and Perron, P. (1988) Testing for a unit root in time series regression. *Biometrika*, 75, 335–46.

Poincaré, H. (1892–1899) *Les méthodes nouvelles de la mécanique céleste*. Three volumes.

Press, W. H., Flannery, B. P., Teukolsky, S. A. and Vetterling, W. T. (1986) *Numerical Recipes: the Art of Scientific Computing*. Cambridge: Cambridge University Press.

Priestly, M. B. (1991) *Non-linear and Non-stationary Time Series Analysis*. New York: Academic Press.

Putnam, R. H. and Woodbury, J. R. (1979) Exchange rate stability and monetary policy. *Review of Business and Economic Research*, 2, 1–10.

Ramsey, J. B. and Rothman, F. (1988) Characterization of the time inversibility of economic time series estimation and test statistics. RR no. 88-39, C. V. Stan Center for Applied Economics, New York University.

Rucker, R. (1983) *Infinity and the Mind: the Science and Philosophy of the Infinite*. New York: Bantam Books.

Samuelson, P. (1965) Proof that properly anticipated prices fluctuate randomly. *Industrial Management Review*, 6, 41–9.

Schulmeister, S. (1990) An essay on exchange rate dynamics. Discussion Paper IIM/LMP 87–8, Wissenschafts Zentrum Berlin für Social-Forschung, Berlin.

Schuster, H. G. (1989) *Herministic Chaos: an Introduction*. Weinheim: VCH Verlagsgesellschaft.

Smith, L. A. (1988) Intrinsic limits on dimension calculations. *Physics Letters A*, 133, 283–8.

Stewart, I. (1989) *Does God Play Dice? The New Mathematics of Chaos*. Oxford: Blackwell.

Subba Rao and Gabr, A. (1980) Test for linearity of stationary time series. *Journal of Time Series Analysis*, 1 (1), 145–58.

Takagi, S. (1988) Forward and spot exchange rates. *Journal of Monetary Economics*, 14, 319–38.

Takagi, S. (1991) Exchange rate expectations. *IMF Staff Papers*, 8 (1), 156–83.

Takens, F. (1981) Detecting strange attractors in fluid turbulence. In D. A. Rand and L. S. Young (eds), *Dynamical Systems and Turbulence, Volume 898 of Lecture Notes in Mathematics*. Berlin: Springer-Verlag.

Wickens, M. R. (1984) Rational expectations and exchange rate dynamics. In T. Peters, P. Praet and P. Reding (eds), *International Trade and Exchange Rates in the Late Eighties*. Amsterdam: North-Holland.

Index